INTERNATIONAL
CAPITAL MOVEMENTS
AND THE
DEVELOPING
WORLD

INTERNATIONAL CAPITAL MOVEMENTS AND THE DEVELOPING WORLD

The Case of Taiwan

Chich-Heng Kuo

New York
Westport, Connecticut
London

Copyright Acknowledgments

The author and publisher gratefully acknowledge permission to reprint extracts from the following:

Gustav Ranis, "Industrial Development," in *Economic Growth and Structural Change in Taiwan: The Postwar Experience of the Republic of China*, edited by Walter Galenson. Copyright © 1979 by Cornell University Press. Used by permission of the publisher, Cornell University Press.

"Direct Foreign Investment in Taiwan," by Gustav Ranis and Chi Shive, Walter Galenson, ed., *Foreign Trade and Investment: Economic Growth in the Newly Industrializing Asian Countries*, © 1985 (Madison: The University of Wisconsin Press) and Taiwan copyright © Mei Ya Publications, Inc.; used by permission of the publisher.

Shirley W. Y. Kuo, *The Taiwan Experience*. Reprinted by permission of Westview Press from *The Taiwan Experience*, by Shirley W. Y. Kuo. Copyright © Westview Press, Boulder, Colorado, 1983.

Financial Statistics, Part I: *Financial Statistics Monthly* (Paris), 1990, Tables I.12 and I.21. Reprinted by permission of the original publisher, Organisation for Economic Co-operation and Development .

Library of Congress Cataloging-in-Publication Data

Kuo, Chich-Heng.
    International capital movements and the developing world : the case
of Taiwan / Chich-Heng Kuo.
       p.   cm.
    Includes bibliographical references and index.
    ISBN 0-275-92969-8 (alk. paper)
    1. Capital movements—Taiwan. 2. Investments, Foreign—Taiwan.
3. Financial institutions—Taiwan. 4. Capital movements—History.
I. Title.
HG5798.K86 1991
332'.042—dc20   90-28078

British Library Cataloguing in Publication Data is available.

Copyright © 1991 by Chich-Heng Kuo

Library of Congress Catalog Card Number: 90-28078
ISBN: 0-275-92969-8

First published in 1991

Praeger Publishers, One Madison Avenue, New York, NY 10010
An imprint of Greenwood Publishing Group, Inc.

Printed in the United States of America

The paper used in this book complies with the Permanent
Paper Standard issued by the National Information Standards
Organization (Z39.48-1984).

10 9 8 7 6 5 4 3 2 1

TO MY FATHER AND MOTHER

PRICE $45.00 ISBN 0-275-92969-8. 224 pages. October 1991

Review copies are available by calling (203) 226-3571

Reviewers please inform your readers that they can order the book
with a credit card by calling: 1-800-225-5800 ID # 701.

Contents

Tables and Figures

Acknowledgments

I would like to express my sincere and special thanks to Professor William A. Lovett for his tireless and valuable guidance during my study at Tulane University School of Law. Beginning in fall 1984, Professor Lovett wisely guided my studies at Tulane. It would have been impossible for me to finish this book without his strong support and recommendations. I have been able to benefit from his excellent scholarly knowledge in the fields of both economics and law. I also profited from his experience and thinking on the subjects of international trade and finance.

In addition, I would like to acknowledge the assistance of my good friend Robert J. Ward, Jr., in the preparation of this book. His kindness and competence in helping me and my family during our stay in the United States are highly appreciated. I also benefited a great deal from his useful guidance regarding my writing.

Finally, my warmest gratitude goes to my wife for her support and sacrifice during the preparation of this treatise.

Introduction

After World War II, international trade and international capital movements were perceived increasingly as important means for fostering economic growth. The General Agreement on Tariffs and Trade (GATT) has been more successful than expected in helping developing countries to benefit from the freer world trade system, while allowing them to protect and develop their own economies at the same time. In addition, the International Monetary Fund (IMF) has emphasized the goal of freer flows for international capital with respect to current-account transactions because the original drafters of the IMF were concerned that restrictions on international capital flows could impede current-account business and trade transactions. But meanwhile controls on long-term international capital movements and investments have been regarded more as a matter of sovereignty, thus making the issues of freeing international capital movements considerably more complicated for broad regulation under international agreements. Today, the most advanced developed countries (and strongest newly industrializing countries) are using a more liberal approach toward international capital movements mainly because the financial markets and capital markets in these countries are becoming more fully developed, and their sound economic and political situations further assure stable and reliable capital sources, with limited controls on international capital movements. This helps explain how, in recent years, because the United States is a relatively safe place to park investment funds, it has been able to finance a large foreign trade deficit with an influx of foreign investment. Nonetheless, most developing countries still use foreign exchange controls to a certain degree to prevent speculative capital flows and to retain sufficient domestic capital sources for local development needs. Due to underdeveloped financial and capital markets as well as creditworthiness problems, the means and amounts of borrowing abroad by the majority of developing countries have been limited, particularly after the world debt-overload crisis broke out in 1982. Since then the financial strains of many developing countries have been exacerbated because the multinational banks lending to developing countries have decreased in number.

Although every country is pursuing industrial policies aimed at fostering economic growth to suit the specific economic situations in each individual country, the experiences of managing international capital movements are rather similar, that is, there has been a weighing of the advantages of free as opposed to control schemes with varied degrees of restrictions. Some argue that a minimum of controls, if possible, on international capital movements is desirable in order to prevent a distorted economic order, while fostering more foreign investment and encouraging a stronger balance of payments for individual developing countries. Others, on the other hand, want more national regulation to shape and speed up, hopefully, the industrial development process, with less reliance on foreign investment. Thus, how to regulate international capital movements consistently with IMF and other international organization rules and policies is a crucial subject for developing countries.

Because of similar policy problems with respect to controls on international capital movements, it is beneficial for all countries to learn from one another's experiences, so as ultimately to pursue the best policy choices. To understand the regulatory scheme and policy options of any specific country, however, it is necessary to review briefly the evolution of the IMF and the current world financial market trends. The successful economic development of Taiwan, the Republic of China, has proven that a poor country can help itself by employing wise policy tools and sound management of its financial system in contrast to the many troubled countries with serious debt overloads. The most important part of this study of Taiwan's economic success is that the story provides lessons for most developing countries as to how and why controls on international capital movements might work, as well as how and why these controls are now being relaxed. This study reviews the current aspects of international capital movements, and attempts to provide some regulatory and policy suggestions for other developing countries by illustrating the experience of Taiwan.

Chapter 1 of this study briefly reviews international capital flows by exploring the motivations of those different kinds of capital movements, thus providing a fuller picture of the current international capital flows. A cost-and-benefit analysis of controls on international capital movements follows to discuss the reasons behind the use of a control regime. Since the IMF has played a key role in liberalizing international capital movements, a review of the evolution of the IMF rules with respect to foreign exchange arrangements will provide the general regulatory framework in which a nation may try to restrict international capital movements. The various national strategies toward international capital movements have been grouped under different stages of economic development and social systems in order to explore the fundamental policy guidelines of each individual country. Finally, standards for national performance and capital markets are suggested to evaluate the economic efficiency of the controls used.

Chapter 2 provides the background for the Taiwanese economic development as well as the basic environment of encouraging and restricting international capital movements. This chronicle of economic development for Taiwan indicates policy changes from time to time, and a gradual shift to a more liberal approach toward controls on international capital movements. Since foreign direct investment in Taiwan has strongly contributed to the nation's economic development and has been the major stream of capital inflow, the review and assessment of these foreign capital inflows and their impact on the economy are essential in illustrating how a developing nation can attract foreign capital inflows, thereby stimulating economic development. Moreover, because the operations of the nation's financial system are crucial to channeling foreign capitals into domestic uses, an overview of financial operations in Taiwan can provide an understanding of how these controls on international capital flows functioned.

The strong encouragement of inward foreign direct investment and strict foreign exchange controls on outward transactions have been key factors in the successful economic development of Taiwan. Chapter 3 of this study analyzes the regulatory scheme of encouraging capital inflows, that is, encouragement of inward foreign direct investment and restrictions upon capital outflows (i.e., foreign exchange controls). The fiscal, financial and other incentives with respect to foreign direct investment in Taiwan are reexamined in detail. And the comprehensive exchange control regulations are classified into inflow and outflow controls, with emphasis on financial stability. Complications arising from mainland China's threat to the security of Taiwan (the Republic of China) also are discussed to explain the necessity of imposing controls on international capital movements, as well as of keeping a high and safe foreign exchange reserve level in Taiwan.

Chapter 4 examines current developments in Taiwan with respect to controls on international capital flows. The year of 1986 was a turning point for policy change in Taiwan. Because of the large accumulated foreign exchange reserves and the recent appreciation of the New Taiwan dollar, since 1986 the government has used a series of policy tools to cool down the inflationary pressures in Taiwan. These new measures also are aimed at helping to head off rising protectionism abroad. Thus, a liberal but gradual approach toward less inward and more outward foreign direct investments has been initiated, and partial liberalization of foreign exchange controls and banking operations have been undertaken as well. The trend toward freer movements of international capital in Taiwan is evident and inevitable. Nonetheless, the liberalization movement has been criticized as insufficient and inefficient. Some say it is insufficient because too many restrictions on outward capital flows still remain, and because the foreign exchange deposit accounts only deferred the time of surrendering the foreign exchange to the Central Bank. This is why the public has never been allowed to hold foreign exchange earned. It is arguably inefficient because expectations of the appreciation of the New Taiwan dollar has diverted the public away from holdings in foreign currencies. Furthermore, some remaining questions are posed to analyze the possible causes which are impeding the new reforms.

Chapter 5 focuses on the experience of Taiwan in providing lessons for economic development in other nations. Another successful newly industrializing country, South Korea, also is taken into comparison because of a similar successful utilization of foreign capital, but with some interesting differences in detail. The heavy foreign borrowing policy of the Korean government is considerably different from the strong foreign direct investment policy in Taiwan, but both have resulted in great economic achievements. These contrasting examples should provide valuable lessons to other developing countries. These two success stories indicate that the argument for some controls on international capital movements for developing countries is sustainable and desirable in order to help provide a stable financial system and manageable foreign exchange resources for economic development. Finally, the efficient utilization of foreign capital, either through lending to large conglomerates or by fostering the growth of many small and medium-sized domestic businesses, also offers important lessons for the developing countries.

The Taiwanese economic achievements have been called a "miracle." The effective policies and regulations employed certainly have encouraged strong foreign direct investment in Taiwan on the one hand. On the other hand, the comprehensive foreign exchange control regulations have prevented speculative capital, such as capital flight, from escaping abroad substantially. In short, the Taiwanese legal scheme and policy operations have retained most of the scarce capital resources for domestic uses which are vital to the nation's economic development. Today, the problem of increasing plenty has caused some policy changes, but the impacts of those changes are more positive than adverse. It may be concluded that when an economy has become more mature and self-sustaining, some liberalization of international capital flows is not only desirable but necessary. In light of current worldwide financial strains, the successful case of Taiwan could help lead the way for other developing countries to follow.

INTERNATIONAL
CAPITAL MOVEMENTS
AND THE
DEVELOPING
WORLD

1

Overall Aspects of International Capital Movements

After World War II, two significant agreements were implemented to facilitate freer trade and enhance the mobility of world resources—the General Agreement on Tariffs and Trade (GATT) and the Bretton Woods Agreement of the International Monetary Fund (IMF). Over the past thirty years, GATT has substantially reduced tariff barriers on international trade and cut nontariff barriers to some extent. Thus, a freer international trade system has been undertaken under the auspices of GATT (compared to the 1930s prewar period), at least among industrial nations and for the benefits of developing nations. In contrast, the IMF, which was designed to foster mobility of international capital and stabilize the international exchange system has achieved somewhat less success.

The phenomena of international capital movements has been a subject of international and national concern for a long time. From an individual country's point of view, the concern has stemmed from the impact of international capital flows, inward or outward, on the domestic economy. In the international forum, concern has arisen from the mobility of capital and the stabilization of an international exchange system. Although the IMF created a quasi-legal regime with respect to international capital movements (at least in regulating current-account transactions) and with respect to an exchange-rate surveillance system, the free movement of all international capital was not a primary objective of the Fund. Today, most developing countries (including socialist and communist countries) still use exchange controls to a certain degree.[1]

Although the volume of international capital movements has increased substantially since the early 1970s, freer flows of international capital remain a goal in many advanced industrial countries. An overview of major streams of international capital movement is necessary to realize how the contemporary international monetary system operates and how the financial restraints of developing countries function. A cost-and-benefit analysis of controls of international capital movements also is examined in order to understand the reasons for imposing controls.

The control measures which a country could engage have varying purposes and goals. Based on a 1986 Organisation for Economic Co-operation and Development (OECD) survey, all these control measures can be grouped as (1) individual authorization requirements; (2) general exchange controls; and (3) various administrative practices, among others. A further discussion of the dimensions of control measures also is included in this study to indicate the best choice of control measures. Finally, policy considerations for the choice of control measures are reviewed as an underlying factor in shaping the control-choice decision.

The rules of the IMF are an important part of the game. Although the articles of the IMF agreement have been amended twice since the birth of the Fund, the articles involving international capital movements remain untouched. Nonetheless, since the world debt overload crisis broke out in 1982, multinational bank lending to developing countries has been declining. Creditworthiness problems as well as underdeveloped capital and financial markets also have impeded capital inflows into developed countries. Borrowing from the IMF and the World Bank has become more important for many developing countries seeking external finance.[2] The IMF has enhanced its surveillance power to oversee the adjustment programs of developing countries in order to assure coordination between the IMF and the individual countries.

Controversies over the subject of capital control have long existed. Countries with different stages of economic development have continued using different strategies for regulating international capital movements. For instance, a country with a well-established financial market, ample capital supplies, and sound macroeconomics tends to favor freer flows of capital, and vice versa for less developed countries. To recent debt-over-loaded countries, the shortage of external finance and capital flight problems remain as major concerns; thus the freer movements of capital for them have not really been feasible. A review of current national strategies and the standards for national performance will be helpful to understand the operations of different regulatory regimes.

INTERNATIONAL CAPITAL MOVEMENTS AND REASONS FOR RESTRICTIONS

Review of International Capital Movements

Strictly speaking, any form of international capital movement involving private enterprise is profit seeking or attempting loss avoidance,[3] that is, seeking to obtain some "benefit," whether by way of maximizing returns or minimizing losses. The return to be maximized need not be direct interest yields alone but may also be transactional profit. For example, international bond issues, portfolio investments, commercial bank lending, banking and corporate export credits, and direct investment are major playing cards in international capital flows. However, there are other kinds of capital movement that are not necessarily based on such business judgments—for example, speculation and hedging, capital flight, as well as precautionary diversification, etc. Thus many complications can arise under differing regulatory regimes.

Various kinds of capital flows are involved in the game from one country to another through world financial centers, such as New York, London, Tokyo, Frankfurt, Brussels, Zurich, and Toronto, in conjunction with different currencies being exchanged.[4] Theoretically, the free flow of international capital can maximize the world's production.[5] However, various barriers which impede international capital movements exist in various channels of international capital flows for different national reasons. To discern the different means of control for international capital movements, along with the different regulatory schemes in individual countries, an overview of the major international capital flows is essential.

The first type of international capital movements to be examined is international bond issuances. There are two kinds of international bond issues—foreign bonds and Eurobonds. The former refers to the issuance of bonds in one country (host country) by a foreign issuer. The bond is underwritten by one or more syndicates in the host country and is intended to borrow from the residents of the host country. For example, the German government issues US$10 million in bonds in the New York market, denominated in U.S. dollars and underwritten by Morgan Guaranty Company. In contrast, "Eurobonds" refer to a situation where the issuer issues the bond in any country's market and is underwritten by different syndicates from different countries. Since the issuances of Eurobonds are not confined in one specific country, its issuances often are exempt from any one nation's withholding taxes and other regulatory restrictions.[6] For example, the French government might issue US$50 million in bonds in

London and Frankfurt, denominated in U.S. dollars, which is underwritten by the Bank of England, Citicorp, and the Creditbank Luxemburgoise.

The volume of international bond issuances has increased substantially since the early 1970s and accelerated since the early 1980s. During the period of 1972–86, the growth of foreign bonds has been moderate, while Eurobond issuances grew rapidly (see Table 1.1).[7] However, international bond issues by developing countries accounted for only a small portion of total issuances, mainly due to creditworthiness problems in most of those nations.

The rapid growth of the international bond market in the early to mid-1980s was caused by the following factors: (1) lower inflation rates in some key industrial countries, compared to the 1970s when the 1974 and 1978 Organization of Petroleum Exporting Countries (OPEC) crises caused substantial inflation and high interest rates; (2) a slight but sound recovery of world economies in 1983; (3) the relatively high yields of bond holdings compared with declining interest rates in major world financial markets; (4) new types of financial instruments, such as floating-rate notes, which provided more flexible and profitable bond holding; and (5) less restrictions on bond issuances in certain major markets, such as removal of the withholding tax on bondholdings by foreigners.[8] The borrowers of international bond markets include sovereign borrowers, commercial banks, corporations, and international organizations. In addition to traditional straight debt instruments, there are other types of instruments used in international bond markets, such as floating-rate notes, convertible bonds, warrants, original issue discount bonds, and currency-hedged bonds.[9] In 1985, the total international volume of straight bond issuances was US$92.5 billion; for floating-rate notes issuances, US$58.4 billion; for convertible bonds and warrants, US$11.4 billion; and others accounted for US$5.4 billion.[10]

A second kind of international capital movement is international portfolio investment. International portfolio investments in stock markets provide a major potential source of risk capital. The basic idea of portfolio investment focuses on sharing profits of an enterprise. It differs from direct investments in which the investors participate in the operation and management of the enterprises. Thus, the normal case is that individual portfolio investors hold less than 5 percent of the total shares of a corporation, thereby the investors are able to avoid any operational risk and are more easily able to liquidate their investment with freedom and convenience.

In recent years, portfolio investments from pension funds have grown rapidly in the OECD areas. During 1984, U.S. pension funds had attracted US$16 billion in foreign commitments as the largest institutional purchases of equity. The second largest purchasers of foreign stocks (equity) are the U.S. life insurance companies. Due to the fairly strict regulation of the insurance industry and more extensive diversification of investments in international bond issuances, the life insurance companies invest a smaller sum of foreign stock (equity) than pension fund purchasers.[11]

The motivations for international portfolio investments concentrate on higher returns and risk diversification, not only to avoid specific country risks but also to avoid exchange risks. However, the underdeveloped stock markets in developing countries, capital insecurities, plus regulatory barriers to potential foreign investors all contribute to the reasons why rather little portfolio investment goes to less-developed countries.[12]

A third flow of international capital is international commercial bank lending. International bank lending expanded rapidly during the 1970s and had played a key role in recycling the surpluses generated by the oil price rise. However, bank lending to developing countries has decelerated since 1982, when the so-called debt-overload crisis broke out.[13]

Today international bank lending to developing countries is more selective and cautious.[14] Coordinated efforts have been made to keep capital adequacy levels higher than they were during the late 1970s. In the United States, the passage of the International Lending Supervision Act of 1983 signaled the national concern over international bank lending. In Japan, consolidated monitoring procedures have been adopted, and in the Federal Republic of Germany, consolidated supervision has been mandated by legislation. Meanwhile, it is highly desirable for banks to reestablish adequate reserves in light of market reactions as well as supervisory responses. In general, banks in continental European countries are maintaining "earmarked reserves." Those banks experiencing payment difficulties from the debt overload countries are required to keep their reserves high enough to absorb losses equivalent to a fifth or more of their exposure to such countries.[15] As a result, international medium- and long-term loans to developing countries (excluding OPEC areas) have continued to decline from the peak of US$37.6 billion in 1982 to US$23.9 billion in 1983, and decelerated even more to US$18.9 and 14.1 billion in 1984 and 1985 respectively. In the first half of 1986, the volume of international medium- and long-term bank loans to developing countries was as low as US$2.9 billion.[16]

Another form of international capital movements is export credits offered by banks or nonfinancial institutions. Banks and corporations are the two major sources of credits for financing of private commercial trade. Banks can benefit from accumulating claims on foreigners on the basis of returns. More often, it is the practice of banks to serve their customers by

Table 1.1
International Bond Issues, by Country, 1972–1986 (in millions of U.S. dollars)

	1972	1974	1978	1981	1983	1984	1985	1986(H)
OECD Areas								
Eurobonds	5550	3254	11578	26281	45597	75754	122954	82459
Foreign Bonds	2299	3831	14867	15843	21437	21020	22648	14836
U.S.								
Eurobonds	2031	105	1265	6110	6114	21491	36348	21223
Foreign Bonds	182	84	374	697	1241	1462	3195	3417
Canada								
Eurobonds	371	126	828	5533	3866	4488	6980	7084
Foreign Bonds	1072	1962	3930	5448	2908	1761	2505	770
Japan								
Eurobonds	32	153	1500	4625	6953	11002	14897	11618
Foreign Bonds	-	95	1292	2096	6678	6035	6203	3466
Germany								
Eurobonds	51	-	324	110	2451	1661	3063	4902
Foreign Bonds	73	133	21	133	470	403	105	21
France								
Eurobonds	172	207	775	2278	6103	7020	10240	4896
Foreign Bonds	74	340	529	841	1231	1524	1185	479
U.K.								
Eurobonds	777	143	776	1229	1525	4736	14987	6606
Foreign Bonds	111	198	672	156	553	261	266	255
Switzerland								
Eurobonds	-	12	84	-	845	496	864	912
Foreign Bonds	-	30	-	-	-	88	-	-
Sweden								
Eurobonds	171	25	242	947	3360	3984	4494	2940
Foreign Bonds	55	87	500	785	758	2446	1609	563

OPEC								
Eurobonds	85	–	1209	200	338	425	650	390
Foreign Bonds	–	63	684	242	78	107	134	–
Other Developing Countries								
Eurobonds	775	142	2007	3245	1989	2871	6441	987
Foreign Bonds	352	740	1912	986	753	1230	1473	1151
India								
Eurobonds	–	–	–	282	60	215	280	166
Foreign Bonds	–	–	–	–	–	83	93	83
South Korea								
Eurobonds	–	–	–	280	442	729	1328	330
Foreign Bonds	–	19	56	43	105	327	372	308
Malaysia								
Eurobonds	25	–	20	–	541	950	1741	–
Foreign Bonds	–	–	20	–	344	191	261	–
Thailand								
Eurobonds	–	–	25	55	195	173	800	–
Foreign bonds	–	–	44	44	59	111	62	–
Africa								
Eurobonds	257	50	144	–	329	618	721	–
Foreign Bonds	13	–	338	92	203	396	57	–
International Organizations								
Eurobonds	524	–	168	1568	1857	2460	4311	2039
Foreign Bonds	1601	609	3250	3443	4718	5403	6622	2000
Subtotal								
Eurobonds	6934	3396	14961	31294	50098	81717	135431	86742
Foreign Bonds	4252	5243	20713	20514	27050	27801	31025	17993
Total Issuances	11186	8639	35674	51808	77148	103518	166456	104735

Note: 1986 (H) = period ending June 1986.

Source: Financial Statistics, Part I: *Financial Statistics Monthly* (Paris: OECD, 1990), Tables I.12 and I.21.

issuing letters of credit, thus extending financial credit on commercial trade. The underlying reason for cooperation in granting credit for foreign customers is to entice sales and profit from sales. Nevertheless, financial credit is not necessarily linked to exports. A small, less-well-established importing firm also may rely on external financing for importation needs, and corporate financial credit can tackle these needs.[17]

At the end of 1986, officially supported export credits of the developing countries totaled US$206.7 billion, of which US$170.6 billion were nonbank trade-related credits.[18] The increasing volume of export credits offered to developing countries has been helpful to meet adjustment program needs in individual countries, without so much disruption of international trade.[19]

Another dimension of international capital movement is foreign direct investment. Foreign direct investment is defined as "a lasting interest in an enterprise operating in the countries, with the purpose of having an effective voice in the management."[20] Foreign direct investment may involve the remittance of funds on an equity basis, retention of profits earned in the host country, the transfer of real resources (notably intangibles like technology), or an intracompany loan.[21]

In a recent United Nations survey, the growth rate of international direct investments was 15 percent per annum in the 1970s in current U.S. dollar terms. During 1970–80, the reported volume of outward foreign direct investments was US$42 billion.[22] Since the year 1981, the United States has shifted gradually from the position of the main source of foreign direct investment to the position of a major recipient of such flows.[23] Although direct foreign investment in developing countries was rising from US$6 billion in 1977 to US$14 billion in 1981, it declined to US$9.9 billion in 1983 due to the ensuing recession and the debt crisis of 1982.[24]

A new form of foreign direct investment was described recently by OECD Development Center, which referred to "(1) joint investment in which foreign held equity does not exceed 50 percent; (2) various international contract agreements which involve at least an element of investment from the foreign firm's point of view with or without equity participation."[25] However, the impact of the new forms of foreign direct investments on international capital movements is questionable. For instance, licensing agreements can be reached without any capital flows between the home country and host country.

There are many kinds of international capital movement which may be caused by factors other than normal profit seeking, and include loss avoidance. The most clearly manifest one is speculation and hedging. Arthur Bloomfield stated that "speculation involves the deliberate assumption of an exchange risk, i.e. of an uncovered exchange position, with a view to profit (or at least hedge risk) from an anticipated movement in exchange rates." For example, speculation in the forward market in 1934–39 caused the capital inflows to the United States of the U.S. funds held abroad in the form of deposits.[26]

A second cause of international capital movement other than profit seeking is the so-called "confidence problem."[27] Kenneth Dam defined the confidence problem as "countries (and individuals) holding reserves in foreign exchange who might lose confidence in the future value of a principal currency and decide to convert holdings of that currency into gold or other currencies." Once the external liabilities of a country accumulate to an unaffordable extent, such as a debt overload or a huge trade deficit, the confidence problem may become acute, easily worsened by any payment deficit of the reserve center. When Britain "went off gold" in 1931 and the United States "closed the gold window" in 1971 are cited as examples. By the same token, in the late 1970s foreign holders (including individual and country holdings) of the U.S. dollar were trying to switch to the increasingly popular deutsche mark and Japanese yen with a view to diversifying their foreign exchange reserves. This is another example of the confidence problem causing unusual movements of international capital.

A third cause of international capital movement other than profit seeking is anticipation of exchange depreciation. Anticipation of exchange depreciation may cause some currency holders to purchase other currencies (including other financial instruments) and/or gold in order to avoid expected losses.[28] To cope with the worsening U.S. trade deficit, five major industrial nations (G-5)—United States, United Kingdom, Germany, France and Japan—held a meeting in New York on 22 September 1985 and concluded that the exchange rates of non-dollar currencies should appreciate against the U.S. dollar to reflect the growing current-account surpluses of the United States' trade partners.[29] Thus, U.S. corporations have shifted to international bond markets for short-term Euronotes and Eurocommercial paper as part of their external finance. Meanwhile, foreign investors have shown more interest in U.S. Treasury securities and corporate bonds.[30]

One of the most important underlying causes of international capital movement other than profit seeking is political instability and capital flight. Political upheaval, threats of revolution, dismal economic performance, and speculative greed all have been said to encourage capital flight. Since World War II, the United States has been regarded as a safe country by worldwide investors. A substantial part of capital inflows to the United

States can be classified as capital flight, or at least as precautionary diversification. For example, in early 1986, Morgan Guaranty estimated that net capital flight from eighteen major borrowing countries totaled US$198 billion. This huge amount of capital flight has played a significant role in the increase of the total debts from these countries to US$450 billion.[31]

Among the many types of international capital movement, there are so-called "normal" and "abnormal" distinctions. A normal capital movement refers to one "taking place from low to high interest rate (or return) countries." And an abnormal capital movement refers to one "occurring in the opposite direction, or upstream."[32] The rationale for this distinction is that "under normal economic and political conditions," capital holders seek to maximize their returns by moving capital from low-yield markets to high-yield markets—in other words, "downstream flows." If capital moves in the opposite direction, it is assumed that there are some kinds of abnormal factors causing "upstream flows." Those "abnormal" factors are capital flight and destabilizing exchange speculation. Another feature of abnormal capital movement is that "they are generally much larger and more volatile, arise more suddenly, and move from countries with deficits on current account to countries with a surplus on current account, rather than vice versa."[33] Nonetheless, to distinguish between normal and abnormal movements will aid in confronting the difficulties of deciding whether the conditions causing the transfers of capital can be effectively regulated. However any precise classification of capital movements on such a basis would be difficult and somewhat arbitrary.[34]

Other classifications of international capital movements, such as "equilibrating" versus "disequilibrating" capital movements[35] and "induced" versus "autonomous" capital movements[36] which are based on foreign exchange reserve considerations, are insufficient to regulate day-by-day international capital movements, which in turn operate by free-market momentums. Due to the high mobility of capital and the complexity of today's global financial market, it is difficult to ascertain what causes many particular capital flows from one country to another. To classify a specific capital movement under the form it takes and to regulate it accordingly usually is more constructive than to explore the motivations of those making the movements.

Reasons for Restrictions

Official restrictions on international capital flows are used for different purposes. When the balance of payments fall into disequilibrium and an economy becomes more vulnerable to external forces, the authorities are likely to impose restrictions on trade and capital movements. For example, in their reconstruction periods following World War II, most European countries were using restrictive exchange controls to maximize the use of scarce dollar reserves. The United States later used moderate and temporary restrictions, which included the Interest Equalization Tax (IET) and the Voluntary Foreign Credit Restraint Program (VFCRP) to limit capital outflows to improve its balance of payments from September 1964 to January 1974.[37]

In general, temporary or permanent controls can be rationalized as follows: (1) to help insulate the domestic financial market and capital market from potentially large and unwanted international movements of funds which are deemed to be disturbing to the economy by the authorities; (2) to curb imported inflation or deflation by insulating the domestic money supply from potentially large movement of short- and long-term funds; (3) to keep the exchange rates more stable and to restore public confidence by preventing or limiting speculative capital movements; (4) to foster domestic economic growth and to encourage domestic industries by imposing controls to reduce the purchases of imported goods; (5) to provide a more effective solution to the balance of payments problem; (6) to limit the international role of a domestic currency; (7) to prevent capital outflows from countries with underdeveloped markets and/or capital shortages by using selected longer-term capital controls which are permitted under the articles of IMF Agreement; and (8) to remove undesirable side effects of peculiar economic and regulatory developments abroad and vice versa.[38] For debt-overloaded countries, restrictions on capital movements also might help to prevent loss of domestic assets which could otherwise be used by the society to foster economic growth and to meet adjustment needs. If capital were completely free to be transferred outside of a particular country, a country's hopes of repaying international loans could be jeopardized.[39] Thus, control on capital movements may enable a country to economize scarce capital for domestic uses.

Moreover, to cope with the interest-rate differential between domestic and foreign markets, control over capital flows is important for the authorities to influence the course of the money supply and the total credit flows. Meanwhile, capital flows are in themselves an important policy target, since capital flows greatly affect a country's international exchange reserves or the degree of exchange-rate adjustment, depending on whether the exchange rates are relatively fixed or flexible.[40]

The costs of controls have been raised as follows: (1) The value of a domestic currency is distorted against foreign currencies, leading to misallocation of domestic resources; (2) the prices of imported products are raised, thus creating the burden on domestic consumers; (3) monitoring a control's operation involves substantial administrative cost; (4) ensuing illegal transactions can incur substantial costs; and (5) controls may induce retaliation from other countries, thus adding to the burden on the domestic economy.[41] In recent years, the United States has advocated the freer flow of international capital in order to sustain the freer trade system in the world. In August 1988 the omnibus trade bill was passed by the Congress of the United States, the measures of exchange control to keep the exchange rate at certain level would be another concern for trade-deficit countries. Needless to say, to remove exchange control is another way to avoid the criticism of hampering international trade.

The legal regime created by Article VIII of the IMF Agreement does not prohibit restrictions on international capital movements, nor on transactions that underlay monetary payments and transfers. But a member country which accepts the status of Article VIII is obligated to impose no restrictions on the making of payments and transfers for current-account transactions, nor to engage in discriminating currency arrangements and multiple currency practices. These policies are supposed to assure convertibility of its currency. Most recently, Spain became the sixty-first member country which accepted the Article VIII status,[42] and yet about forty of these countries still use capital controls to some extent. In contrast, the transitional arrangements of Article XIV of the IMF Agreement provide that a member country may retain general restrictions on international payments and transfers for current-account transactions, including multiple exchange practices.[43] Roughly 100 countries are still governed by Article XIV status, thus the transitional arrangements have enabled most developing countries to take advantage of discriminatory foreign-exchange controls over current- and capital-account transactions.[44] This illustrates how most of the developing countries have retained controls on international capital movements.

MEASURES AND OBJECTIVES OF CONTROL

General Survey of Control Measures

In a 1982 OECD survey, the controls on international financial operations are grouped as follows: "a. individual authorization requirements, including legal prohibitions; b. exchange control measures (other than individual authorization) and administrative practice; and c. other control measures, including the use of minimum reserve requirements and taxes."[45]

Individual authorization is referred to as "corresponding closest to the [restrictions] in the sense of the Code, i.e., an absolute legal or regulatory prohibition of an operation or a requirement for case-by-case authorization to make transactions or to complete the accompanying transaction." Such measures are designed to limit capital flows by directly controlling the number of transactions and/or transfers. For example, one country could have regulated the loan of foreign countries by requiring prior authorization before taking out the loan.

The second category of capital controls refers to "other administrative regulations which are needed to govern the means, timing, nature and/or cost of undertaking transactions and transfers." By regulating foreign-exchange operations, the authorities have been able to limit the volume of transactions or transfers. Examples include such measures as surrender requirements, balance of net positions, special currency circuits, prudential regulation (designed to improve the protection of deposits by limiting the foreign-exchange exposure of lenders), and interest-rate controls which relate specifically to international loan, credit, or deposit operations (i.e., the imposition of ceiling or negative rates, or the prohibition of interest payments). Most of these measures are considered to be a "frustration" under Article 16 of the Code, that is, "international arrangements likely to restrict the possibility of affecting transactions or transfers." For instance, one country could have required its residents to purchase foreign securities via a specific semiofficial agency thereby limiting the outflows of the domestic capital.

The third category of controls refers to those measures which "applied to international financial operations including measures whose primary purpose is to achieve the amount or costs of capital flows where capital control is also intended." The dividing line between the second and third category is blurred. Nonetheless, the third group involves "financial operations," such as minimum-reserve requirements, the withholding tax, and credit expansion limits. These measures also could constitute, under certain circumstances, "frustrations." For example, a government could have raised the withholding tax on dividends to a high rate level in order to frustrate foreign investors, thus restricting capital inflows.

All measures, whether directly or indirectly affecting international capital flows, also have the effect of limiting the volume of transactions and/or transfers. The degree of their impact on the volume depends, for the first category, upon how flexible they are applied, and for the second and third categories, upon the undertaken conditions and the form of controls.[46]

Dimensions for Control Measures

The choice of controls is based on different policy objectives and cost/benefit analyses. The effects of controls depend on different social backgrounds and stages of economic development. For most mature industrial countries, with well-established financial markets, control measures tend to be moderate or negligible. In most developing countries (including socialist countries), with less-developed financial and capital markets as well as foreign reserve shortages, significant control measures generally are used.

A major dimension of capital controls is effectiveness versus flexibility. Basically, controls should be applied with some flexibility to cope with changing domestic and foreign conditions. But in many countries with rigid control systems, the flexibility of controls may not be feasible. In those countries, a set of priorities normally is used in applying control on transactions and settlements; thus, the authorities don't have leeway to deal with a specific case.[47] For example, most developing countries are capital-importing countries, and domestic outward investment is either prohibited or discouraged. By so doing, these countries can effectively prevent capital outflows without applying the policy flexibly; this policy can restrict profitable foreign investments abroad.

A second dimension of control measures is direct or indirect controls. Some of the control measures are intended to have direct impacts on international capital movements. The obvious one is exchange control regulations which regulate the operation of foreign exchange. For example, the prior-approval requirement for remittance is the most-often-used measure for developing countries to regulate the operation of the foreign-exchange market. Other kinds of control measures, such as taxation or fees, may have indirect impacts on capital flows. The choice of these control measures often is intended to regulate capital flows with quantitative restrictions in addition to its fiscal purpose. The Interest Equalization Tax (IET), which was used by the United States to alleviate the influx of foreign capital, can be cited as a further example.

A third dimension of control measures is temporary or permanent controls. Temporary control measures are set to deal with certain circumstances during a specific period of time.[48] For instance, Canada used voluntary guidelines on capital outflows when the U.S. dollar was under speculative pressure in the early 1970s. The United States used the Voluntary Foreign Credit Restraint Program (VFCRP) to supplement the IET in 1965 as another example of temporary control measures. In addition, under the IMF Article XIV transitional arrangements, the use of multiple exchange rates is supposedly considered as a temporary control measure although many countries have used them for more than thirty years.[49] Permanent regulations often are used for the purpose of more lasting policy objectives. For example, to prevent capital outflows, prior approval of remittances commonly is required in developing countries. However, the implementation of this requirement may be varied in different period of time to cope with the changes in domestic and external markets.

Another dimension of control measures is whether to limit the range of controlled sectors or not. Countries may select some specific sectors as the target of control. For example, the countries with a view to preventing foreign control of key domestic enterprises may adopt certain controls on foreign portfolio investments in these areas.[50] The prohibition of foreign direct investment into specific industries is another example. However, some of the control measures may apply to all the residents of a specific country, such as the aforesaid prior approval of remittances. Those control measures which do not specifically apply to bank lending, deposits, portfolio investments, or direct investments often are based on unlimited range of consideration, that is, generally applying to all residents.

Finally, there is a choice between bank and nonbank control measures. Some of the control measures, such as minimum-reserve requirements and interest-rate controls, are operated through financial institutions (banks). Other control measures, such as export/import licensing and investment approval, are not necessarily carried out by financial institutions. The criterion for choosing bank or nonbank operations also depends heavily upon whether the financial market is well established or not. Those countries with well-established financial markets or government-owned (or heavily regulated) banking institutions are likely to choose bank control measures, whereas these countries not so well established economically tend toward nonbank control measures. In a country with more fully developed financial markets, banking may be trusted to fulfill most of the purposes of the controls, that is, bank control measures may be expected to achieve the policy goals. In a nation with underdeveloped financial markets, nonbank control measures may also be needed to regulate capital flows more effectively.

In short, the choice of control measures involves the timing, technique, and nature of controls. Since one control measure often is an advantage for one policy goal but a disadvantage for other policy considerations, the effectiveness of a control measure also is a crucial question. For example, by imposing export licensing, the authorities may secure a source of foreign reserves. But this practice also impedes an export expansion policy. Thus, the exchange-control authorities should choose the best way to minimize the adverse impacts and to maximize the desirable effects of controls by adopting the most appropriate extent, range, and limitations on these measures.

Policy Considerations

Controls on international capital movements are taken by different countries for various policy reasons. The most-often-claimed policy reason is for balance of payments support. For example, a deteriorating balance of payments, such as an increasing trade deficit, would normally cause the depreciation of the given domestic currency. This may cause domestic inflation, distress, or disruptions. To prevent the balance of payments from generating huge deficits (or cumulating undue surpluses), a nation may try to impose controls on outflows or inflows of international capital. For instance, the Swiss government has used controls on heavy capital inflows (or sterilization measures) to limit the rising Swiss franc or to prevent excessive monetary stimulus.[51]

Many countries are more concerned over their capital outflows. According to a 1980 OECD survey, even some of these countries, such as Greece, New Zealand, Portugal, and Turkey, use controls on capital outflows. The policy consideration of these countries is the fear of a drain on foreign-exchange reserves, where extensive capital outflows would be seen as leading to undesirable results,[52] such as decreasing foreign-exchange reserves and the depreciation of domestic currency. For instance, the outward investments from New Zealand are subject to the approval of the Reserve Bank and the authorities favor investment projects which can benefit the current-account balance, that is, exports.[53]

For most developing countries, because of painful capital shortages and underdeveloped capital markets, imports of capital for domestic investment are necessary. There is simply little justification to export scarce capital for another nation's use. For example, a capital-importing country's policy aim could have targeted to satisfy domestic needs of capital for resources and development. Thus, little legislation encouraging outward loans and investment would be enacted.

In some countries, policy considerations dictate regulation of inflows of foreign capital, quite apart from the problem of balance of payments. Fears of foreign control over the domestic economy or protection for domestic industries from foreign competition are dominant in their policy thinking, particularly for infant industries. Authorities may prohibit foreign investment in some specific sectors, delay or regulate interest or dividend payments to foreign investors, or restrict the remittance of investing capital and profits earned by foreign investors, thus impeding capital inflows and outflows.[54] The equity requirement used by South Korea in reviewing foreign direct investments is a typical case.[55]

Another policy consideration is national security. Infant and defense industries often are excluded from the list of foreign direct or portfolio investment—such as steel or petroleum industries, because of the importance of these sectors to the growth of national defense in developing countries. National security reasons also are at the root of the controls on capital outflows because large foreign-exchange reserves may be required to assure the payment of defense needs abroad, such as the purchase of arms; therefore restricted capital outflows are desirable.

In addition, various international commitments, such as bilateral agreements, treaties, or international organization agreements may be taken into consideration by policymakers. The conditionality discipline of the IMF often requires a member country to make efforts in its economic adjustment in order to obtain a standby arrangement with the IMF. The adjustment process may alter tariffs on imports, increase domestic interest rates, and perhaps involve more integration with the international financial market. All these factors can impact on national policies and may lead to a liberalization of controls.[56] A recent trade negotiation between the United States and Taiwan in which the latter agreed to open its insurance market to U.S. firms in Taiwan provides a good example.

Another fundamental consideration is whether a country should adopt an export-expansion or import-substitution policy. A nation with an export-expansion oriented strategy is likely to encourage more foreign direct investment to produce goods for the international market. On the other hand, a nation with import-substitution economies is likely to restrict foreign direct investment to protect domestic industries from foreign competition. Thus, under an export-expansion policy, more incentives are given to attract foreign investment and technology. Most East Asian newly industrializing countries belong to this group, and the encouragement of foreign direct investment is more strongly urged in these areas.

For some developing countries, securing supplies of energy and raw materials is another reason to impose controls on international capital movements. For non-oil-producing countries, scarce supplies of energy and raw materials can be vital to these nations' economies. To allocate scarce foreign exchange in the order of priority, controls on foreign exchanges may be necessary. For example, in Taiwan from the 1950s to early 1980s, almost all foreign currency payments abroad had to be channeled through the Central Bank. This requirement was intended to ensure that all foreign currency payments follow an order of priorities established by the Council of Economic Planning and Development, thereby safeguarding sufficient foreign currencies necessary for the purchase of raw materials and oil.

Another consideration is the stability of the domestic financial system. To stabilize the domestic financial system, it may be necessary to use some measures of control on international capital movements. A substantial capital outflow or inflow can strain a nation's financial system due to the drain of loanable funds or the creation of an excessive money supply. Moreover, in most developing countries, bank deposits are uninsured, and interest rates are artificially lower than international financial markets, not to mention frequent inflationary pressure caused by fiscal deficits. The potential for capital flight could be catastrophic if there were no controls on international capital outflows.[57] Finally, a rapid drain of foreign-exchange reserves could cause the balance of payments situation to worsen thereby causing grave inflation and depreciation.

Another consideration for advanced industrial countries may be full employment objectives. It often is argued that capital outflows from industrial countries to developing countries may relocate jobs to lower-wage-paying countries. To limit excessive job losses in industrial countries, these industrial countries may impose restrictions on certain types of capital outflows, such as overseas direct investment. France has used authorization requirements to regulate outward foreign direct investment to areas outside French previous colonies.[58]

In recent years, another policy consideration of the developing countries may be observed in trying to head off the rising protectionism in the industrial countries. Trade negotiations often include the issues of openness of domestic markets for foreign investors, such as in the banking and insurance industries, as well as the reduction of tariffs and other trade barriers. The open trade practices advocated by the Reagan Administration have been extended to the banking operations in some developing countries for U.S. multinational banks. To gain more leverage in these trade negotiations, the developing countries may liberalize part of their foreign-exchange controls to offer a more open market for foreign investors. For instance, Singapore and Hong Kong were able to keep benefits of the Generalized System of Preference (GSP) from the United States because of the relative openness of their markets as compared to South Korea and Taiwan.[59]

In short, the control measures which a country could adopt may vary by different policy considerations, which are based in turn on the different economic and social backgrounds of the nations. For instance, the inflation rate in Taiwan during 1946–48 was at an annual 500 percent and then up to 3,000 percent in the first half of 1949. The inflation rate was brought down from 69.9 percent in 1951 to 11.4 percent by 1965. This successful anti-inflation policy contributed greatly to a sound economic development over the past thirty years. Thus, a low inflation rate was and will be an important policy consideration for Taiwan especially, as well as for other developing nations.[60]

RULES AND REGULATIONS UNDER THE IMF

Roles of the International Monetary Fund

The IMF is an international organization, as well as a fund for money and other assets. The member countries are eligible to "borrow" from the Fund and "repay" their "loans" under the agreement.[61] The purposes of the Fund are set forth in Article I of its charter:

a. To promote international monetary cooperation through a permanent institution which provides the machinery for consultation and collaboration on international problems.

b. To facilitate the expansion and balanced growth of international trade, and to contribute thereby to the promotion and maintenance of high levels of employment and of real income as well as to the development of the productive sources of all economies.

c. To promote exchange stability, to maintain orderly exchange arrangements among members, and to prevent competitive exchange depreciation policies.

d. To assist in the establishment of a multilateral system of payments with respect to current transactions between members and to the elimination of foreign exchange restrictions which hamper the growth of world trade.

e. To give confidence to members by making the Fund's resources temporarily available to them under adequate safeguards, thus providing them with the opportunity to correct maladjustments in their balance of payments without destroying of national or international prosperity.

f. In accordance with the above, to shorten the duration and lessen the degree of disequilibrium in the international balance of payments of members.[62]

Under the articles of agreements of the IMF, the role assigned to the Fund is as follows:[63]

1. Monitoring changes in par values or in exchange arrangements where par values are not effective. The second amendment of the articles terminated the power to approve or disapprove par values unless at some future time a system of par values is reinstated by nearly unanimous agreement. But the "surveillance" mandated in new Article IV does give the Fund some authority to evaluate the adequacy of exchange rates.

2. Administering what can be called a "code of fair practice" in the field of foreign-exchange rates and international financial transactions. This important power includes approval or disapproval of payment restrictions or discriminatory practices.

3. Providing financial resources to member countries to assist them in dealing with payment balances. The framing of the terms on which resources should be made available became one of the most difficult controversies, but also gave rise to some successful elements in the evolution of the Fund.

4. Developing relations with member countries and providing, or associating with them to obtain, information needed by the Fund to carry out its responsibilities. The Fund was given the power to require that certain kinds of information be provided, even if the member regards it as sensitive and has not published it.

The Fund may request member countries to realign their currency and can discourage member governments from pursuing domestic economic policies that are at odds with international exchange-rate stability. On 2 March 1979, the Fund adopted guidelines, implementing conditionality, to which member countries should pay heed when drawing on the resources of the Fund. Due to the 1980s debt crisis and worldwide financial constraints (see Table 1.2),[64] drawing from the Fund has become a more important source of external finance for many debt-overloaded countries, thus enhancing the surveillance role of the Fund.[65]

In April 1986, both the IMF Deputies of the Group of 10, which represents major industrial countries, and the Department of the Intergovernmental Group of 24 on International Monetary Affairs, representing developing countries, agreed that the function of surveillance is central to the Fund's role and should be enhanced, particularly through close scrutiny of the policies of the member countries.[66]

Bretton Woods Agreement

The original drafters of the Bretton Woods Agreement were concerned about the revival of world trade, thus one of the primary objectives was to eliminate restrictions on payments for current-account transactions (Article VI, Section 3). Member countries may impose capital controls when necessary and no consultation or approval by the Fund is required under the framework of the Bretton Woods Agreement. With respect to international capital control, the U.S. Treasury Department was focused on the settlement of international balance on current-account transactions when the Bretton Woods Conference was held in 1944.[67]

The Fund's articles explicitly permit member countries to regulate international capital movements. Section 3 of Article VI provides: "Mem-

Table 1.2

Trade and Current-Account Balances and Foreign-Exchange and Gold Reserves, 1988 (in billions of U.S. dollars)

	Foreign Exchange	Gold	Current Account	Exports	Imports	Trade Balance
Latin America and Caribbean						
Brazil	4.44a	0.83	-1.45a	33.78	16.05	11.16a
Mexico	3.63	0.78	-2.91	20.77	19.59	1.75
Argentina	2.50a	1.33	-1.25	8.94	5.32	4.04
Venezuela	2.21	3.49	-4.69	9.63	12.66	-1.35
Chile	2.32	0.47	-0.81a	7.05	4.73	1.23a
Peru	0.39	0.52	-1.13	2.70	3.08	-0.06
Colombia	2.30	0.34	0.37a	5.04	5.00	1.87a
+Ecuador	0.29	0.13	-0.60	2.19	1.71	0.59
Bolivia	0.08	0.27	-0.20	0.60	0.60	0.06b
Uruguay	0.37	0.80	-0.12a	1.41	1.16	0.11a
Paraguay	0.18	0.009	-0.13	0.51	0.57	-0.07
Guyana	0.006a	n.a.	n.a.	0.24a	n.a.	n.a.
+Costa Rica	0.50	0.006	-0.38a	1.32	1.41	-0.07
+Panama	0.05	n.a.	0.73	0.28	0.75	-0.18
+Honduras	0.04	0.006	-0.27a	0.77a	0.90a	-0.03a
Guatemala	0.15	0.16	-0.44a	1.08a	1.56	-0.36a
Salvador	0.12	0.14	n.a.	0.59a	0.99a	n.a.
+Nicaragua	0.17b	n.a.	n.a.	0.30a	0.93a	n.a.
+Jamaica	0.11	n.a.	-0.09a	0.76	1.45	-0.03a
+Dominican Republic	0.19	0.006	-0.27a	0.89	1.85	-0.84a
Trinidad & Tobago	0.01	0.02	-0.25a	1.39	1.12	0.35a
Africa						
Nigeria	0.48	0.21	-0.56	7.37	3.91	2.42
Algeria	0.67	1.70	-0.14a	8.61a	7.04a	2.41a
+Morocco	0.41	0.21	-0.18a	3.60	4.77	-1.07a
+Tunisia	0.65	0.06	-0.21	2.40	3.69	-1.09
Libya	2.75	1.10	n.a.	n.a.	4.88a	n.a.
+Mauritania	0.33	n.a.	-0.15a	0.43a	0.24a	0.43a
+Senegal	0.007	0.09	n.a.	n.a.	n.a.	n.a.
+Sierra Leone	0.005	n.a.	-0.02a	0.11	0.15	0.03a
+Liberia	0.002	n.a.	-0.19a	0.38	0.31a	-0.42
+Ghana	0.16	0.07	-0.10a	0.98a	0.99a	-0.13a
+Cameroon	0.11	0.009	n.a.	0.81a	1.72a	n.a.
+Togo	0.17	0.003	0.05	n.a.	n.a	-0.02
+Central African Republic	0.07	0.003	-0.08	n.a.	n.a.	-0.07a
+Congo	0.002	0.003	0.22a	n.a.	n.a.	0.46a
+Zaire	0.14	0.14	-0.69	0.98a	0.76a	0.56
+Sudan	0.009	n.a.	0.23	0.50a	0.87a	-0.43a
+Uganda	0.04	n.a.	-0.13	0.42a	0.48a	-0.17a

Table 1.2 (continued)

	Foreign Exchange	Gold	Current Account	Exports	Imports	Trade Balance
Kenya	0.18	0.02	-0.49a	1.07	1.99	-0.71a
+Tanzania	0.06	n.a.	n.a.	0.29a	0.92a	n.a.
+Mauritius	0.33	0.02	-0.08a	0.99	1.26	-0.15
+Madagascar	0.17	n.a.	n.a.	0.33	n.a.	n.a.
+Malawi	0.10	0.003	-0.007a	0.29	0.40	0.10a
+Zambia	0.10	0.003	-0.14a	1.18	0.84	0.26a
+Zimbabwe	0.13	0.12	-0.05a	1.43a	1.21a	0.39
+Botswana	1.65	n.a.	0.009	1.42	1.03	0.59
+South Africa	0.58	1.06	1.27	21.55	18.76	5.22

Middle East

	Foreign Exchange	Gold	Current Account	Exports	Imports	Trade Balance
Israel	2.98	0.31	-0.10a	9.61	15.03	-3.81a
+Egypt	0.94	0.74	-0.32a	5.85	23.30	-4.33a
+Jordan	0.08	0.23	-0.35a	0.93a	2.71a	-1.47a
+Iraq	n.a.	n.a.	n.a.	9.01a	7.42a	n.a.
+Iran	n.a.	n.a.	n.a.	n.a.	9.57	n.a.
Syria	0.16a	0.25	-0.19	1.35	2.22	-0.87a
Saudi Arabia	8.34	1.40	-9.60a	23.20a	20.11a	5.34a
Kuwait	1.02	0.77	4.71	7.16	5.35	1.91
+Lebanon	0.70	2.81	n.a.	0.59a	1.88	n.a.
Bahrain	0.89	0.05	-0.15a	2.27	2.64	-0.01a
United Arab Emirates	3.08	0.25	n.a.	n.a.	8.52	n.a.
Oman	0.75	0.09	-0.85a	2.63	2.20	2.04a
+Yemen (Saana)	0.19	0.01	-0.38	n.a.	n.a.	-0.52
+Turkey	1.71	1.16	1.50	10.19	13.27a	-1.80

Asia and Pacific

	Foreign Exchange	Gold	Current Account	Exports	Imports	Trade Balance
South Korea	9.17	0.10	14.16	60.70	51.81	11.45
Indonesia	3.68	0.95	-1.19	19.47	19.17	5.73
+Philippines	0.71	0.87	-0.37	7.03	8.72	-1.09
Thailand	4.46	0.76	-1.67	15.72	19.54	-2.07
Malaysia	4.56	0.72	1.88	21.11	16.55	5.64
+Bangladesh	0.72	0.02	-0.29	1.29	3.05	-1.44
+Sri Lanka	0.17	0.02	-0.34a	1.48	2.26	-0.47a
+Pakistan	0.29	0.59	-0.56a	4.52	6.59	-2.32a
India	3.08	3.19	n.a.	13.31	19.17	n.a.
Nepal	0.16	0.05	-0.28	0.19	0.69	-0.48
China	13.04	3.87	0.30	47.54	55.28	-1.66a
Taiwan	73.90	10.18	13.54	60.50	49.76	10.74
Singapore	12.53	n.a.	1.66	39.31	43.87	-2.35
Japan	67.26	7.39	79.63	264.86	187.38	94.99
Australia	9.65	2.25	-10.95	33.07	36.07	-1.11
+New Zealand	2.10	0.006	-0.76	8.78	7.34	2.02

Table 1.2 (continued)

	Foreign Exchange	Gold	Current Account	Exports	Imports	Trade Balance
Eastern Europe						
Poland	1.53	0.14	-0.37a	13.96	13.96	-0.79a
Hungary	1.39	0.49	0.12a	9.95	9.95	-0.17a
Yugoslavia	1.71	0.58	1.25a	12.663	12.66	0.08a
Western Europe						
Denmark	7.60	0.50	-1.80	27.78	25.92	2.06
Norway	9.05	0.36	3.68	22.44	23.22	-0.11
Sweden	5.76	1.85	-1.20	49.75	45.63	4.48a
Finland	4.37	0.60	-3.00	21.75	21.13	1.14
Iceland	0.21	0.02	-0.19a	1.42	1.60	-0.05a
Ireland	3.51	0.11	-0.92b	18.72	15.57	2.62a
United Kingdom	30.55	5.79	0.40	145.17	189.34	-36.51
West Germany	39.63	29.02	48.58	323.37	250.57	78.64
Netherlands	10.81	13.40	5.34	103.19	99.44	8.17
Switzerland	17.87	25.39	5.88a	50.62	56.49	-5.53a
Belgium	6.17	10.27	2.92a	92.10	92.29	-0.16a
France	16.62	24.95	-4.08a	96.00	178.85	-9.25a
Spain	26.31	4.28	-0.14a	40.34	60.53	-12.98a
Italy	24.15	20.33	-4.64	128.53	138.59	-0.77
Portugal	3.78	4.90	-0.63	10.64	10.64	-5.14
+Greece	2.62	1.04	-0.96	6.53a	13.17a	-6.07
+Cyprus	0.68	0.14	-0.09a	0.71	0.71	-0.78a
Austria	4.99	6.45	-0.70	31.03	36.22	-5.83
North America						
+United States	12.90	79.83	-134.72	321.60	459.57	-126.29
Canada	10.04	5.23	-9.11	116.84	115.21	8.45

Notes:

n.a.: not available.

+: Countries under serious financial strain or lacking sufficient foreign-exchange and gold reserves.

a: year of 1987.

b: year of 1986.

Gold value based on SDR 304.86 per ounce.

Foreign exchange and current account are based on the SDR; other units are based on the U.S. dollar.

Source: IMF, *International Financial Statistics, 1988 Yearbook*, various country tables.

bers may exercise such controls as are necessary to regulate international capital movements, but no member may exercise these controls in a manner which will restrict payments for current transactions or which will unduly delay transfers of funds in the settlement of commitments."[68] Under Article VI, Section 1(a), moreover, the Fund may request a member "to exercise control to prevent the use of Fund resources for financing a large or sustained capital flow." An executive board decision adopted in 1956 provided:

Subject to the provisions of Article VI, Section 3, (1) members are free to adopt a policy of regulating capital movements, for any reason, due regard being particularly close to the general purpose of the Fund and without prejudice to the provisions of Article VI, Section 1; (2) they may for that purpose, exercise such controls as are necessary, including making such arrangements as may be reasonably needed with other countries, without approval of the Fund.[69]

The articles of the agreement were a compromise of U.S. and British views. In light of postwar balance of payments deficits, the British government was concerned with speculative capital outflows out of deficit countries. Due to the prewar Nazi Germany practice of using controls as a measure of international economic "aggression," the U.S. Treasury regarded the limitation on the use of exchange controls as part of planning for peace within the United Nations system.[70] The agreement then was drafted to permit member countries to use controls on capital movements, but no controls were to be imposed on current-account transactions. Because of the difficulty of defining "current" and "capital" accounts, the articles have empowered the Fund with discretion.

Another significant provision is Article XIV, Section 2, which exempts the obligation of members to make their currencies convertible as defined in Article VIII, Sections 2, 3, and 4. Member countries who avail themselves under this provision may "maintain (and adapt to changing circumstances) restrictions on payments and transfers for current account transactions."[71] Although this provision does not require the prior approval of the Fund,[72] the executive board decided that

in view of Article I (iii) and Article IV, Section 4 (a), members availing themselves of the transitional arrangements must seek the prior approval of the Fund for any introduction or adoption of multiple rates of exchange under Article XIV, Section 2. The Fund would satisfy itself that the introduction of a multiple rate of foreign exchange by a member that had been occupied by an enemy was dictated by "changing circumstances," and that in either case the introduction or adoption of restrictions was consistent with the promotion of exchange stability, the maintenance of orderly exchange arrangements, and the avoidance of competitive exchange alterations.[73]

The impacts of the decision are cited as follows: (1) The Fund's jurisdiction over the introduction or adoption of multiple rates of exchange is affirmed. (2) Member countries can take advantage of the postwar transitional period of Article XIV, Section 2, until the situation improves such that there is no need for restrictive exchange measures. (3) To promote exchange stability is a fundamental consideration in the understanding of Article XIV, Section 2, and Article VIII, Section 3.[74]

Since the distinction between "current" and "capital" accounts is difficult to define, the Fund's role in supervising the practices adopted by members to restrict capital movements has been hampered. In addition, speculative capital could be transferred fairly easily through current-account channels, such as trading payments. Although in recent years the liberalization of international capital movements has been advocated among industrialized countries, it was not originally a primary objective of the original drafters of the Bretton Woods Agreement.

Post–Bretton Woods Agreement Era

In 1971 when the United States closed its "gold window," the Bretton Woods fixed exchange-rate system collapsed.[75] In 1972, one publication of the American Society of International Law stated:

The Bretton Woods drafters substantially overestimated the degree to which it was possible to segregate capital flows from trade flows and thus the degree to which it would be possible to regulate or control the former without impeding the latter. There was a tendency to underestimate the economic benefits from the freedom of international capital movements related to the freedom of trade. On both economic welfare and administrative growth, the presumption contained in the present Fund Articles of Agreement in favor of acting on capital rather than on trade flows when attempting to maintain exchange parity in terms of balance-of-payments difficulties is not appropriate.[76]

On 1 April 1978, the second amendment revised the statement of Article IV as follows: "Section 1 General Obligations of Members: Recognizing that the essential purpose of the international monetary system is to provide a framework that facilitates the exchange of goods, services, and capital among countries." It is argued that this cause appears to favor the freedom of capital movements.[77] However, the Outline of Reform did not recommend any substantial regulatory change or extension of the jurisdiction of the Fund over capital movements.

Although after the Bretton Woods era there has been no significant change in the role of the Fund regarding capital movements, the Fund's surveillance over members' exchange rate stability[78] has caused an indirect impact on international capital movements. In addition, under Article VIII, Section 5, and Rule L-3, member countries are obligated to inform the Fund "in detail" about the imposition, change, and removal of all control measures regarding international capital movements. Thus it is argued that the surveillance power of the Fund under Article IV of the Agreement can be used against capital control measures with far-reaching implications. Thus, the Fund should make financial resources available only to countries relaxing controls.[79] However, as worldwide financial strains persist, it would be difficult to insist that member countries, especially developing countries, which adopt some measures of control over capital movements are not tackling the problem of adjustment, and are thus inconsistent with the articles of the agreement, which require the Fund to "pay due regard to the circumstances of members."[80]

Another important surveillance power of the Fund is to oversee the foreign-exchange-rate policies of the member countries. Under Article IV, Section 3(b), and the Executive Board Decision No. 5392-(77/63), a member country should not use manipulating exchange rates or the international monetary system "to prevent effective balance of payments adjustment or to gain an unfair competitive advantage over other members."[81] Nonetheless, a member country is allowed to intervene in the foreign-exchange market to correct the disruptive short-term movements in the exchange value of its currency provided that other members' interests have been taken into consideration. In order to decide whether a member country is adopting a foreign-exchange-rate policy consistent with the Fund's policy, the Fund needs to examine the member's balance of payments condition, including foreign-exchange-reserves position and external indebtedness as well as other policies which can foster economic growth and stabilize the financial system. However, under the managed (or dirty) floating-exchange-rate system, it is conceded that the Fund's surveillance over the foreign-exchange policies of the member countries is ineffective and needs to be strengthened.[82] In fact, unless a nation is undertaking an adjustment program supported by the Fund, there is hardly any impact of the Fund's surveillance power over the country's national policies, because the value of a national currency is presumably decided by supply and demand in foreign-exchange markets. This represents the conventional justification for resisting the Fund's influence on national foreign-exchange policies under the managed (or dirty) floating-exchange-rate system. Indeed, the most important role of the surveillance power of the Fund is to "help re-establish normal financial relations between debtor countries and their creditors" via multiuser rescheduling arrangements.[83]

ALTERNATIVE NATIONAL STRATEGIES

Controversies over Controls on Capital Movements

The pros and cons of controls on international capital movements have long existed. At the time the Bretton Woods Agreement was drafted in 1944, the postwar weakness of sterling was anticipated and the British view thus favored comprehensive controls on capital transactions:

It is widely held that control of capital movements, both inward and outward, should be a permanent feature of the post-war system at least so far as we [British] are concerned. If control is to be effective, it probably involves the machinery of exchange control for all transactions, even though a general open license is given to all remittances in respect of current trade. but such control will be more difficult to work . . . by unilateral action if movements of capital can be controlled at both ends. The system contemplated should greatly facilitate the restriction of international credit for loan in ways . . . to have a means of distinguishing (a) between movements of floating funds and genuine new investment for the developing world's resources, and (b) between governments which will help to maintain equilibrium from surplus countries to deficit countries and speculative movements or flight out of deficit countries or from one surplus country to another.[84]

Under the Keynes Plan for a Clearing Union, the major concerns on capital movements were "the flight of funds for political reasons or to evade domestic taxation or in anticipation of the owner [of the funds] turning refugee."[85] Thus, it was argued that an International Clearing Union could facilitate the controls of capital movements more effectively.[86] By the same token, those who advocated controls at the time of the second amendment argued:

Countries will cooperate in actions designed to limit disequilibrating capital flows and in arrangements to finance and offset them. Actions that countries might choose to adopt could include . . . the use of administrative controls, including dual exchange market and financial incentives.[87]

These "disequilibrating capital flows" were still perceived mainly as capital flight under the Keynes Plan, thus the controls on international capital movement are logically needed.[88]

By contrast, under the Stabilization Fund plan originally proposed by the United States (or White Plan), freer capital movements were proposed by the United States as persisting surpluses were expected in 1944:

Foreign exchange controls usually constitute an interference with trade and capital flows. . . . Insofar as an international stabilization fund can reduce the necessity for such controls and can prevent the use of such controls where they are not necessary, it will serve to substantially increase foreign trade of nations and encourage the flow of production capital.[89]

The U.S. point of view was stated as follows:

Countries will not use controls over capital transactions for the purpose of maintaining inappropriate exchange rates or, more generally, of avoiding appropriate adjustment action. Insofar as countries use capital controls, they should avoid an exceeding degree of administrative restriction which could damage trade and beneficial capital flows and should not retain controls longer than needed.[90]

Thus, the United States was more concerned about operation of the freer trade system which could have been hampered by capital control.

However, it is difficult to distinguish between capital flows based on speculative considerations and those based on business judgments. Moreover, some economists have suggested that, in some cases where a country is experiencing capital flight, measures such as minimizing trade deficits or offering investment incentives might achieve economic goals more successfully than restricting international capital movement through control measures.[91]

Although the IMF did not give full consideration to the freedom of capital flows, other rules regarding liberalization of capital movements could be seen in other international agreements, such as bilateral agreements, friendship and commercial treaties, as well as multilateral agreements, including the OECD Code of Liberalization of Capital Movements.[92] International capital movements have been gradually liberalized, at least among most of the industrial countries, for the past thirty years. Nevertheless, the individual country's strategies toward it differ, mainly based on the country's own circumstances such as economic development, balance of payments, political stabilization, and ideological tendencies.

By the end of 1985, among 148 member countries of the Fund, 30 countries were free from restrictions on international capital movements (5 countries still adopted import surcharges), 29 countries restricted capital-account transaction payments, and 89 countries had controls over both current- and capital-account transaction payments.[93] Thus most countries, particularly developing countries, prefer to use controls on international capital movements in order to best utilize scarce capital resource and prevent capital flight. Since the world debt crisis broke out in 1982, the adjustment programs under the Fund's auspices have recommended more liberal foreign-exchange regimes for debt-overloaded countries. Nevertheless, it is argued that before fiscal deficits have been controlled, the domestic interest rates should be raised to the same level of international financial market rates, because a low interest rate and liberal monetary growth will sustain domestic inflation, instability, and capital flight. Furthermore, relatively high interest rates abroad will induce capital flight if the controls on foreign exchange are lifted. The case of Argentina in the late 1970s and early 1980s is one example.[94] In light of worldwide financial strains and widespread debt overloads in developing countries, controls on international capital movements probably will prevail in areas outside the industrial countries.

Industrialized Country Strategies

For matured industrial countries (MICs), capital formation is a lesser concern and financial markets are well developed compared with those of less-developed countries (LDCs). The strategies of the MICs can be seen in the Code:

(a) members shall progressively abolish between one another, . . . restrictions on movements of capital to the extent necessary for effective economic cooperation. . . . (e) members shall endeavor to avoid introducing any new exchange restrictions on the movements of capital or the use of non-resident owned funds and shall endeavor to avoid making existing regulations more restrictive.[95]

However, the general liberalization of international capital flows has not been achieved among MICs until recent years. As examples, the Interest Equalization Tax and the Voluntary Foreign Credit Restraint Program were used by the United States during 1963–74;[96] and before 1979, Japan still retained formidable barriers to both capital inflows and outflows. Many types of Japanese financial instruments, for instance, were not open to foreigners.[97]

In general, most MICs are now free-market oriented. The policies of this group are aimed at moderate recovery and noninflationary growth. Domestic price stability, controlling the growth of government spending, reducing fiscal deficits, and fostering the maintenance of market forces compose the main policy objectives. Since the United States plays a key role in international financial activities, the U.S. federal deficit has been "a threat to domestic and international financial stability."[98] Furthermore, in the past several years, notwithstanding growing trade deficits of the United States,[99] the relatively high interest rates in the United States and the uncertainty of the restless world environment have encouraged large capital inflows into the United States.

In addition, a new wave of protectionism could be developing in the United States and other MICs, aimed to correct unfair trade practices, save domestic industries, and foster more employment opportunities; and yet, capital controls among MICs have eased.[100] A recent study by the Fund's research department warned that the adoption of protectionist trade measures by industrial countries could be a serious threat to direct investment, because such measures "discourage new export-oriented investment in those sectors where developing countries have the greatest comparative advantage."[101] However, one can contend that limited protectionist measures could be useful to foster more stable, balanced growth for the MICs, which could help assure a sound market also vital to the development of newly industrializing countries (NICs) and LDCs. Nevertheless, more protectionist measures could be used against some MICs, such as Japan and Germany, and more successful NICs, such as Korea, Hong Kong, and Taiwan, which are enjoying a substantial trade surplus with other MICs (such as the United States). From a practical standpoint, the impacts of modest protectionist measures will not affect foreign direct investment in LDCs as a whole, provided that overall economic recovery can be improved for most nations.

Since 1982, international bank lending to developing countries has declined substantially, and the flows of official development assistance also have maintained a range of 0.35 to 0.40 percent in 1985 compared to 0.5 percent in the 1960s.[102] This trend indicates a more conservative attitude toward international bank lending and official assistance to developing countries.[103] Since the New York meeting of G-5 on 22 September 1985, the coordinated efforts to reduce interest rates have significantly alleviated the interest burden of indebted countries. On 4–6 May 1986 in Tokyo at the 12th annual economic summit, the Tokyo Economic Declaration called for:

closer cooperation among multilateral financial institutions, a resumption of commercial bank lending, flexibility in rescheduling debt, and "appropriate" access to export credits for developing countries urged the adoption by the industrial countries that would foster technological innovation, structure change and expansion of trade and foreign investment.[104]

The joint declaration indicates the possible policy shift for MICs to encourage financial flows to LDCs in order to foster structural change and adjustment, thereby achieving a more stabilized world financial market for recovery and growth.

Newly Industrializing Country and Less-Developed Country Strategies

The NICs and LDCs are traditionally capital-importing countries. The Supplement of the World Economic Outlook of the IMF in 1985 pointed out that those "capital-importing countries . . . are still in relatively early stages of recovery from the disturbances of the past decade, including the [1980s] international debt crisis and the severe global recession."[105] To some degree, this group of countries adopted more restrictive views regarding capital movements to prevent capital flight and used limited resources to foster economic development. These countries tend to encourage direct investment with different degrees of restrictions. For the more successful NICs, foreign-exchange control policies are liberal while the foreign direct investments have become two-way traffic, that is, inward and outward investments. To the indebted LDCs, the restrictions are likely to be severe in part due to the lack of external finances to meet development needs and the overbearing protection of domestic markets.

As observed by one report of the Fund, generally NICs and LDCs have been "pursuing a strategy aimed at reestablishing international credit-worthiness and at restoring the momentum of domestic growth. . . . They have been trying to narrow their current account deficits and to implement domestic policies designed to improve the performance of their economies."[106]

Since 1982, due to the world debt crisis and the lack of external finance, there are some changes in the exchange rates of many developing countries related to the adjustment process. In some developing countries, real exchange rates have been changed in response to domestic growth policies, such as reducing inflation or fostering real output growth. For those countries which use pegged arrangements with strong intervention by authorities, the real exchange rate has changed little since the imposition of controls.[107]

A report of the Group of 24, which represents developing countries, during the meeting of 19–21 August 1985, called for, inter alia, the following changes in the international financial system as part of the strategies of developing countries:[108] (1) An annual allocation of at least 15 billion SDRs (Special Drawing Rights) is warranted, with the allocation linked to the financing needs of developing countries. (2) The debt problem should be alleviated through imaginative solutions involving debt restructuring and relief. (3) Industrial countries should discourage capital outflows from developing countries facing acute capital flight problems, interest rates should more closely reflect the real cost of funds, protectionism in industrial countries should be rolled back, market access should be improved for developing country exports, and official capital flows to developing countries should be expanded. (4) The World Bank should not place undue emphasis on policy-based lending or on linking the quantity of bank assistance to the length of term. (5) Adoption of target zones for the exchange rates of major industrial countries could help achieve the objective of exchange-rate stability and a sustainable pattern for balance of payments. This implied that monetary policy for exchange-rate stability should complement the use of fiscal policy to counter inflationary and deflationary pressures as well as the use of other policy instruments. Intervention, for example, could be used on a meaningful scale, without confining it to lending against the wind, toward the end of exchange-rate stability, as a complementary measure to other policies, and sometimes in coordination with other countries. (6) The high conditionality in the IMF (from the compensatory financing facility) should be reversed, and access should be restored to a 100 percent quota.

In view of the persisting strains in the world economic environment and the fact that the IMF and the World Bank have mobilized financial support for growth-oriented adjustment programs, for these indebted countries, adjustment that takes the form of increases in exports, savings, investments and economic efficiency has been and will be encouraged.[109] Adjustment policies are also necessary to induce a return of flight capital, direct foreign investment, and other non-debt-creating flows.[110]

Generally speaking, most NICs and LDCs should be able to confront the problems of debt overload and development needs. But on the one hand, adequate external financing is crucial to meet their adjustment needs. On the other hand, especially for some Latin American countries, proper policy measures to prevent capital flight out of the country also are essential in order to stabilize their financial systems. How to free capital flows in order to finance domestic needs, while preventing capital flight at the same time, is a major concern for developing countries today. With respect to some NICs which achieved stronger economic development than others, such as Korea, Singapore, and Taiwan, they have spurred their strategies of outward investments and are more likely to liberalize capital movements in the foreseeable future than their counterparts.

Socialist and Communist Country Strategies

A general law of classical Marxist thought is that the accumulation of constant capital by the capitalists will cause an inevitable decline in the average rate of profit and a growing concentration of capital into fewer and fewer hands. Some contemporary neo-Marxists have abandoned the law of declining profit and shifted to advocate that the capitalists will take more surplus out of the developing countries than they invested. Thus, for developing countries, the normal state of their economies is exploitation and stagnation.[111] Furthermore, the theory that capitalists would exploit the benefits of the worker also contributed to a restrictive attitude toward private capital markets.

Another distinguishing feature of socialist and communist countries is a centrally planned economy. The exchange earnings of socialist countries are subject to state controls and distributions. In all members of the Council for Mutual Economic Assistance (CMEA), foreign trade usually is handled through state-run organizations, and government approval is required. Under a few circumstances, foreigners are allowed to hold individual domestic currency which is subject to a special exchange rate.[112]

A common currency, the transferable rouble, has been used among CMEA countries since 1964. The creation of the International Bank for Economic Cooperation (IBEC) laid down the basis for multilateral settlement among CMEA countries. The International Investment Bank (IIB) provides medium- and long-term investment credit under certain conditions. The value of goods exchanged are determined in transferable roubles. The accounting and credit activities of the IBEC and IIB also are recorded in transferable roubles. Since the transferable rouble is only a unit of accounting for bookkeeping and valuation purposes, there is no need to exchange the transferable roubles to the currencies of individual member countries, and vice versa. Only under certain circumstances, such as joint investments or joint enterprises, are transfers from a national currency into transferable roubles required, but again with the purpose of evaluating the final settlements of the transferable roubles.[113]

Although some bilateral treaties between CMEA countries and Western countries were signed to provide trade credit, given the centrally planned economies of the CMEA countries and their fear of exploitation by Western countries, the current- and capital-account transactions between West and East are limited with restrictions.[114]

Standards for National Performance and International Capital Markets

Different countries use varied strategies toward international capital movements. Nonetheless, the international capital market as it exists today has made many national economies more and more interdependent with each other. Whether integration of international capital markets will provide a more suitable global environment for economic growth or not depends on individual national performance to achieve desired results. This section will examine the importance of the integration of international markets under different national levels of performance, as well as the possible impacts of international capital flows to individual countries' economies.

The main argument for the integration of the international capital markets is that international capital can move from where it is plentiful to where it is scarce, thereby maximizing national and world productivity, thus making the efficiency of capital use the most important standard for national performance. It is arguable that international capital outflows from developing countries to avoid taxation, depreciation, and/or controls, etc., does not follow the rule of comparative advantage. But others argue that restrictions on international capital flows will not help the allocation of international capital resources better than on comparative advantage flows.[115]

Under the standard for most efficient use of capital, any country which borrowed from abroad through any international capital flow channels should use the best domestic policies to utilize the capital fully as well as to maximize the returns on this capital. Many argue that a nation with an outward-oriented economy is likely to achieve the best use of foreign borrowing. This view—of the economic scale of production and technology provided by the outward-oriented economies—is consistent with the rule of comparative advantage, whereby the maximum profits of the capital can be obtained. In contrast, a nation with an inward-oriented economy has tended to encourage import-substitution industries and to protect domestic industries by restricting foreign direct investment, raising import tariffs, controlling the prices on primary products, and investing in public sectors, perhaps without sufficient efficiency evaluations, thereby reducing capital/output ratios.[116] In any event, a nation with a free-market-oriented economy can better benefit from international capital market integration than a nation with a heavily controlled economy.

A second standard for national performance on the international capital market is economic growth. Because most of the developing countries depend on primary products for international trade, the inflows of foreign capital enable the less developed countries to purchase capital goods, such as machinery and technology, which cannot be produced domestically but are vital to the economic development of these countries.[117] Even for industrial countries, such as United States, capital inflows have kept the balance of payments from worsening due to the huge trade deficits and government budget deficits. Although an international capital market to finance economic development is desirable, the creditworthiness problems of less-developed countries are impeding their ability to borrow from the international market. Moreover, the problem of debt servicing has further worsened the developing countries' borrowing perspectives.[118] Indeed, the international capital movements under review in this study are dominated by industrial countries, and, unless the developing countries can earn their own creditworthiness, the IMF and the World Bank should continue to be an intermediary between private banks and less-developed countries which face severe financial strains. In recent years, the IMF has borrowed from the international market to help refinance the debt-overloaded developing countries under the so-called "rescue packages" in Mexico, Brazil, Argentina, and Yugoslavia. The World Bank also has participated in syndicate international medium-term bank loans to developing countries.[119]

This standard may be incomplete, however, insofar as it only considers the needs of the international capital market for international capital inflows into developing countries, whereas the disadvantages of capital outflows from developing countries are neglected. This is one of the reasons why the strategies of newly industrializing countries and less-developed countries are focusing on more capital inflows without lifting controls on capital outflows.

A third standard for national performance and international capital market is the marginal efficiency argument. This argument focuses on the structural differences between different financial systems. Because the competitive specialization of financial institutions in the United States is high compared to the European market, the U.S. market has an advantage of marginal efficiency in attracting foreign capital.[120] Some say high U.S. budget deficits and elevated interest rates are important, too. Thus European investments, and recently Asian investments from Japan, Taiwan, and South Korea, are gaining a huge market share in the United States. This argument can only explain the international capital markets in the United States and developed countries, however, and has no direct impact on the allocation of international capital to developing countries.

A fourth standard of national performance on the international capital market is balance of payments adjustment. The inflows of international capital to a specific country can help a nation to achieve the balance of payments by financing its deficits.[121] To improve the balance of payments, a nation may choose to prevent capital outflows or encourage capital inflows or both while there is a deficit on the balance of payments (and vice versa). For instance, the U.S. Interest Equalization Tax and Britain's Capital Issues Committee were cited as examples of attempting to prevent capital drains.

In the developing world, balance of payments adjustment is more complicated. In 1980, the World Bank initiated the program of structural adjustment lending (SAL) to revive the medium-term balance of payments in developing countries while achieving economic growth. The SAL provided by the World Bank combined with the IMF conditionality are offering the developing countries not only external financing but also a program of structural change to revive the developing countries' medium- and long-term balance of payments problems.[122]

It is conceded that external financing is needed for balance of payments adjustment, particularly in the event of a sudden disruptive price hike in commodities, such as the OPEC crises. The inflows of international capital can be used to finance trade and other current-account deficits, thereby restoring the balance of payments. Nevertheless, huge inflows of foreign capital may jeopardize the independence of national monetary policies.[123] Moreover, there is a potential danger of a sudden disruptive stop of capital inflows.[124] In recent years, the huge amount of private bank lending to developing countries also caused other serious concerns such as the risk of destabilizing the international financial system, should major borrowers default; and the encouragement of borrowing to finance deficits rather than adjustments.[125] Thus, the restoration of the balance of payments via external financing is not without costs. Nonetheless, developing countries, particularly non-oil-producing countries, are still suffering under rela- tively high oil prices, weak exports to industrial countries, growing protectionism in industrial countries, and high interest rates. In short, it will be necessary for the IMF and the World Bank to continue playing a key role in reviving the developing countries which are facing balance of payments problems.[126]

Another standard for national performance on the international market is international trade performance. The international trade of a country refers to foreign-exchange earnings and economic growth, at least with respect to export-oriented countries. The important connection between the international trade performance and international capital market lies in the needs for export credits. As aforementioned, officially supported export credits in developing countries reached US$206.7 billion by the end of June 1986. It is argued that export credits have helped the develop- ing countries in restructuring their economies in light of the declining international private bank lending to developing countries. The following characteristics of the export credits have had positive impacts on debt- overloaded countries that have undertaken an adjustment program: (1) The practices that new export credits will be suspended or limited before the debtor countries have fulfilled rescheduling arrangements for previous loans provide a better basis for new debt issuing, that is, a debt-overload situation in the case of bank lending is not likely to happen; (2) export credits only finance the serious import demand of the borrowing countries instead of financing the deficits from balance of payments, thus limiting the possible abuses of funds; and (3) export credits can finance the borrowing countries without interrupting international trade.[127] Since export earnings have been the largest source of foreign exchange for developing countries, especially the export-oriented countries, taking away the worldwide export credits would have worsened the economic growth of those developing countries.

The importance of export credits to developing countries has been perceived as one of external finance. It also is important to industrial countries which accounted for 66 percent of world exports and 69 percent of world imports.[128] This backup system is vital to fostering international trade between industrial and developing countries.

Under these standards for national performance on the international capital markets, industrial countries are able to benefit most from the integration of the international capital markets because the mobility of capital can maximize the returns while the social costs, such as capital flight, are negligible due to the stable financial and political environment. The second group of countries which can benefit from the integration of international capital markets is the newly industrializing countries, particularly the export-oriented countries since their creditworthiness is better than less-developed countries, and the export-promotion policies of the NICs have raised their capital/output ratios as well. For less-developed countries, particularly the debt-overloaded countries, the integration of international capital markets can be helpful in financing their adjustment needs provided that the IMF and World Bank continue to play an intermediary role of smoothing international capital flows. In line with socialist and communist country ideologies, the integration of international capital markets will enhance "capitalism's" capacity of exploitation because national immigration laws will continue to prevent shifts in labor forces from one country to another, and the free flows of capital will only create an opportunity for capitalism to exploit low-wage labor.[129] One conclusion can be drawn that the more mature and free-market oriented a nation's economy is, the more the advantages stemming from the integration of international markets (or allowing for the free movement of international capital) can be appreciated.

NOTES

1. See *IMF Annual Report on Exchange Agreement and Restriction, 1986* (Washington, D.C.: IMF, June 1986), pp. 568–73.
2. The importance of the IMF and the World Bank in financing developing countries

facing balance of payments problems can be seen from the increasing number of loans from the World Bank and high number of standby arrangements with the IMF. The loans approved by the World Bank to developing countries totaled US$13.2 billion in 1986 compared with US$5.8 billion in 1977. The IMF standby arrangements and extended arrangements amount to SDR (Special Drawing Rights) 5.1 billion and the undrawn balance amounted to SDR 2.8 billion at the end of 1986. (See *The World Bank Annual Report 1986*, Washington, D.C.: World Bank, 1986, p. 8; *IMF Survey*, 9 February 1987, p. 46.)

3. Under the General List of International Capital Movements established by the Code of Liberalization of Capital Movements of the OECD, a comprehensive catalogue of nongovernmental operations which involve the transfer of capital from one country to another was drafted. It covers operations which combine transactions between residents of different countries as well as any capital transfers resulting directly therefrom and envisaged thereunder by the parties concerned. The forms of international-capital movements were classified as follows (see *OECD, Code of Liberalization of Capital Movements*, Paris: OECD, 1982 and 1986, Annex D, pp. 99–105):

a. direct investment: Investment for the purpose of establishing lasting economic relations by making particular investments which give the possibility of exercising an effective influence on the management thereof; b. liquidation of direct investment; c. admission of securities to capital markets; d. buying and selling of securities; e. buying and selling of collective investment securities; f. operations in real estate; g. buying and selling of short-term treasury bills and other short-term securities normally dealt in on the money markets; h. credit directly linked with international commercial transactions, or with the rendering of international services; i. financial credits and loans; j. operation of accounts with credit institutions; k. personal capital movements; l. life insurance arising under insurance contract; m. sureties and guaranties; n. physical movement of capital assets; and o. disposal of non-resident-owned blocked funds.

4. Lloyd B. Thomas, Jr., *Money, Banking and Economic Activity*, 2nd ed. (Englewood Cliffs, N.J.: Prentice-Hall, 1982), p. 538.

5. Peter H. Lindert and Charles P. Kindleberger, *International Economics*, 7th ed. (Homewood, Ill.: Richard D. Irwin, 1982), p. 440.

6. See Morris Mendelson, "The Eurobond and Foreign Bond Markets," in *International Finance Handbook*, Vol. I, ed. by Abraham M. George and Ian H. Giddy (New York: John Wiley & Sons, 1983), Section 5.1, pp. 29–31.

7. Table 1.1 indicates the trend of international bond issuances. A disproportional distribution of international bond borrowing between developed countries and developing countries is clearly manifest.

8. Maxwell Watson, Donald Mathieson, Russell Kincaid, and Eliot Kalter, *International Capital Markets, Developments and Prospects*, IMF Occasional Paper No. 43 (Washington, D.C.: IMF, February 1986), pp. 58–72.

9. Straight debt bonds are similar to ordinary debt notes with fixed-yield rates, terms, and specific currency requirements etc. Floating-rate notes are essentially short-term notes with an automatic rollover. Convertible bonds are considered as a straight bond plus an option. Warrants may be convertible into equity or other bonds. Original discount bonds' appreciation in value as maturity approaches is not taxable at all or is taxable only at the capital gains rate until the bonds are liquidated. Currency-hedged bonds are designed to permit intramarket penetration and currency hedging. (For further analysis, see Morris Mendelson, "The Eurobond and Foreign Bond Markets," pp. 29–31.)

10. *Financial Market Trends*, Special Feature: *Prudential Supervision in Banking* (Paris: OECD, August 1986), p. 41.

11. In New York, insurance companies are forbidden to hold more than 1 percent of their assets abroad, plus up to 10 percent in Canadian securities; British insurance companies are prohibited from buying in a stock exchange market which is not approved by the Department of Trade. (Donald Lessard and John Williamson, *Financial Interme- diation Beyond the Debt Crisis* (Washington, D.C.: Institute for International Economics, September 1985), pp. 50–51.

12. In Philippines and Thailand, withholding taxes on dividends are substantial; Brazil and Peru limit foreign investment to a special mutual fund; Mexico allows holding of a few specific stocks in addition to the Mexican Fund; Argentina and Venezuela impose a minimum holding period requirement; Colombia, Kenya, India, Indonesia, Pakistan, and Zimbabwe are essentially closed to foreign investments. (See Lessard and Williamson, *Financial Intermediation*, pp. 58–59.)

13. International bank lending to developing countries picked up to almost US$700 billion during the decade between the early 1970s and the early 1980s and by 1982 resulted in the global debt crisis. In addition to recycling the surpluses of oil exporting countries, the relative ease of the U.S. monetary policy and regulations, prosperous prospects of developing countries (especially the group of newly industrializing coun- tries), as well as the lack of interbank financial data have been said to have caused the 1980s debt crisis. (See John H. Makin, *The Global Debt Crisis, America's Growing Involvement*, New York: Basic Books, 1984). By the end of 1986, the total debt of debt-overloaded countries around the world reached an estimated US$850 billion. For a detailed analysis, see William A. Lovett, *World Trade Rivalry: Trade Equity and Com- peting Industrial Policies* (Lexington, Mass.: Lexington Books, D. C. Heath, 1987),Table 4-1, pp. 138–42.

14. "Developments in International Banking and Capital Markets in 1985," *Bank of England Quarterly Bulletin* 26, no. 1 (March 1986), p. 58.

15. Watson et al., *International Capital Markets*.

16. *Financial Statistics*, Part I: *Financial Statistics Monthly* (Paris: OECD, various issues).

17. Edward E. Leamer and Robert M. Stern, "Problems in the Theory and Empirical Estimation of International Capital Movements," in *International Mobility and Move- ment of Capital, A Conference of Universities—National Bureau Committee for Eco- nomic Research*, ed. by Fritz Machlup, Walter S. Salant, and Lorie Tarshis (New York: National Bureau of Economic Research, 1972), p. 171.

18. *Statistics on External Indebtedness: Bank and Trade-related Non-bank External Claims on International Borrowing Countries and Territories, at End-June 1986, (to- gether with revised data for End-June and End-December 1985)* (Paris and Basel: BIS/OECD, January 1987), Table I.

19. Miranda Xafa, "Export Credits and the Debt Crisis, Recent Trends, Current Policy Issues," *Finance and Development* (Publication of the International Monetary Fund and the World Bank) 24, no. 1 (March 1987), pp. 19–22.

20. Emilio Mayer, *International Lending: Country Risk Analysis* (Reston: Reston Publishing, 1985), p. 132.

21. Lessard and Williamson, *Financial Intermediation*, p. 15.

22. *Transnational Corporations in World Development, Third Survey* (London: Graham & Trotman, United Nations, 1985), Table II-2.

23. Since 1983, the foreign capital inflow into the United States has increased substantially. The total amount of capital inflow was US$84.9 billion in 1983 while the total amount of capital outflow was US$49.8 billion. In 1988, the ratio was 219.3 to 82.1,

with foreign investment in the United States increasing to US$58.4 billion and U.S. investment abroad decreasing to US$17.5 billion (*Survey of Current Business*, various issues, Table 1, Washington, D.C.: U.S. Dept. of Commerce, International Transactions, March 1990).

24. Lessard and Williamson, *Financial Intermediation*, Table 3.

25. Charles Oman, *New Forms of International Investment in Developing Countries* (Paris: OECD, 1984), p. 12. The new forms include licensing agreements, management, services, and production-sharing contracts, as well as subcontracting and turnkey operations.

26. Arthur I. Bloomfield, *Capital Imports and the American Balance of Payments, 1934–39: A Study in Abnormal International Capital Transfers* (Chicago: University of Chicago Press, 1950), p. 30.

27. The confidence problem was proposed by Prof. Kenneth W. Dam and was narrowly defined to foreign reserve adequacy. (See Kenneth W. Dam, *The Rules of the Game: Reform and Evolution in the International Monetary System* (Chicago: University of Chicago Press, 1982), pp. 9–10.

28. Bloomfield, *Capital Imports*, p. 33.

29. The "G-5 Plaza Agreement" (or Communiqué), *IMF Survey* (Washington, D.C.: 7 October 1985), pp. 296–97.

30. "U.S. Capital Flows," *World Financial Markets*, Morgan Guaranty Trust Company of New York, January 1986.

31. Barnaby J. Feder, "Capital Flight Adds to Burden of Debtor Nations," *New York Times*, 9 June 1986, p. 26.

32. Bloomfield, *Capital Imports*, pp. 30–32. See also Marco Fanno, *Normal and Abnormal International Transfers* (St. Paul: University of Minnesota Press, 1939), Chapters ii–iii; Charles P. Kindleberger, *International Short-term Capital Movements*, Reprint (New York: A. M. Kelley, 1965), pp. 155–59; Gottfried von Haberler, *Prosperity and Depression*, Enl. ed. (New York: United Nations, 1946), pp. 436–41, and *The Theory of International Trade with Its Application to Commercial Policy* (New York: Macmillan, 1937), p. 85.

33. Bloomfield, *Capital Imports*, p. 30.

34. Ibid., p. 31.

35. This classification was proposed by Nurkse. He used interest rate and the balance of payments of the capital-exporting and -importing countries as criteria to focus attention on whether a movement of capital increased (disequilibrating) or decreased (equilibrating) international drains on official gold and exchange reserves. (Ragnar Nurkse, *International Currency Experience: Lessons of Interwar Period*, Princeton: League of Nations, 1947; Bloomfield, *Capital Imports*, pp. 32–34.)

36. An "induced" capital movement is one that in passive response to fluctuations in balance of payments as a whole (or in individual constituent items thereof) tends to offset or equalize these fluctuations. An "autonomous" movement, on the other hand, is one that arises independently of the balance of payments and tends to create a disturbance calling for offsetting adjustments. (See Fritz Machlup, *International Trade and the National Income Multiplier*, Philadelphia: Blakiston, 1943, pp. 130–43; Stephen Enke and Virgil Salera, *International Economics*, New York: Prentice-Hall, 1947, pp. 153–55.)

37. OECD, *Controls on International Capital Movements: The Experience with Controls on International Financial Credits, Loans and Deposits* (Paris: OECD, 1982), p. 33.

38. For detailed analysis of these reasons for controls, see Michael R. Rosenberg, "Foreign Exchange Controls: An International Comparison," in *International Finance Handbook*, Vol. I., ed. by Abraham M. George and Ian H. Giddy (New York: John Wiley & Sons, 1983), Section 2.2.

39. Jeff Gerth, "Mexico's Loss of Assets Threatening Debt Plan," *New York Times*, 9 June 1986, p. 26. However, studies have shown that the capital flight from major debt countries has dropped since the onset of the debt crisis in 1982, in part because governments have adopted more restrictive measures to control the transfer of foreign currency by citizens. (Barnaby J. Feder, "Capital Flight Adds to Burden of Debtor Nations," *New York Times*, 9 June 1986, p. 26.)

40. OECD, *Controls on International Capital Movements*, pp. 48–49.

41. For detailed analysis of these costs, see Rosenberg, "Foreign Exchange Controls," Section 2.2.

42. *IMF Survey*, 15 September 1986, p. 280.

43. Up to the end of 1984, twenty-six IMF member countries still applied multiple exchange practices (see "Executive Board Warns of Harmful Effects Arising from Multiple Currency Practices," *IMF Survey*, 24 June 1985).

44. Joseph Gold, *Legal and Institutional Aspects of the International Monetary System: Selected Essays*, ed. by Jane B. Evenson and Jaikeun Oh (Washington, D.C.: IMF, 1979), p. 66.

45. OECD, *Controls on International Capital Movements*, pp. 14–15.

46. Ibid., p. 15.

47. Jozef Swidrowski, *Exchange and Trade Controls, Principle and Procedures of International Economic Transactions and Settlements* (Cambridge: University Printing House, 1975), p. 29.

48. OECD, *Controls on International Capital Movements*, p. 49.

49. See note 41.

50. See note 12 for other examples.

51. Until 1979, the Swiss authorities imposed controls on capital inflows including a ban on the payment of interest deposits by foreigners, imposition of substantial commission charge, and restrictions on inflows of foreign bank notes. (See "Occasional Paper 45 Examines Swiss Role as Financial Center," *IMF Survey*, 30 September 1986, p. 299.)

52. OECD, *Controls on International Capital Movements: The Experience with Controls on International Portfolio Operations in Shares and Bonds* (Paris: OECD, 1980), p. 23.

53. OECD, *Investing in Developing Countries: OECD/DAC Member Countries' Policies and Facilities with Regard to Foreign Direct Investment in Developing Countries*, 5th Rev. ed. (Paris: OECD, November 1982), p. 88.

54. Richard W. Edwards, Jr., *International Monetary Collaboration* (Dobbs Ferry, N.Y.: Transnational Publisher, 1985), p. 452.

55. In South Korea, normally foreign direct investment projects are required to have 50 percent equity from domestic participation. A more detailed discussion will be given in Chapter 5 of this study.

56. See Wilfred L. David, *The IMF Policy Paradigm, The Macroeconomics of Stabilization, Structural Adjustment, and Economic Development* (New York: Praeger, 1985), pp. 13–33.

57. See Mohsin S. Khan and Nadeem Ul Haque, "Capital Flight from Developing Countries: An Examination of the Phenomenon and the Issues It Raises," *Finance and Development*, March 1987, p. 2.

58. OECD, *Investing in Developing Countries*.

59. *New York Times*, 3 January, 1987, p. 30; Taiwan graduated from the GSP on 1 January 1989.

60. Shirley W. Kuo, *The Taiwan Economy in Transition* (Boulder: Westview Press, 1983), pp. 16–17.

61. Dam, *Rules of the Game*, p. 101.

62. Gold, *Legal and Institutional Aspects*, p. 77.

63. Paraphrased from Frank A. Southard, Jr., *The Evolution of the International Fund*, Essays in International Finance, No. 135 (Princeton: Department of Economics, Princeton University, December 1979), p. 2.

64. Table 1.2 indicates the current worldwide financial strains.

65. See Sidney Dell, *On Being Grandmotherly: The Evolution of IMF Conditionality*, Essays in International Finance, No. 144 (Princeton: Department of Economics, Princeton University, 11 October 1981).

66. "Fund Analysts Compare G-10 and G-24 Reports," *IMF Survey*, 30 June 1986, p. 199; "An Essential Review ... Article IV Consultations Provide Framework for Surveillance of Fund Member's Policy," *IMF Survey*, September 1986, p. 206.

67. "U.S. Documentary, Questions and Answers on the International Monetary Fund (June 10, 1944," in J. Keith Horsefield, ed., *The International Monetary Fund, 1945–1965: Twenty Years of International Monetary Cooperation*, Vol. III (Washington, D.C.: IMF, 1969), p. 136.

68. Article XXX(b) of the Agreement provides the following definition of payments for current-account transactions:

Payments for current account transactions means payments which are not for the purpose of transferring capital, and include, without limitation:

a. all payments due in connection with foreign trade, and other current business, including services, normal short term banking and credit facilities;

b. payments due as interest on loans and net income from other investments;

c. payments of moderate amounts for amortization of loans or for the repatriation of direct investments; and

d. moderate remittances for family living expenses.

The Fund may, after consultation with the members concerned, determine whether certain specific transactions are to be considered current account transactions or capital account transactions.

69. Executive Board (E. B.) Decision, No. 5411/56/39.

70. Secretary of the Treasury Morgenthau stated in "Bretton Woods and International Cooperation," *Foreign Affairs* 23 (1945): 185:

The decade of the 1930s was almost unique in the multiplicity of ingenious schemes that were devised by some countries, notably Germany, to exploit their creditors, their customers, and their competitors in their international trade and financial relations. It is necessary only to recall the use of exchange controls, competitive currency depreciations, multiple currency practices, blocked balance, as well as other restrictive and discriminatory devices to find the causes for inadequate recovery in international trade in the decade before the war. These monetary devices were measures of international economic aggression, and they were the logical concomitant of a policy directed toward war and its consequences.

71. Article XIV, Section 2, Exchange Restrictions:

In the post-war transitional period, members may, notwithstanding the provision of any Articles of this Agreement, maintain and adapt to changing circumstances (and, in the case of members whose territories have been occupied by the enemy, introduce where necessary) restrictions on payments and transfers for current international transactions. Members shall, however, have continuous regard in their foreign exchange policies to the purpose of the Fund; and as soon as conditions permit, they shall take all possible measures to develop such commercial and financial arrangements with other members as will facilitate international payments and the maintenance of exchange stability. In particular, members shall withdraw restrictions maintained or improved under this Section as soon as they are satisfied that they will be able, in the absence of such restrictions, to settle their balance of payments in a manner which will not unduly encumber their access to the resources of the Fund.

72. However, an advance notice is required where a member country intends to impose restrictions on payments and transfer for international current-account transactions that are not authorized by Article VI, Section 3, and Article XIV, Section 2. (E. B. Decision, No. 144-152/51, August 1952); Horsefield, *IMF 1945–1965*.

73. E. B. Decision, No. 649 (57/33) (26 June 1957); Selected Decision, 3rd (1965), pp. 84–92. See Horsefield, *IMF 1945–1965*, pp. 262–66; also Gold, *Legal and Institutional Aspects*, p. 394.

74. Gold, *Legal and Institutional Aspects*, pp. 395–96.

75. Dam, *Rules of the Game*, p. 247.

76. *Long-term International Monetary Reform: A Proposal for an Improved International Adjustment Process*, Occasional Paper (Washington, D.C.: American Society of International Law, 1972), pp. 33–34.

77. Edwards, *International Monetary Collaboration*, p. 456.

78. The Fund's surveillance powers as they relate to exchange-rate policies are stated in Article IV, Section 3(b):

The Fund shall exercise firm surveillance over the exchange rate policies of members, and shall adopt specific principles for the guidance of all members with respect to those policies. Each member shall provide the Fund with the information necessary for such surveillance, and when requested by the Fund, shall consult with it on the member's exchange rate policies.

79. See Edwards, *International Monetary Collaboration*, p. 458. The Fund's discretion under Article IV, Section 3 (a), has been further defined by a set of guidelines regarding the conditions to be accepted by member countries to draw on the resources of the Fund. Thus, the member's burden of adjustment has been emphasized by the Fund. (See Dell, *On Being Grandmotherly*.)

80. Article IV, Section 3 (b), as amended on 1 April 1978 provided that the Fund shall adopt principles for the guidance of members and in applying those principles, the Fund shall pay due regard to the circumstances of the members.

81. Principles for the Guidance of Member's Exchange Rate Systems, Executive Board Decision (77/63).

82. One report of the Deputies of the Group of 10 requested full cooperation among member countries and the Fund as well as more candid assessments of national policies and of their domestic and international impacts. "Deputies of the Group of 10 Issue Report on Functioning of the Monetary System," *IMF Survey*, July 1985, pp. 6–8.

83. "Enhanced Surveillance," *IMF Survey*, September 1986, p. 267 (box).

84. Horsefield, *IMF 1945–1965*, Documents, 3:47.

85. Ibid.

86. Ibid.

87. Outline of Reform, paragraph 15, C-20 Documents, pp. 12–13.

88. See Dam, *Rules of the Game*, pp. 80, 88–99, 248.

89. Horsefield, *IMF 1945–1965*, Documents, 3:47. The Canadian plan also suggested:

To abandon as soon as the member country decides that conditions permit, all controls on foreign exchange transactions, other than those required effectively to control capital movements, with other member countries; and not to impose any additional restrictions, except for the purpose of controlling capital, without the approval of the Union (Horsefield, p. 118).

90. Outline of Reform, para. 15, C-20 Documents, p. 12.

91. Edwards, *International Monetary Collaboration*, pp. 458–59.

92. Ibid. The examples listed by Edwards include treaties concerning the reciprocal Encouragement and Protection of Investors between Egypt and the United States, (29 September 1982); the Convention of Establishment between France and the United States (25 November 1959); the treaty establishing the Caribbean community (4 July 1973); the treaty establishing the Latin American Integration Association (12 August 1980).

93. See IMF, *Annual Report on Exchange Agreement and Restriction, 1986* (Washington, D.C.: IMF, 1986), Summary Features of Exchange and Trade System in Member Countries, pp. 568–73.

94. Sebastian Edwards, "Sequencing Economic Liberalization in Developing Countries: The Order of Policy Is An Important, But Difficult, Aspect of Adjustment," *Finance and Development*, March 1987, pp. 26–29.

95. Article I, "General Taking," *OECD, Code of Liberalization of Capital Movements*.

96. However, it is arguable that IET and VFCRP were not restrictive measures to control the capital movements, because (1) there was no direct restriction on capital movement and the United States did not prohibit the use of any foreign direct investment or other forms to transfer the funds, and (2) during the period of 1963–74 capital outflows from the United States were still substantial in spite of those restraints.

97. See Jeffrey A. Frankel, *The Yen/Dollar Agreement: Liberalizing Japanese Capital Markets* (Washington, D.C.: Institute for International Economics, 1984).

98. "World Economic Outlook, 1986," *IMF Survey*, 5 May 1986.

99. The trade deficit of the United States increased from US$25.5 billion in 1980 to the peak of US$160.3 billion in 1987, with a little downturn in 1988 and 1989 with respective trade deficits of US$111.9 billion and US$91.6 billion. (*Survey of Current Business*, March 1990, Table 1; *International Financial Statistics 1989*, Washington, D.C.: IMF, 1989.)

100. "Protectionist Pressures Persist, but Capital Controls Ease in '85," *IMF Survey*, September 1986, pp. 273–77.

101. IMF Research Department, *Foreign Private Investment in Developing Countries*, Occasional Paper Series No. 33 (Washington, D.C.: IMF, January 1985), p. 20.

102. "Managing Director's Address . . . Adjustment Process not Inimical to Growth, Protecting Human Needs," *IMF Survey*, 14 July 1986, pp. 218–22.

103. The so-called Baker plan was proposed by U.S. Treasury Secretary James Baker to provide debt-overloaded countries external finance for adjustment needs (*IMF Survey*, 1 November 1985, p. 349). However, according to the Bank for International Settlements (BIS) report, up to June 1986 there continued to be no sign of any return to spontaneous lending to the problem debtor countries, in spite of Baker's request in October 1985 (*Wall Street Journal*, 27 October 1986, p. 46). See also M. S. Mendelson, "Baker on Trial," *Bankers*, September 1986, pp. 29–33. Mendelson questioned the practical workability of the Baker proposal due to factors such as the economic uncertainty in debt overload developing countries, rescheduling conditions, and U.S. domestic policy considerations—the need to reduce federal budget deficits, trade imbalances, and wariness as a result of former experience with foreign aid.

104. "Leaders of Seven Major Industrial Nations Agree on Coordinations of Economic Policies," *IMF Survey*, 19 May 1986, p. 157.

105. "WEO 1985 . . . How Capital Flows and World Oil Prospects Affect the Outlook for Developing Nations," *IMF Survey*, 13 May 1985, p. 148.

106. "World Economic Outlook, 1986," 5 May 1986, *IMF Survey*, p. 132.

107. "Annual Report of 1985 of the Fund's Executive Board," *IMF Survey*, October 1985, p. 292.

108. Paraphrased from "Report of Group of 24 Calls for Basic Changes in International System," *IMF Survey*, September 1985, pp. 2–12.

109. "Managing Director's Address," *IMF Survey*, pp. 218–22; "Managing Director's Statement . . . Resolution of Developing Countries Debt Problems Demand Rapid Growth, Open Trading System," *IMF Survey*, 28 October 1985, pp. 317–23.

110. K. Burke Dillon, C. Maxwell Watson, G. Russell Kincaid, and Chanpen Puckahtickom, *Recent Developments in External Debt Restructuring*, Occasional Paper No. 40 (Washington, D.C.: IMF, October 1985), p. 9.

111. Franklin R. Root, *International Trade and Investment*, 5th ed. (Cincinnati: South-Western Publishing, 1984), pp. 388–92.

112. See R. W. Edwards, *International Monetary Collaboration*, Chapter 9, for further analysis.

113. Imre Vincze, *The International Payments and Monetary System in the Integration of the Socialist Countries* Copyright (©) 1884 by Kluwer Academic Publishers (Dordrecht, Holland, 1984), pp. 132–36.

114. See R. W. Edwards, *International Monetary Collaboration*, p. 373.

115. Charles P. Kindleberger, "The Pros and Cons of an International Capital Market," in Charles P. Kindleberger, *International Money, A Collection of Essays* (London: George Allen & Unwin, 1985), pp. 226–27.

116. Bela Balassa, "The Adjustment Experience of Developing Economics after 1973," in *IMF Conditionality*, ed. by John Williamson (Washington, D.C.: Institute for International Economics, 1983), pp. 166–68.

117. See Michael DaCosta, *Finance and Development: The Role of International Commercial Banks in the Third World* (Boulder: Westview Press, 1982), pp. 7–25.

118. The debt-servicing problems in developing countries are caused by: (1) ambitious government expenditure programs; (2) investment projects with inadequate returns; (3) the lack of controls or monitors of foreign borrowing; and (4) domestic policies and/or exogenous factors which cause reduced foreign-exchange reserves. (Bahram Nowzad, "Debt of Developing Countries," in *Adjustment and Financing in the Developing World: The Role of the International Monetary Fund*, ed. by Tony Killick (Washington, D.C.: IMF/Overseas Development Institute, 1982), p. 156.

119. Xabier Gorostiaga, *The Role of the International Financial Centres in Underdeveloped Countries*, trans. by Annette Honeywell (New York: St. Martin's Press, 1984), p. 120.

120. Kindleberger, "Pros and Cons," pp. 229–31.

121. Ibid., pp. 233–34.

122. Stanley Please, *The Hobbled Giant, Essay on the World Bank* (Boulder: Westview Press, 1984), pp. 17–41.

123. Kindleberger, "Pros and Cons," pp. 236–39.

124. In mid-1928, as an example, long-term capital suddenly ceased to flow into Germany and other developing countries. (Charles P. Kindleberger, *Keynesianism vs.*

Monetarism, and Other Essays in Financial History (London: George Allen & Unwin, 1985), pp. 316–17.

125. Michael DaCosta, *Finance and Development*, pp. 86–87.

126. Brian Tew, "The Position and Prospects of the International Monetary System in Historical Context," in *Adjustment and Financing in the Developing World*, ed. by Killick.

127. Miranda Xafa, "Export Credits and the Debt Crisis, Recent Trends, Current Policy Issues," *Finance and Development*, March 1987, pp. 19–22.

128. According to a GATT report, the total value of world imports and exports were US$2,000 billion and US$1,922 billion respectively in 1985. ("Manufacturers Assume Growing Role in Trade, Offering Promise for Developing Countries," *IMF Survey*, 15 December 1986).

129. Susan Strange, "Interpretations of a Decade," in *The Political Economy of International Money: In Search of a New Order*, ed. by Loukas Tsoukalis (London: Royal Institute of International Affairs; Beverly Hills: Sage, 1985), pp. 25–35.

2

Introduction to the Economy of Taiwan

Taiwan is an island nation with limited resources. The total area encompasses 35,898 square kilometers (14,000 square miles)—about the size of Massachusetts. The population is 19 million. Over the past thirty-five years, the Taiwan economy has shifted gradually from an agricultural economy to an industrialized economy, with increasing export orientation.[1] By the year of 1987, export earnings reached the peak of 50.7 percent of the GNP.

The outward-oriented policies were introduced in the early 1960s in light of small domestic markets and limited resources in the island. These policy measures also were designed to encourage private entrepreneurs to develop small and medium businesses, and thereby to explore domestic and foreign markets. Thus, foreign trade has been important for the successful economic growth in Taiwan. The per capita value of exports and imports has increased sharply from US$46.1 in 1962 to US$5,571 in 1988, attributed partly to the appreciation of the Taiwan dollar against the U.S. dollar (see Table 2.1).

As one of the newly industrializing countries, Taiwan has achieved a substantial economic growth during the past thirty years. Between 1963 and 1972, the average real growth rate of gross national product (GNP) was over 10.8 percent and was 8.4 percent during the period of 1973 to 1980. Although in 1981 and 1982 the growth rates declined substantially due to the worldwide recession, an 11.7 percent and 11.9 percent growth rate in 1986 and 1987 as the result of export boom in these two years, together brought the GNP to US$144.5 billion by the end of 1989 (see

Table 2.1
Trade as Percentage of Taiwan's GNP (in millions of U.S. dollars)

Year	GNP Amount	GNP Growth Rates	Exports Growth Rates	Exports/ GNP %	Imports Growth Rates	Imports/ GNP %	Total Trade GNP%	Per Capita$
1952	3646	12.0	–	8.1	–	14.2	22.3	37.9
1953	3985	9.3	35.1	8.6	8.7	13.8	22.4	38.7
1954	4367	9.5	-26.9	6.5	20.0	14.9	21.4	35.4
1955	4720	8.1	32.2	8.3	-4.8	12.6	20.9	36.5
1956	4980	5.5	52.9	9.1	52.6	16.0	25.1	33.8
1957	5342	7.4	25.4	9.6	9.6	14.7	24.3	37.9
1958	5693	6.7	5.1	10.3	6.6	16.7	27.0	38.8
1959	6134	7.7	47.8	12.5	50.2	20.8	33.3	37.9
1960	6530	6.3	4.5	11.3	28.2	18.9	30.2	43.4
1961	6977	6.9	30.9	13.8	19.4	20.9	34.7	47.1
1962	7524	7.9	11.8	13.4	-5.6	18.8	32.2	46.1
1963	8230	9.4	52.1	17.8	19.0	18.9	36.7	59.3
1964	9242	12.2	30.7	19.5	18.5	18.7	38.2	71.4
1965	10260	11.1	3.6	18.7	29.9	21.7	40.4	80.9
1966	11184	8.9	19.3	21.2	11.9	20.9	42.1	90.5
1967	12366	10.7	19.5	21.7	29.5	23.7	45.4	110.1
1968	13488	9.2	23.2	23.9	12.1	26.7	50.6	125.6
1969	14701	8.9	33.0	26.3	34.3	27.0	53.3	162.1
1970	16359	11.4	41.2	29.7	25.7	29.7	59.4	207.2
1971	18468	12.9	39.1	35.0	21.0	32.5	67.5	263.2
1972	20926	13.3	45.0	41.8	36.3	35.5	77.3	363.6
1973	23608	12.8	42.8	46.8	43.9	41.5	88.3	536.5
1974	23873	1.2	25.2	43.7	82.9	51.5	95.2	802.8
1975	24893	4.9	-5.7	39.3	-14.7	42.6	81.9	704.2
1976	28251	13.9	53.8	47.3	27.7	45.1	92.4	967.6
1977	31090	10.2	14.6	48.9	12.0	43.9	92.8	1073.1
1978	35413	13.6	31.9	52.4	26.1	45.9	98.3	1399.1
1979	38410	8.2	23.6	53.5	30.5	52.3	105.8	1786.7
1980	41147	7.3	22.9	52.9	33.5	54.1	107.0	2241.5
1981	43493	6.2	16.5	52.2	9.4	50.1	102.3	2438.0
1982	44930	2.9	4.2	50.6	-5.5	45.4	96.0	2245.8
1983	48472	8.0	16.3	54.0	10.6	45.0	99.0	2441.9
1984	53573	9.6	19.8	57.6	7.0	46.1	103.7	2777.2
1985	56108	4.4	1.5	55.4	-7.9	42.6	98.0	2656.0
1986	70190	10.6	23.2	60.4	14.3	39.9	97.4	3307.0
1987	98100	12.4	13.2	60.1	21.5	41.9	100.8	4527.0
1988	106166	6.8	1.4	57.1	27.8	46.5	105.4	5571.0

Notes:
   GNP at 1981 constant prices.
   Exports and imports at current prices.

Source: Republic of China, Executive Yuan, *Taiwan Statistical Data Book, 1989* (Taipei: Council for Economic Planning and Development, Executive Yuan, 1989), various tables.

Figure 2.1
Taiwan Economic Growth Rate, 1953–1989

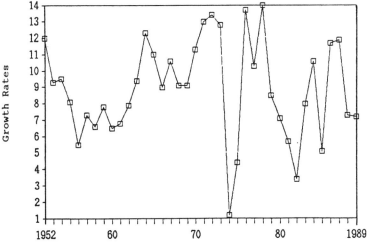

Source: Republic of China, Executive Yuan, *Taiwan Statistical Data Book, 1989* (Taipei: Council for Economic Planning and Development, 1989), Table 1-1b.

Figure 2.1). "Growth with stability" has been a vital factor underlying government policy formation. Except for the years of 1973 and 1974, commodity prices have remained more stable than most other nations in the region.

Two important factors have contributed to Taiwan's successful story— strong flows of foreign direct investment into Taiwan and effective exchange control. A sound balance of payments has been well managed. (See Table 2.2.) The significance of foreign direct investment is with mostly free-market-oriented inflows, and its contribution to the Taiwan economic development is far more important than external finance through international bank lending. Although the government has become more selective toward foreign direct investments and increasingly gives priority to technology-intensive industries, ample other opportunities, such as Western fast-food chain stores, car rental businesses, the insurance industry, etc., are also available for foreign investments. On the other hand, foreign-exchange control has played a key role to prioritize foreign investment and to prevent domestic capital flight and other speculative

Table 2.2
Taiwan's Balance of Payments, 1978–1989 (in millions of U.S. dollars)

	1978	1980	1983	1984	1987	1989
Current Account	1639	913	4412	6976	17999	11384
Merchandise Exports	12602	19575	25028	30185	53298	65874
Merchandise Imports	-10413	-19498	-18760	-20952	-33012	-49672
Trade Balance	2189	77	6268	9233	20286	16202
Other Goods, Services and Income (Inflow)	1824	3052	3804	4550	8179	3546
Other Goods, Services and Income (Outflow)	-2346	-3947	-5617	-6637	-9770	-3860
Balance of Services, Other Goods, Income	-478	-805	-2187	-1913	-1591	-314
Total Balance: (Goods, Services, Income)	1667	818	4455	7146	18695	10884
Direct Investment (net)	110	124	130	131	11	-5347
In Taiwan	213	466	405	559	1223	2241
Abroad	-113	-324	-265	-428	-103	931
Portfolio	20	45	41	-50	-371	-902
Net Errors and Omissions	-125	-363	-352	-408	-305	430
Total Change in Reserves	-61	-1092	-3478	-3939	-31822	243
Foreign Exchange Reserves				15664	76748	73224

Sources: Republic of China, Executive Yuan, *Taiwan Statistical Data Book, 1988* (Taipei: Council for Economic Planning and Development, Executive Yuan, 1988); Republic of China, Taiwan District, *Balance of Payment Statistics* (Taipei: Central Bank of China, various issues); Republic of China, Ministry of Economic Affairs, *Statistics on Overseas Chinese & Foreign Investment, Technical Cooperation, Outward Investment, Outward Technical Cooperation, the Republic of China* (Taipei: Investment Commission, Ministry of Economic Affairs, various years).

flows, thereby assuring scarce capital for domestic use, particularly during the first stage of economic development. However, the exchange control regulations have been liberalized gradually since the late 1970s, and the allowance of direct investment abroad is now playing a more significant role in the economic development.

This part of the study will review Taiwan economic development, foreign direct investment in Taiwan, and the operation of financial systems in Taiwan with a view to providing a background for policy and regulation.

ECONOMIC DEVELOPMENT

Transitional Period, 1945 to the Early 1950s

Between 1895 and 1945, Taiwan was a colony of Japan. Due to the Pacific war, some parts of Taiwan were disrupted and the infrastructure which developed under the Japanese regime was slightly damaged. In 1945, Taiwan was returned to the Republic of China following the unconditional surrender of Japan. During this period of time, Taiwan was able to rehabilitate the nation from the war and reconstruct its economy. One of the major factors to which this stage of development is attributed is the influx of skilled personnel from the Mainland in 1949 (as the Kuomintang lost its civil war with the Communists). This sudden increase in population caused a strain upon resources, thus worsening the external account deficits, mainly resulting from the decline in agricultural exports.[2] But the arrival of mainlanders with more experience in administrative technique and management was valuable in creating stronger administrative and private entrepreneurial conditions underlying economic growth.[3]

The government also paid heed to painful lessons from the Mainland and adopted a series of new policies to curb hyperinflation.[4] In 1949, to restore public confidence and to prevent capital flight, foreign currencies were only allowed to convert partly into exchange settlement certificates (ESCs) and partly in cash.[5]

In light of the shortage of domestic capital, a multiple-exchange-rate system was employed in 1951. The system offered preferential rates to those imported goods for public sectors, plants which also applied to the imports of important raw materials, as well as intermediate inputs for private sectors.[6] The use of multiple exchange rates not only encouraged manufacturing and production but also paved the way for the first phase of development—primary import substitution. The policy aims at this stage were focused on social and economic stabilization.

Primary Import Substitution and the Transition to Export Substitution, 1953–62

The year 1953 was a starting point. The per capita income reached the peak of the prewar period and the government announced the first four-year plan for economic development. The decade from 1953 to 1962 was observed by economists as a period of rapid growth. The average real growth rate of GNP was 7.3 percent per annum.[7]

At this stage the policies were aimed to foster domestic capital formation and encourage the development of import-competing goods industries. Exchange control measures, such as multiple exchange rates, pre-authorization requirements, and import licensing, etc., were used to prevent capital flight and other speculative capital flows. High protective tariffs also helped to curb the demand of foreign goods and prevent a drain on scarce foreign-exchange resources. Under these policy considerations, a moderate inflation rate and overvalued domestic currency[8] could be seen as the result. Moreover, over half of total industrial production was produced initially by state-run enterprises. The import-substitution policy provided a basis for the gradual development of private entrepreneurs in light industries.[9]

A successful land reform program was conducted as early as 1951 when the Rent Reduction Act was promulgated. In 1953, the Land-to-the-Tiller Enforcement Act was introduced. These two legislations accompanied by public land lease-to-own policies provided more incentives for agricultural production and helped transfer capital from many private land owners to industrial production. As a result, during 1952–63, agricultural production increased 59.5 percent and private industrial production quintupled.[10]

In 1960, the Nineteen-Point Reform was announced to liberalize previous exchange controls and international trade as well as encourage production. This gave more leeway for market forces and paved the way for export-oriented policies.[11] During the 1960s, domestic currency also was depreciated against the U.S. dollar from NT\$5 to NT\$40 per U.S. dollar.[12] Following the declaration of Nineteen-Point Reform, the Taiwan Sugar Company, a top export-earning company, then sold its ESCs below the market price and incorporated the official basic exchange rates, thereby stabilizing exchange rates. After the lift of multiple exchange rates in 1961, the exchange rates then stabilized through the early 1980s.[13] Other measures such as a tax rebate system for exports, reduction of import licensing categories, preferential interest rates for exports, and outright export subsidies, etc., were implemented. These reforms allowed Taiwan to utilize foreign resources (raw material and capital) and domestic labor to create a new phase of stronger economic development.

Primary Export Substitution and Gradual Exhaustion of the Labor Surplus, 1963–72

The period from 1963 to 1972 was the most rapid and steady economic growth period with 10.8 percent annual growth rate of GNP.[14] The first export processing zone operated in 1965 to facilitate exporting industries, and the entrepreneurs were able to utilize the ample labor force to compete in international markets. During this period of time, the infrastructure ground was sufficient to support export-oriented industries. Other measures such as bond factories and export finance also began to facilitate exports. The stabilized environment attracted foreign investors who then significantly contributed to the successful economic development.[15]

The shift of industrial structure from domestic raw-material-based industries, such as sugar, to imported raw-material-based industries, such as textiles, leather, and wood production, was evident. The share of industrial products in exports rose to 83.3 percent in 1972, compared with 41.1 percent in 1963.[16] The international trade of Taiwan suffered deficits from 1952 through 1970, except for a marginal surplus in 1964, but capital inflows more than offset these deficits. In 1971, Taiwan began to enjoy a trade surplus with other countries as a whole, with 1974 and 1975 being exceptions due to the OPEC crisis and worldwide recession. Meanwhile, the predominant role of agricultural products was being gradually replaced by industrial products. By the end of the decade, the labor market was tightening up due to the boom of labor-intensive industries.[17] A slogan that "agriculture supports industry, industry fosters agriculture" signified an effort to achieve an even development of agriculture and industry. For instance, the Forestry Research Institution, the Agriculture Experiment Station, and the Food Industry Research and Development Organization were set up to strengthen the linkage between agricultural and nonagricultural sectors.[18] In the late 1960s, a so-called second land reform was introduced through land consolidation and mechanization to solve the problem of labor scarcity. And a gradual shift from labor-intensive industries to labor-saving industries also began to be instituted.

Secondary Export Substitution and the Oil Crises, 1973–84

The first OPEC oil crisis emerged in 1973 and was a shock to the Taiwan economy due to its nature as a small outward-oriented economy and a shortage of natural energy resources. The trade deficits in 1974 reached US$1.3 billion, the largest ever, and the inflation rate was near 47.5 percent, compared to 8.1 percent in 1973. There were several factors considered as the cause of inflation in 1974: (1) the huge trade surplus in 1973 increased by 37.9 percent the money supply; (2) the shortage of domestic energy supply; and (3) the collapse of Bretton Woods and the pegged exchange-rate system in 1973.[19]

In the beginning, the government absorbed most of the shock by subsidizing the state-run China Petroleum Company and other state-run enterprises to control the price of basic needs. In 1973, the government tried to curb inflation by restricting credits, introducing energy conservation measures, and by stronger import restrictions on raw materials and petroleum. In January 1974, the Economic Stabilization Program was devised to cool the economy more effectively. The measures then used included one-time large increases in the controlled prices of petroleum products, electricity, transportation fees, freight costs, etc., thereby reflecting the actual cost of manufacturing.[20] By September 1974, the credits offered by financial institutions began to ease and prices had stabilized, but economic recession remained. The Ten Great Projects which were undertaken then stimulated domestic demand and created more employment.[21] These fiscal incentives gave more momentum for private enterprises. As worldwide recoveries were seen in 1976, the Taiwan economy began to pick up pace with exports, and industrial production grew rapidly. After the booming year of 1978, the second OPEC crisis caused economic growth to slow down again mainly due to worldwide recession and stagnation in the early 1980s. In 1982, economic growth declined to a low point of 3.3 percent.[22]

Since July 1983 brought oil price cuts and the apparent recovery of the U.S. economy, the Taiwan economy itself began to grow more rapidly with export expansion. At the same time the industrial structure shifted from labor-intensive industries to technology- and capital-intensive industries.[23] The machinery manufacturing, optical industry, and information and electronic industries, as well as other more sophisticated industries, evolved as the chosen strategic industries to replace traditional labor-intensive production. In 1984 electronic products were the number-one exports instead of textiles. A slogan of "growth with stabilization" was created to reflect the cautious attitude of government toward international challenges and competition.

Internationalization and Liberalization, 1985 and Onward

There are several factors which have caused the internationalization and liberalization the Taiwan economy. First, to sustain economic growth, internationalization and liberalization have further expanded foreign markets and secured supplies of raw materials. Secondly, as the trade surplus accumulated beginning in the 1970s, outward foreign direct investment began to grow in the early 1980s. During 1989, for instance, approved outward foreign direct investment reached the peak of US$93 billion.[24] Thus, a more internationalized and liberalized environment is necessary to cope with the exigence of a rapidly developing economy. Third, the status of Hong Kong after 1997 remains uncertain, and Taiwan may eventually be able to replace its international role of finance and trade. Fourth, in light of Communist China's attempts to isolate Taiwan economically and politically, the development of substantial economic and business ties with other nations would be a way to combat such threats.[25]

Under the Ninth Taiwan Economic Mid-term Development Plan, 1986–2000 (in Chinese), the fundamental economic development guidelines are as follows: (1) liberalization: to give more leeway for market force functions, to reduce unnecessary administrative intervention, to provide fair competition for industries, to enhance the efficiency of resources, and to strengthen economic structures; (2) internationalization: to expand the space of economic activities, to open domestic and foreign markets, to stimulate domestic and foreign competition, to enhance international economic, technological, and cultural exchange in order to foster substantial foreign relationships with other nations; and (3) systematization: to amend and perfect economic and social regulations, to maintain social harmony, and to improve the national interest and welfare of the people. The most recent policy changes and their impacts will be discussed in Chapter 4.

FOREIGN DIRECT INVESTMENT

Two of the most striking features of the Taiwan economic miracle were relatively free inflows of foreign direct investments combined with effective regulations to prevent capital flight. Among other modest channels of capital flows, the Taiwan stock market has only a twenty-nine-year history, and the listed Taiwan stocks only amounted to US$1 billion up to December 1984. However, substantial upward movements occurred thereafter. At the end of 1989, there were 181 listed companies with capital

amounting to US$16.9 billion. Foreign borrowing went up to 6.7 billion
(by 1986), and the external debt service ratio remained low at only
6.5 percent. During 1974–86, the international bond issuance amounted
to only US$380.4 million, of which US$70.4 million was foreign bond
issues.[26] Foreign direct investment, however, has been the major capital
inflow which contributed significantly to the development of the Taiwan
economy. The total amount of foreign direct investment (including overseas Chinese) from 1952 to 1986 reached US$10.9 billion. This section
will review the inflow of foreign direct investment in Taiwan and its
impacts on Taiwan economic development.

Historical Review

During the 1950s due to the shortage of capital, domestic and external,
U.S. aid played a key role to finance most of the early public investment
in Taiwan.[27] The difficulty of capital formation comes from two aspects:
postwar reconstruction and the need for large military expenditures.[28]
Although in 1954 and 1955 the statutes for Investment by Foreign Nationals and the revised statutes for Investment for Overseas Chinese were
enacted, foreign investors were still hesitant to invest and the government
attitude toward foreign investment was rather conservative. The main
issues then considered by the government were: (1) the repatriation of
foreign invested capital and earnings which would have an adverse impact
on the stabilization of the domestic capital market; and (2) the risk of
foreign control of domestic industries.[29] Meanwhile, foreign investors
were reluctant to invest in a small domestic-market-oriented economy and
the country risk was relatively high during the 1950s. In the early 1960s,
with a more stabilized outlook, policy changes, and better economic
performance, foreign direct investment began to take place on a larger
scale and gradually fill the gap left by the cessation of U.S. aid.[30]

The measures then used to encourage foreign investment included a
five-year exemption from corporation income tax for new investors, or
acceleration of asset depreciation; a maximum of 25 percent of corporation
income tax after the five-year tax holiday; exemption or deferment of
payment of custom duties on imported machinery and equipment; exemption or reduction on stamp and business taxes for export transactions; and
acquisition of plant sites in government-designated industrial land.

In 1965, the Kaohsiung Export Processing Zone was set up to foster
exports for domestic and foreign direct investment. The Nantz and
Taichung Export Processing Zones were set up in 1969. The government

provided the so-called "one-step service" in the export processing zones and simplified investment application in order to induce foreign investors.

The stock exchange market began to operate in February 1961, which provided a channel for individual corporations to attract domestic capital. However, until the early 1980s, the stock market played a role of little importance to foreign investments due to restrictive regulations and limited venture capital. At the beginning, there were only 18 companies with a total registered capital of US$135 million. In 1985, the Ministry of Finance proposed a package that allowed multinational investors in the United States, Japan, and European countries to invest directly in the Taiwan stock market. In addition, foreign investors could buy stock listed in the Taiwan stock market via special permission from the Ministry of Finance. For instance, the government approved a special joint venture project which allowed Nissan Motor Company of Japan to purchase 25 percent of the shares belonging to Yue Loong Motor Company, the largest auto manufacturer in Taiwan in July 1985. This was the first time the Taiwan stock market accepted direct investment from a foreign company based overseas.[31] Thereafter, Australia BTR Nylex Corporation was given permission to purchase stocks issued by three listed firms in Taiwan—China General Plastics Corporation, Asia Polymu Corporation, and Tai Ta Chemical Company. The share prices of the transactions was set by open market operation.[32] Beginning in January 1988, foreign nationals have been allowed to participate in securities transactions through investment in local securities firms and the management of these firms.

In 1980, the Hsinchu Science-based Industrial Park joined the line to attract foreign direct investment with a view to foster the development of high-technology industries. Under the operation plan of the Park, there are three stages to be accomplished. In the first stage, only foreign investors were invited to operate in the following fields: (1) first-line industries; (2) innovation design and improvement of production techniques; (3) information generation for direct use in the industrial sector to design new products; and (4) development of alternative raw materials for key sectors in the Taiwan economy. In the second stage, local firms were included to set up joint ventures with foreign enterprises or through technology transfers and cooperation with local scientific institutions. At the third stage, local firms are also invited to set up operations in the Park thereby transferring the technology and skill learned from foreign investments. The experience of the cooperative relationships between local and foreign firms will assure a successful transfer.[33] The law which regulates foreign direct investment in the Park has been amended to extend a ten-year tax holiday to offer extra advantages to firms engaged in high technology.

By the end of 1988, sixty plants had operated in the Park. The industries to which foreign direct investment went included computers, electronics, telecommunications, precision instruments, and special materials. The major companies include Wang Laboratories (CRT monitors), RCA (integrated circuits), and Texas Instruments (assorted electronic components).

During the period 1952–89, total foreign direct investment reached US$10.9 billion, of which 84 percent or US$9.2 billion was invested by foreign investors (not including overseas Chinese). As divided into industries, electronic products accounted for US$2.7 billion, chemical industries accounted for US$1.7 billion, and service industries accounted for US$1.4 billion.[34] Of this foreign direct investment, 28 percent (US$3,070 million) came from the United States, 27 percent (or US$2,983 million) from Japan, and 15 percent (or US$1,62.3 million) from European countries (see Table 2.3 and Table 2.4).

The first large foreign direct investment was made by Mobil Oil of the United States in 1960. The company invested in the chemical industry to produce urea material as a supplier of the Taiwan Fertilizer Company. The

Table 2.3
Foreign Direct Investment in Approval, by Industry, 1952–1989 (in millions of U.S. dollars)

	Oversea Chinese	Foreign Private	Total
Total	1733.7	9216.2	10949.9
Agriculture and Forestry	4.4	1.2	5.6
Food & beverage processing	63.3	435.4	498.7
Electronics & electric products	73.8	2684.5	2758.3
Fishery and livestock	22.5	8.1	30.5
Textiles	105.0	110.1	215.1
Garment & Footwear	28.6	37.1	65.7
Leather & Fur Products	23.0	31.1	54.1
Lumber & Bamboo Products	9.8	10.6	20.3
Paper & paper products	42.5	44.5	87.0
Chemicals	65.6	1643.4	1709.0
Plastic & Rubber Products	45.5	322.1	367.6
Nonmetallic mineral products	292.3	194.0	486.4
Basic Metals & Metal products	51.4	709.2	760.5
Machinery, equipment & Instruments	48.3	880.8	929.1
Transportations	78.2	200.0	278.1
Constructions	94.5	43.1	137.4
Banking and Insurance	160.5	370.0	530.5
Foreign Trade	52.6	346.7	401.3
Service	423.7	1017.4	1441.7
Others	36.1	123.6	159.7

Note: The total amount of foreign direct investments in 1989 doubled the total amount in 1986 with a rapid growth in service and technology-intensive industries.

Source: Statistics on Overseas Chinese & Foreign Investment, Technical Cooperation, Outward Investment, Outward Technical Cooperation, the Republic of China (Taipei: Investment Commission, Ministry of Economic Affairs, various issues).

Table 2.4
Foreign Direct Investment in Approval, by Investing Region, for Selected Years, 1952–1989 (in millions of U.S. dollars)

	1952	1960	1965	1970	1974	1978	1980	1983	1986	1989	Total
Overseas Chinese											
Hong Kong	1.1	0.7	2.7	8.3	21.7	16.5	17.9	10.1	12.1	71.8	556.0
Japan	–	0.2	0.3	1.2	3.0	4.5	3.1	0.8	2.3	27.0	127.2
Others	–	0.2	3.5	20.2	55.9	55.2	201.6	18.2	50.4	78.5	1050.5
Private Foreigners											
U.S.	–	14.0	31.1	67.8	38.8	69.8	110.1	93.3	138.4	343.0	2717.9
Japan	–	0.3	2.1	28.5	38.9	50.3	86.1	196.8	253.6	640.6	2855.7
Europe	–	–	–	10.7	14.8	4.5	14.4	20.7	139.6	531.4	1662.3
Others	–	–	1.9	2.1	16.3	12.1	32.8	64.6	174.0	426.0	1980.6
Total	1.1	15.5	41.6	138.9	189.4	212.9	466.0	404.5	770.4	2418.3	10949.9

Sources: Republic of China, Executive Yuan, *Taiwan Statistical Data Book, 1988* (Taipei: Council for Economic Planning and Development, Executive Yuan, 1988), Tables 12-2, 12-3, and 12-4; *Statistics on Overseas Chinese & Foreign Investment, Technical Cooperation, Outward Investment, Outward Technical Cooperation, the Republic of China* (Taipei: Investment Commission, Ministry of Economic Affairs, various issues).

second largest investment was Gulf's investment in lubrication oil and PVC pipes. In 1965, a polyethylene plant was set up by National Distillers & Chemical Corporation. These early-stage investments were concentrated on chemical industries and were mainly to supply domestic demands, that is, import-substitution type. From 1966 onward, the policy changed from import substitution to export substitution, and the domestic economy became more suited for export industries—export processing zones, the science-based industrial park requiring a more skillful and well-educated labor force as well as a developed infrastructure, etc., all allowed export-oriented industries to expand. In 1967, the Hong Kong riots and wage hikes caused U.S. electronic firms to shift some operations to Taiwan. General Instruments was the leading one to invest in Taiwan, followed by TRW and Admiral two years later. Up to the end of the 1970s, RCA, Texas Instruments, Motorola, Ampex, Arvin Industries, Bendix, Corning Glass, Zenith, etc., were also setting up branch plants in Taiwan.[35]

In a survey conducted by the government in the late 1960s, the reasons for foreign direct investment were weighted as follows: political stability measured at 2091 was first, followed by low wage rates (849), attractive domestic market (701), well-educated and dependable labor (625), low cost of energy fuel (577), assurance of a five-year tax holiday (551), and other tax incentives (202).[36] A substantial amount of earnings was reinvested to expand the existing scale of operations thus indicating that the environment for foreign direct investment was rather satisfied.

Another significant facet of foreign direct investment in Taiwan could be seen in that after 1960, with policy changes—reduction of trade licensing catalogs, dismantling multiple-exchange-rate systems, providing fiscal and financial incentives to encourage domestic and foreign direct investment—foreign direct investment began to flow in faster (see Figure 2.2). Given this fact compared to more restrictive policies previously, such as trade barriers to protect domestic industries, the implication is manifest that "a liberal economic policy is a crucial element in enticing foreign direct investment."[37]

According to one study, foreign direct investments related to the exports of Taiwan are significant. However, country origins of foreign direct investment matter less for export destination than the combination of industry characteristics and timeliness. As recently as 1981, manufactured foreign direct investment exports to developed countries declined to 66 percent of the total, and exports to developing countries increased substantially.[38]

In recent years, foreign direct investment has become two-way traffic: inward and outward. For example, a joint venture in Indonesia to explore

Figure 2.2
Growing Foreign Direct Investments in Taiwan, 1953–1989

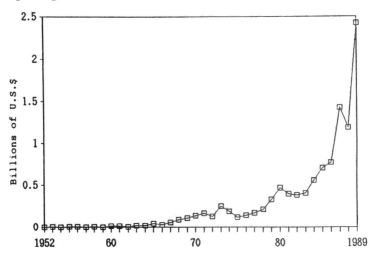

Source: Republic of China, Executive Yuan, *Taiwan Statistical Data Book, 1990* (Taipei:
    Council for Economic Planning and Development, 1990), Table 13-2.

petroleum and a fertilizer plant in Saudi Arabia have been set up. Tatung, the largest electronic manufacturer, set up a branch plant in the United States to manufacture TV sets and electronic fans and also acquired a British television plant. In Southeast Asia, other manufacturers of garment, footwear, and electronic products have set up their own subsidiaries. The outward direct investments are motivated partly to take advantage of low labor costs, partly to avoid import restriction, and partly to penetrate foreign markets.[39] Foreign outward direct investment in the first five months of 1990 reached US$45.6 billion, rising almost six times from the same period of 1989. The question of whether this is the sign of capital drain in the future has caused concern among the authorities.[40]

Foreign Direct Investment and Economic Development

Foreign direct investment has played a significant role in the nation's economic development. First of all, foreign direct investments not only provide external finance for domestic industries, but also bring in know-how (even high technology in recent years), marketing and distribution channels, management skills, etc., thus increasing the competition ability of exporting industries.[41] As an OECD study indicated, foreign direct investments in developing countries "provide a unique combination of long-term finance, technology, training, know-how, managerial expertise and marketing experience." And the returns of foreign direct investment depend on the operational profits of the invested venture rather than fixed interest as in the case of foreign loan debt service.[42]

As noted in the first stage of economic development, foreign direct investments were crucial as an external finance for domestic investments. As the economy turned around to a substantial growth after 1970, the contribution of foreign direct investments to capital formation was only half of the percentage as in the 1950s and 1960s.[43] The role of foreign direct investment, more importantly, emphasized the timing and quality which influence the performance of a domestic economy.[44]

International trade is vital to Taiwan's economic growth. The share of exports and imports in the GNP has remained around 48 to 50 percent since the early 1980s. The average annual growth rate in exports during 1961–70 was 22 percent and 19.2 percent during 1971–81. From 1981 to 1985, however, the export average annual growth rate was reduced to 7.6 percent. Although, as shown in one study,[45] while the contribution of foreign direct investment only accounted for 28.62 and 23.02 percent of exports in 1976 and 1984 respectively, foreign direct investments accounted for 39 percent of the exports in 1987. Thus, foreign direct investments played a significant role in export expansion, because these foreign investors—mainly multinational corporations—have provided a world-wide marketing channel and distribution network for domestic exports.[46]

Secondarily, foreign direct investments provided more employment opportunities. As a 1975 survey shows,[47] the average size of foreign firms was relatively larger than domestic firms. However, in 1987 only 9.1 percent of the total labor force in the manufacturing sector (2,624,358 employees) was in foreign direct investment firms. Another impact of foreign investment was that it contributed to the shift of the labor force from agricultural employment to the industrial and service sectors.[48]

Another important impact of foreign direct investment was the "linking process," and it has been a major concern of domestic industries and the authorities. In this aspect, linkage included the purchase of local materials, new manufacturing and marketing techniques, and training the local labor force, as well as management. Regarding the purchase of local inputs, the impact of foreign direct investment was not so significant, particularly for those 100 percent foreign-owned enterprises. Because these firms were relatively insulated from domestic markets and tended to shop for raw material or intermediate materials abroad, these firms which located in export processing zones were cited as the extreme case. During 1966–74, less than 14 percent of the machinery, equipment, and raw materials were supplied by local producers.[49] Of course, other factors such as shortage of natural resources, the lack of domestic supplies, and the lack of manufacturing techniques to meet the required standards all caused the purchase of domestic inputs at a lower level than expected. However, during 1975–87, the overall purchase of local raw material or semiproducts ranged from 47.28 percent to 50.81 percent. Considering these foreign direct investments were located in export processing zones where the tendency to retain 100 percent foreign ownership was high and where the operations were aimed at exporting, the local purchase ratio was lower than the overall average. Overseas Chinese investments also had a relatively high tendency to use local inputs because the industries in which they invested were textiles and construction. If a foreign firm had been set up for a long period of time, it was likely to use local inputs.[50] In the Taiwan Singer Sewing Machine Company, for instance, the local purchase ratio of the company was zero in 1964 but jumped to 50 percent in 1965. In 1969, except for the needle for the regular straight-style model, all the parts were made locally.[51]

An exceptional case of purchasing local inputs was that of the electronic industries. Since most of the newly established foreign direct investments in the electronic industry were attracted by the cheap and high quality of local supplies, most of them engaged intensively in domestic market purchases even at the establishment stage.[52] The rule of local content had been a crucial element for the authorities to approve foreign direct investment. Under the Categories and Criteria of Productive Enterprises Eligible for Encouragement, as amended on 26 November 1986, among the 468 products which are eligible for encouragement, 44 (9.4%) products are subject to local content requirements. The local content requirements ranged from 30 percent to 80 percent, and most of the local content requirements are applied in the electrical and electronic and well as automobile industries because these two industries are designated by the government as strategic industries and because the quantity and quality of local supplies are adequate to meet the demand. For example, in mid-1985, the authorities called off a project proposed by Toyota partly because both parties could not reach an agreement concerning the issue of local content.[53]

In 1987, foreign direct investment purchase of domestic machinery and equipment rose to a high level of 42.2 percent. This indicates that domestic industry has been more or less successful in upgrading as well as that research and development undertaken with foreign direct investment may have the effect of transferring technical advances to domestic industries.

Some Case Examples

The evolution of foreign direct investment in Taiwan and its impacts on Taiwanese economic development could be illustrated in the following three case examples which represent foreign direct investment in three different stages of economic development.[54]

The first case is a German company which invested NT$18 million to set up a garment manufacturing plant in Taoyuan in 1965. The site of the plant was located in Kui Shan industrial district. The plant began to operate in 1969. In the starting stage all the outputs were exported. In 1970, the firm began to sell in the domestic market (40 percent of the production) with the approval of the government.

Under the Statute of Encouraging Investment, a five-year tax holiday was granted. In 1974, the firm invested another NT$8 million to expand the production lines. However, no extra tax incentive was given because there was no new technology or machinery added.

During the first three years of operation, the company was running at a loss. In 1974, the company began to repatriate retained earnings back to Germany as cash dividends (NT$1.5 billion) and stock dividends (NT$8 million). As requested by the government, the company offered 15 percent of its new stock to the employees, but no employee was interested.

The parent company had sent a general manager, a control manager, and a production manager to oversee the operation and quality control. By 1979, all of the German staff was replaced by native Chinese. An expatriate superintendent visited the plant twice a year for quality-control purposes.

A branch office also was set up for handling business such as purchases, sales, finance, insurance, etc. The company employed 100 white-collar workers and 450 female sewers. In 1979, the monthly wages for female sewers were ranging from NT$3,600 to 5,000 depending on efficiency. A two-month bonus for all employees and other fringe benefits amounted to 3 percent of the base payment.

All of the raw materials were imported from Japan, Hong Kong, and Europe. A bonded warehouse provided duty-free import materials for export production.

The second case was a Japanese firm which invested US$600,000 in 1973 to manufacture electronic items in the Taichung Export Processing Zone. The motivation of the investment was the inexpensive labor force. The investment was increased to US$1 million in 1979.

All of the products were exported—half of the DC micromotors were exported to Japan, with Hong Kong, South Korea, and some European countries following thereafter. The United States bought 70 percent of the digital radio conductors. The exports were growing rapidly from NT$4 million per month in 1974 to NT$25 million per month in 1978.

A five-year tax holiday also was granted and a lower corporate income tax (20 percent) was applied because the industry was specifically encouraged by the government. About 90 percent of the raw materials were imported from Japan and the rest were locally made. The labor force employed from 150 persons in 1973 to 600 persons in early 1979. Among them, 90 percent were female workers for the assembly lines. In 1979, the average monthly wages for workers were ranging from NT$3,800 to NT$8,000 depending on the experience and skill needed. For the regular office personnel, monthly wages were NT$8,500 and NT$25,000 for the general manager. Under the company's own policy, 0.5 percent of its annual export earnings were set up for various fringe benefits.

Since there were similar industries in the export processing zone, the labor force could be shifted easily from one firm to another without technical problems. A labor force shortage occurred in 1979. An improved working atmosphere and more fringe benefits were needed to attract more workers.

A Japanese engineer came to the plant every month to inspect the quality of product. The president of the company visited the plant every year. A local general manager took responsibility for the operation and reported to the parent company.

A third firm is an American pharmaceutical firm. The plant was set up in Chungli Industrial Zone in 1977. The sum invested was NT$15.2 million. The plant started operation in September 1978 and the products were exported to Southeast Asian countries, South Korea, and Japan.

It was an automated plant and only ten employees were hired to oversee the production and quality. Another fifteen employees were responsible for all business administration. Monthly average wages were ranging from NT$6,000 to NT$8,500 for workers and NT$8,000 to NT$20,000 for local office staff. An additional one-month payment was given as a bonus to all employees. The general manager was sent from the parent company and a specialist from the parent company visited the plant three times a year.

All production equipment, except 90 percent of its quality-control system, was locally made, and the raw materials were shipped to Taiwan via air. The reasons for choosing the Chungli Industrial Zone to set up a branch plant were the convenient location, pollution-free environment, and the good water quality. Another project has been undertaken by the company to invest another US$6.5 million at the same site to supply domestic and foreign markets.

Some conclusions can be derived from these case examples: (1) The reinvestment of these three companies indicates that the foreign investors are satisfied with the investment climate in Taiwan and that the operations are profitable; (2) comparing these companies as they set up at different stages of Taiwan economic development, it is evident that the tendency of foreign direct investment in Taiwan has been changing from labor-intensive to technology-intensive industries; (3) the export-oriented foreign direct investment also provides for domestic market needs; (4) labor shortages, especially unskilled labor, are foreseeable in the mid-term; and (5) the forward and backward linkage of foreign direct investment to domestic industries should continue to be reinforced.

THE CENTRAL BANK AND THE FINANCIAL SYSTEM

Roles of the Central Bank of China and the Ministry of Finance

The Central Bank of China was established in 1924. The Statute for the Establishment of the Central Bank of China was enacted in 1928. The Central Bank of China Act was promulgated in 1935 and amended on 8 November 1979. After the government relocated in Taiwan in 1949, the Central Bank authorized the Bank of Taiwan to issue domestic currency and execute other functions. Until July 1961, the Central Bank resumed all the operations stipulated by the Act except for the issuance of domestic currency—the New Taiwan dollar.

Under the Central Bank of China Act, the Central Bank acts as a government bank and administrative agency. The Central Bank dealt with governmental agencies, banking and financial institutions, including domestic and foreign except otherwise provided by the law. The roles of the Central Bank were summarized as follows:

1. To formulate interest-rate policy, to determine various deposit reserves, to act as lender of last resort by providing accommodations to the banking industry, to engage in open market operations, and to carry out national debt management.

2. To hold the international monetary reserves and to undertake the overall management of foreign exchange. In considering the balance of payments situation, the Central Bank may take measures to adjust the demand for and supply of foreign exchange with a view of maintaining an orderly foreign exchange market.

3. To issue national currency as the legal tender for all payments within the territory of the Republic; the Central Bank whenever necessary, can authorize other government banks to issue regional currency on its behalf identical to the national currency. The assets and liabilities pertaining to the issuance of the regional currency shall be for

the account of the Central Bank. Thus, the assets and liabilities of the New Taiwan dollar, a regional currency issued by the Bank of Taiwan since 15 June 1949, belong to the account of the Central Bank.

4. To act as the fiscal agency of the government and as the custodian of all government funds. The Central Bank handles Treasury receivables and disbursements, as well as the floatation and redemption of government bonds and Treasury bills.

5. To supervise all banking institutions in the territory and to undertake the examination of their operations. The Central Bank's examination operation may be performed in conjunction with the bank examination program specially designed by the Ministry of Finance.

6. To collect economic indicators, compile financial statistics, and conduct monetary and economic research with the purpose to coordinate the formation of monetary policies and their subsequent implementations.

The roles of the Central Bank consist of monetary-policy-oriented supervisor confined to overseeing banking institutions. In contrast, the Ministry of Finance plays the role of administrative supervisor covering all the financial institutions, including banks, insurance companies, and security exchange markets. The roles of the Ministry of Finance are summarized as follows:

1. To establish a sound money market, to adjust money demand and supply, and to support the development of the agricultural, industrial, and commercial sectors.

2. To design, draft, and review banking and financial laws and regulations as well as supervise their enforcement.

3. To establish a sound banking system as well as to manage and supervise banks and specific financial systems.

4. To strengthen the security market and to regulate the demand and supply of capital matching the needs of enterprises.

5. To establish a sound management of stock transactions so as to safeguard investors' interests.

6. To supervise the practices of certified public accountants, and to establish a sound accounting system.

Other functions of the Ministry of Finance include domestic and international bond issuance, tax policy incentives, and other fiscal policy formulation. The coordination between the Central Bank and the Ministry of Finance assures a sound system for supervising the operation of the financial network in Taiwan.

Financial Institutions

There are various financial institutions in Taiwan as shown in Table 2.5.[55] Most of the banks are managed by the state, which means that the

Table 2.5
Financial Institutions in Taiwan, End of May 1990

Name	Number of Institutions
Banks (16 local and 40 foreign banks)	56
Medium and Small Business Banks	8
Trust and Investment Companies	8
Credit Cooperatives	74
Credit Department of Farms' Associations	285
Credit Department of Fishery Associations	23
Bills Finance Companies	3
Life Insurance Companies	13
Property and Casualty Insurance Companies	19
Securities Finance Companies	1
Total	490

Source: *Financial Statistics Monthly, Taiwan District, The Republic of China* (Taipei: Economic Research Department, Central Bank of China, 1990).

government owns over half of the total stock. Under the banking law, all the banks must be organized as corporations. In Taiwan, the banking industry is dominated by state-run banks. Total bank assets reached US$64 billion by the end of 1983, of which the state-run banks accounted for 78.9 percent, the privately owned banks accounted for 13.6 percent, while the foreign banks accounted for only 7.5 percent (see Table 2.6).[56] There are some exceptions where the government owns less than half of the stocks. The International Commercial Bank of China, for instance, organized as a privately owned bank on 18 December 1971, aims partly to avoid any potential Communist China takeover. Other examples, such as the Overseas Chinese Commercial Bank and the United World Chinese Commercial Bank, established primarily by overseas Chinese, are safeguarded under the Encouragement of Investment by Overseas Chinese Act.

Under the banking law, the commercial banks may engage in such business as acceptance of deposits, commercial lending, foreign-exchange operations (with the authorization of the Central Bank), issuance of letter of credits (L/C), financial bond issuances, stock and other investments, etc. The government could designate a specific bank (normally an industrial one) to provide certain services for specific purposes. The operations of designated banks differ from other commercial banks and are important in financing of the Taiwan economic developments. The following banks are the major designated banks in Taiwan.

The Bank of Communications

Under the Bank of Communications Act, as amended in January 1979, the bank has been designated as a development bank. The functions of the bank, in addition to the normal commercial bank business operations, are to provide medium- and long-term development credit to industries, to initiate investment in development projects, and to offer financial consultation to industries.

The Farmers Bank of China

The bank has been designated to provide financing for farming and fishing industries, to finance the reconstruction of the rural economy, and to provide for upgrading agricultural products.

The Export-Import Bank of China

The bank was created on 11 January 1977 with a view toward facilitating foreign trade. Its primary function is to provide medium- and long-term credit for exports of capital goods and imports of industrial materials or intermediate goods for export use. An ancillary function is to provide export insurance service. Although foreign-exchange operations, to the extent related to export earnings and import payments, are available, there are no regular commercial bank operations in the Export-Import Bank.

The Land Bank of Taiwan

The bank has been designated to provide land and agricultural financing. The main functions of the Land Bank are to provide agricultural credit, to promote agricultural development, to handle housing programs, and to assist the government in carrying out its land and agricultural policies. The bank also issues land bonds and is in charge of the management of public lands and industrial districts or parks.

The Cooperative Bank of Taiwan

The bank operates as "a central banking institution" for the cooperatives in Taiwan. The bank provides guidelines to refinance cooperatives and to the credit department of the Farmers' Association. Under the authorization of the Central Bank, the Cooperative Bank also examines the operations

Table 2.6

Assets and Deposits in Taiwan's Banks at End of 1983 (in millions of New Taiwan dollars)

	Name of the Bank	Assets	Deposits
1	Direct General of Postal Savings System	347,684	316,084
2	Bank of Taiwan	329,395	278,226
3	Cooperative Bank of Taiwan	234,901	218,476
4	Land Bank of Taiwan	183,448	183,448
5	First Commercial Bank	175,563	138,394
6	Hua Nan Commercial Bank	158,518	139,805
7	Chang Hwa Commercial Bank	152,592	126,642
8	Bank of Communications	119,586	72,466
9	Medium and Small Business Bank of Taiwan	92,718	84,020
10	International Commercial Bank of China (Private)	90,112	38,651
11	City Bank of Taipei	82,621	66,429
12	Farmers' Bank of China	70,931	52,816
13	Central Trust of China	44,919	16,842
14	Kathy Investment and Trust Company (Private)	42,324	36,147
15	Citibank N.A. (U.S.)	35,416	3,867
16	China Investment and Trust Company (Private)		
17	United Overseas Chinese Bank (Private)	28,418	18,122
18	Overseas Chinese Commercial Bank (Private)	24,812	13,885
19	Medium and Small Business Bank of Taipei (Private)	24,676	21,716
20	Asian Investment and Trust Company (Private)		
21	Bank of America, NA & SA (U.S.)	17,543	3,054
22	Chase Manhattan Bank (U.S.)	16,727	518
23	Medium and Small Business Bank of Taichung (Private)	16,012	14,385
24	Continental Bank (U.S.)	14,617	1,137
25	First National Bank of Boston (U.S.)	11,892	512
26	Medium and Small Business Bank of Hsinchu (Private)	11,247	10,035
27	Chung Lain Investment and Trust Company (Private)	10,507	9,050
28	City Bank of Kaohsiung	9,963	6,640
29	Export-Import Bank of China	9,127	-
30	Overseas Chinese Investment and Trust Company (Private)	8,246	7,255
31	Chemical Bank (U.S.)	8,062	327
32	Taiwan First Investment and Trust Company (Private)	7,825	6,407
33	Shanghai Commercial and Savings Bank (Private)	7,665	4,689
34	Land Investment and Trust Company of Taiwan	7,528	1,622
35	Seattle-First National Bank (U.S.)	7,451	396
36	Medium and Small Business Bank of Tainan (Private)	7,321	6,288
37	Irving Trust Company (U.S)	7,286	484
38	Morgan Guaranty Trust Company of New York (U.S.)	7,206	479
39	European Asia Bank (Germany)	6,941	429
40	Bangkok Bank Limited (Thailand)	6,848	326
41	Medium and Small Business Bank of Kaohsiung (Private)	6,746	5,622
42	Lloyds Bank International Ltd., London (U.K.)	6,528	225
43	American Express International Banking Corporation (U.S.)	5,740	190
44	Banker's Trust Company, New York (U.S.)	5,510	96

Table 2.6 (continued)

45	Banque Paribas, Paris (France)	5,149	270
46	China Development Corporation	4,144	-
47	First Interstate Bank of California, Los Angeles (U.S.)	4,002	239
48	Societe Generale (France)	3,589	277
49	Manufacturers Hanover Trust Company (U.S.)	3,373	76
50	Metropolitan Bank and Trust Company of Manila (Philippines)	3,339	340
51	Rainier National Bank, Seattle (U.S.)	3,059	135
52	Dai-Ichi Kungyo Bank Ltd. (Japan)	2,802	1,274
53	Grindlays Bank Ltd., London (U.K.)	2,720	154
54	Hollandsche Bank - Uhire N.V. (Netherlands)	1,851	239
55	The Development Bank of Singapore	1,839	362
56	Medium and Small Business Bank of Hualian (Private)	1,688	1,017
57	Toronto -Dominion Bank (Canada)	1,322	70
58	International Bank of Singapore	1,295	27
59	Medium and Small Business Bank of Taitung (Private)	1,174	939
60	Amsterdam Rotterdam Bank, N.V. (Netherlands)	175	0
61	The Royal Bank of Canada	137	3

Source: *Statistical Operation Data of Financial Institutions in Taiwan, Republic of China, 1983* (in Chinese) (Taipei: Financial Examination Department, Central Bank of China, 1983), Table 1-4.

of the credit cooperatives and the credit departments of both the Farmers' Association and the Fishery Association.

Other Banks

In addition to these designated banks, the Bank of Taiwan, the City Bank of Taipei, and the City Bank of Kaoshiung also act as fiscal agents of local government. The Bank of Taiwan had been operating as the central bank before the Central Bank of China resumed operation in 1961. The domestic currency has been issued by the Bank of Taiwan and is regarded as the national currency. The oldest bank funded in Taiwan is the First Commercial Bank. The First Commercial Bank represents a merger of the Savings Bank of Taiwan (funded in 1890), the Chai-I Bank (funded in 1904), the Commercial and Industrial Bank of Taiwan (funded in 1910), and Hsi-Kao Bank (funded in 1915).

Another group of banks in Taiwan are the foreign banks. There were forty-one foreign banks operating in Taiwan at the end of November 1990. The operations of foreign banks are more restricted than the local banks due to a policy to prevent cutthroat competition in the small domestic market and to close the loophole of the exchange controls. Following the operation of offshore banking centers in Taiwan and the policy of internationalizing the banking industry, the restrictions will be liberalized. The foreign banks in Taiwan are authorized to engage in the following activities: (1) accepting checking accounts, demand deposits, and time deposits no longer than six months with a maximum ceiling in total not exceeding NT$2 billion of 12.5 times its working capital; (2) handling inward and outward remittances; (3) issuing and advising letters of credit; (4) discounting and purchasing export bills; (5) accepting foreign currency and foreign-exchange proceeds deposits; (6) extending loans; (7) offering guarantees for payment in foreign currency; and (8) conducting import and export credit investigation.[57]

Trust and Investment Companies

The second type of financial institution in Taiwan is the trust and investment company. The trust and investment companies are governed under the Rules Governing Trust and Investment Companies and Criteria Governing the Establishment of Trust and Investment Companies as promulgated on 30 November 1970. Since then, eight trust and investment companies have been set up.

The trust and investment companies provide financial services to private industries as follows: (1) medium- and long-term loans; (2) equity investment; (3) guarantees; and (4) trust and agency service for individuals and corporate and institutional customers. The trust and investment companies are allowed only to accept trust funds rather than take deposits, with the case of the China Development Corporation being an exception. These companies also engage in investments with government bonds, treasury bills, company debentures, financial debentures, and stocks and in extending long-term loans to productive enterprises.

Credit Cooperatives

A group of unique but widely used financial institutions in Taiwan are credit cooperatives. The origins of credit cooperatives stem from Japanese agriculture cooperatives. In 1949, the government decided to merge the rural credit cooperatives into Farmers' Associations, resulting in the credit departments of the Farmers' Associations. Since then two categories of credit cooperatives were divided into the credit cooperatives of the cities and the credit departments of Farmers' Associations (or Fishery Associations) of the villages and towns.

The credit cooperatives are regional financial institutions and deal with their members only. The functions of the credit cooperatives are as follows: (1) accepting deposits; (2) extending loans; (3) buying discounted financial notes; (4) accepting bills of sale; (5) collecting and disbursing funds; and (6) financing other operations licensed by the government. Since the scandal of the Cathy Cooperative broke out in 1985, the second largest conglomerate in credit cooperatives and trust companies, the government has tightened the supervision of credit cooperatives as well as trust and investment companies.[58]

The functions of the credit departments of the Farmers' Associations and Fishery Associations are as follows: (1) to accept deposits from and extend loans to their members; (2) to handle remittances; and (3) to serve as agents for the Bank of Taiwan, the Cooperative Bank of Taiwan, the Farmers Bank, the Central Bank, and other government agencies in the supply of agricultural credit. They also function as a township treasury with the power to collect receivables and manage the treasury account. The credit departments also offer short-term credit to the same Farmers' Associations or Fishery Associations.

In Taiwan, commercial banks usually require collateral to secure the repayment of loans. To cope with the needs of the small borrowers, the collateral requirement is relaxed in the case of the credit departments' loans to their members. Another feature of the credit department loans is that they always accompany a package of services, such as the upgrading of agricultural techniques and agricultural machine purchases, in order to assure the proper use of the funds and foster agricultural development. The Farmers' Association also provides borrowers with marketing channels for agricultural products to sustain quality and a reasonable price, thereby assuring the security of outstanding loans and improving the farmer's living standard.

General Directorate of Postal Remittance and Saving System

Another unique financial institution in Taiwan is the General Directorate of Postal Remittance and Saving System. Because this system is operated through the widely spread postal offices, its long business hours and location convenience have attracted huge amounts of savings deposits which are in turn redeposited with the Bank of Communications, the Farmers' Bank of China, the Land Bank of Taiwan, and the Medium and Small Business Bank of Taiwan upon the approval of the Central Bank. As shown in Table 2.6, the System is the leading financial institution in Taiwan in terms of assets and deposits. Nonetheless, it only engages in savings deposits and domestic remittance operations.

Bill Finance Companies

One of the newly developed financial institutions is the bill finance company. The Regulation Governing the Dealers of Short-term Negotiable Instruments was enacted on 23 January 1976. Under this regulation, the functions of the bill finance companies include: (1) the buying and selling of short-term government securities, bank acceptances, negotiable certificates of deposits, commercial papers, and other negotiable instruments as approved by the Ministry of Finance; (2) acting as guarantor, endorser, broker, and underwriter of commercial papers; (3) providing financial consulting service to business firms; and (4) acting as broker for called loans among the financial institutions.[59] There are three bill finance companies: the Chung-Shing Bills Finance Corporation, the International Bills Finance Corporation, and the Chung-Hua Bills Finance Corporation, all of which conduct money-market operations in Taiwan.

Security Finance Companies

The only security finance company, Fuh-Hua Security Finance Company, was funded on 21 April 1980. The security finance company engages in the following activities: (1) providing loans for the purchases of securities; (2) providing accommodation for sales of securities; and (3) serving as custodian of securities. Previously, the loans for the purchases of securities were provided by the Bank of Communications, the Bank of Taiwan, and the Land Bank of Taiwan, and the operations have now been transferred to the security finance company.

Insurance Companies

Other financial institutions, such as insurance companies, have not engaged in money-market operations extensively due to the relatively new and yet-to-be-developed money market. Before 1961, all insurance companies in Taiwan were run by the state. In 1961, the government lifted the ban on the organization of privately owned insurance companies. In addition to the regular insurance business, most privately owned insurance companies engaged in the direct investment of productive enterprises.

Up to April 1990, the assets of life insurance companies (including foreign insurance companies) as well as property and casualty insurance companies totaled US$12.7 and US$1.7 billion respectively. In comparison to the other financial institutions' US$284.2 billion in consolidated assets for the same period of time,[60] the Taiwan insurance market has not yet developed to its potential. The following factors have impeded the development of the insurance market: (1) the opening of new insurance companies was banned by the government to discourage excessive competition and to maintain financial stability; (2) privately owned insurance companies were not allowed to underwrite policies for state-run enterprises; and (3) an insurance company which initiated new insurance services was entitled to enjoy two to three years' exclusive rights to such new services. In late 1986 and early 1987, three American insurance companies were allowed to operate a full-range of programs in Taiwan.

The opening of the insurance market for foreign investors resulted partly due to the lack of competition in the domestic market and partly due to the pressure stemming from the United States. To cope with the coming competition, the government decided to lift all the aforementioned restrictions in order to provide an equal basis for competition.[61]

The insurance companies, like other financial institutions, are subject to the supervision of the Ministry of Finance and the examination of the Central Bank. A government reinsurance fund was set up in 1956 under the management of the Central Trust of China and supervised by the Ministry of Finance. The Central Reinsurance Corporation was organized on 31 October 1968 under the direct supervision of the Ministry of Finance. The Central Reinsurance Corporation engages in the following businesses: (1) 5 percent direct participation in each policy issued by domestic insurance companies; (2) reinsurance on all first surplus on the home market, second surplus and facultative business, and business ceded by foreign insurers (for reinsurer); and (3) verification of statistics and research of the insurance industry.

State Operation

Most of the financial institutions in Taiwan were state run due to the shortage of capital in the 1950s and the policy of the government to control the financial sectors thereby fostering economic development more effectively. Due to the relatively new financial institutions in the field of the bills finance companies and the security finance company, it is not surprising that the operations of the money market and the stock market lagged behind economic growth. These state-run financial institutions provided a basis for restoring public confidence, thereby encouraging savings and capital accumulation in the 1950s and 1960s. Furthermore, the financial institutions, as the nature of state enterprises, have effectively executed exchange controls and other government policies, thus contributing to stabilized economic growth in the past three decades. However, under the two guidelines of internationalization and liberalization, reforms are inevitable for coping with domestic and foreign market needs as such issues as foreign-reserve influx and foreign-exchange-rate realignment more and more dominate domestic policies where proper answers are being contemplated.

The Operation of the Financial System

As noted above, most of the financial institutions in Taiwan are state-run enterprises subject to the supervision of the Central Bank as well as the

Ministry of Finance. The operations of the financial system are policy-oriented. However, a review of the operations of these financial institutions will provide a better understanding of the framework of their regulatory background.[62]

Interest-Rate Determination

The determination of interest rates has been an important monetary policy tool. Before 1961, the interest rates were set by the Central Bank. In July 1961, the Central Bank began setting the upper limits for the interest rates of various deposits as well as the range of interest rates on various loans. Beginning in 1981, under the Essential Points of the Interest Rate Adjustment for Banks, as promulgated on 7 December 1981, the interest rates of deposits and loans were determined by the Bank Association, an organization designed to coordinate the business of the banks. The range of interest rates was determined subject to the approval of the Central Bank. Since the liberalization of interest rates to cope with economic development needs was announced by the government, the Central Bank has continued to support the interest rates which were proposed by the Bank Association. The interest rates applied to local and foreign banks equally. In practice, foreign banks are gaining more leeway in deciding their interest rates because the domestic banks are bound by the policy guidelines of the government in handling commercial loans and deposits. This also helps explain the inefficiency of domestic bank operations.

Adequate Reserve Requirements

Under the current Central Bank of China Act, the adequate-reserve levels are set up as follows: (1) checking deposit, 15–40 percent; (2) demand deposit, 10–35 percent; (3) savings deposit, 5–20 percent; and (4) time deposit, 7–25 percent. Due to the profound impacts of the ratio changes, the Central Bank is not likely to change the reserve levels very often.[63] The financial institutions with reserve assets in the Central Bank are required to settle their reserve requirements every week or ten days. The Central Bank could refinance their reserve deficits within the limited ceiling (35 percent of reserve requirements). A penalty charge is imposed if the borrowing exceeds the limited ceiling.

The Discount Window Operation

Under the Central Bank Act of China, in order to fulfill the role of the lender of last resort, the Central Bank may discount real bills and banker's acceptances. In addition, the Central Bank may make loans against collateral in the bills, or against government bonds and obligations. According to the Ruling Guidelines of the Rediscount and Temporary Advance to Financial Institutions, the following financial instruments are eligible for discounted financing: (1) industrial and commercial bills with maturity not exceeding 90 days; and (2) agricultural bills with maturity not exceeding 180 days. Temporary financing requires the period of borrowing less than 90 days and the provision of collateral.

Bank Lending

The attitude of bank lending toward private enterprises or industries in Taiwan has been conservative and collateral requirements have been commonly used, that is, mortgages. These lending practices have been adopted mainly due to the lack of a credit-checking system and a sound money market. How to tap the pool of savings and channel into productive enterprises, particularly the small and medium businesses, has been widely discussed in recent years.

Commercial Bank Lending. In a survey conducted by the Bank of Taiwan in 1981, one-third of the funding of businesses was provided by the owners, two-thirds of the funding was provided by creditors—of which half of the external financing was from the so-called unorganized money market (black market), and the rest from commercial bank lending.[64] This indicated the inefficiency of the commercial banks in Taiwan in tapping the large pool of savings[65] and channeling the savings into the private enterprises. The risk of the black market is high and as a result, the interest rates also are higher than official interest rates. Since the black-market banking activities are not regulated by the authorities and not under the supervision of the Central Bank and the Ministry of Finance, further data is not available to evaluate the adverse impacts on the economy. However, the black-market lenders adopted more flexible standards to provide short-term loans on an unsecured basis as well as the use of postdated checks as collateral. Small and medium businesses tended to borrow heavily from the black market due to creditworthiness problems under the commercial banking standard. In contrast, under the survey conducted by the Bank of Taiwan in 1980, private enterprises comprising working capital of more than NT$100 million that depended on borrowing from the black market only accounted for 3.8 percent of the total outside financing. Thus, the banking system provided financing for large enterprises that was much more significant than that to small businesses. To cope with this inefficiency, a plan has been proposed by the Ministry of Finance to legalize small-scale banking services which were dealing in the black market with a view to curbing black-market activities and to providing sound financing to small and medium businesses.[66]

Again, in recent years, the so-called underground investment company which provides high interest rates to attract huge amounts of money to reinvest in the stock and real estate markets has not only disrupted the operation of the financial system but also encouraged the public to join the speculative money game. The operation of underground investment is illegal under banking law which prohibits any individual or company to take deposits without the bank license. More than 100 cases concerning underground investment-company activities have been prosecuted by the general attorney. Investors who parked their money in these underground investment companies suffered losses when the bankruptcy of underground companies occurred during 1989 and early 1990. As when stock prices dropped, the collapse of underground investment companies and securities exchange firms may cause another financial storm in Taiwan.

Other short-term loans to private enterprises include buyer usance and export-promotion loans. The usance loans are granted to finance imports. The banks could refinance the imports by accessing the U.S. money market via the U.S. banks or tapping Eurodollar markets. For the basic commodities, the banks could refinance exports from the fund of the Central Bank. The export-promotion loans are subsidized loans with relatively low interest rates.[67] The Central Bank provides the fund to the banks and the banks grant the loans on export letter-of-credit basis. The export-promotion loans will be paid off when the L/Cs are negotiated by the lending banks. The L/Cs are designated to lending banks for negotiation. The foreign banks have additional US$1 million per day per bank to be granted for preshipment export-promotion loans.

Export-Import Bank Lending. The Eximbank was set up primarily to provide medium- and long-term credit for the export or import of machine or other capital goods which require a longer period of payment (normally more than one year) as distinguished from the export-promotion loans of the commercial banks.

The sources of the fund provided by Eximbank are supported by the government, and also by the issuances and sales of financial bonds in domestic and foreign financial markets. In addition to financing the exports and imports of capital goods, the Eximbank also provides credit lines for selective foreign banks to refinance their customers in purchasing machinery or other capital goods made in Taiwan. Other services of the Eximbank include guaranteeing the exporter's working capital requirements for overseas construction jobs and export insurance.[68]

Development Bank Lending. Under the Bank of Communications Act, the Development Bank shall assist the government in accelerating the economic development of the country by providing financial assistance to and investment incentives in manufacturing, mining, and transportation industries. The Development Bank accepted deposits from the public and tapped various government development funds thereby refinancing the industries. As expected, the lending of the Development Bank is closely related to government policies and has financed the start-up stage of the so-called strategic industries as well as the upgrade of technology level. The Development Bank also invested in venture capital companies and supported big projects as designated by the government, such as the US$200 million joint venture for making Very Large-Scale Integrated (VLSI) semiconductors.

Agricultural Lending. The Agricultural Credit Planning and Coordination Committee was established in July 1970 to oversee the agricultural credit programs, determine interest for agricultural loans, and allocate funds for agricultural credit. In 1972, the Committee announced the Regulation Governing Large-Scale Integrated Farming Operations Loan Program to encourage large-scale joint farm operations (also known as second land reform). The sources of funds came from the Medium- and Long-term Credit Social Fund of the Central Bank and the United Agricultural Credit Fund of the Council for Agricultural Planning and Development. These loans carried relatively lower interest rates to lure the merger of farming fields.[69]

Another important project of agricultural credit was the accelerated Rural Development Loan Program, which was established in January 1973 with the purpose of achieving the balanced development between agricultural and industrial sectors. In October 1975, the Committee provided a package of loan projects including rural infrastructure loans, capital investment loans, and working capital loans. The rural infrastructure loans were restricted to the government agencies and Farmers' Association. The funds came from the Treasury, the Central Bank, Council for Agricultural Planning and Development, agricultural banks, and township Farmers' Associations.

Money-Market Operations

Before 1975, there was no organized money market in Taiwan. Under the Regulation Governing the Dealers of Short-term Negotiable Instruments as promulgated on 5 December 1975, the Bank of Taiwan, International Commercial Bank of China, and the Bank of Communications jointly organized the first bills finance corporation, Chung-Shing Bills Finance Corporation on 20 May 1976, and the International and Chung-

Hua Bills Finance Corporations followed in late 1976 and early 1978. The shareholders of these three corporations included banks, government, and private enterprises.

The money market has been dominated by commercial paper (90 percent of which was issued by the business and industrial enterprises to raise short-term working capital). A guarantee from a financial institution or backing by the bank's line of credit is required to assure the creditworthiness of the issuers. A trade bill also can be traded in the money market under a discount rate. Since a bank credit is not required in the case of trade bills, the trade bill has been a growing instrument of trade in the money market. Other instruments traded in the money market include banker's acceptances, negotiable certified deposits, and treasury bills. Until the early 1980s the bankers' acceptances accounted for less than 5 percent of the market share and were not widely accepted by the commercial community. Most of the negotiable certified deposits were held by commercial banks as a liquid asset and the secondary market trading was sluggish due to the low yield of interest rate. Treasury bills were issued by the government with caution due to the traditional budgetary surplus concept. Recently, the government began to shift from a surplus budget to a deficit budget.[70] The issuance of treasury bonds is the way to tap the idle money of public investment and to ease the increasing money supply caused by the foreign trade surplus. For instance, the government issued US$2.4 billion worth of public bonds in the fiscal year of 1988 to tap money into public investment projects.[71] Whether the treasury bill will be another growing sector in money-market trading remains uncertain because the excessive government tax revenues have reduced the needs for issuing treasury bills and the distribution system of treasury bills has yet to be fully liberalized.

The interest rates in the money market are determined by market forces instead of government fiat. Beginning in January 1978, the Central Bank started an open market operation and the interest rates in the money market became an important indicator for the short-term interest-rate determination. However, the Central Bank plays a key role in the money-market operation. Thus, a policy-oriented interest-rate system is still inevitable.

Foreign-Exchange Market

The current foreign-exchange system became effective on 1 February 1979 when the government adopted a managed floating-exchange-rate system to replace the so-called Foreign Exchange Concentration System. Before the new system was used, the NT dollar was pegged to the U.S. dollar and all foreign exchange earnings had to surrender to the Central

Bank via the appointed banks. Under the old system, the earnings of foreign exchange could cause a sudden increase in the domestic money supply with inflation pressure. Furthermore, the pegged exchange rates could cause overvaluation of the NT dollar and had an adverse impact on the nation's exports. Currently, the exchange operations are more flexible than before, that is, the exchange rates are based on a basket of foreign currencies[72] and the foreign-exchange holders may deposit their foreign exchange in a special, interest-earning deposit account. By doing so, some argue that speculative capital movements are encouraged, especially after the government lifted most of the foreign-exchange controls in July 1987.

The foreign-exchange market is open for all authorized dealers (normally foreign-exchange-appointed banks), and the dealers are obligated to report their transactions immediately to the Foreign-Exchange Center. The foreign-exchange market includes three submarkets: the bank-customer market, interbank market, and Central Bank–appointed bank market. There is no swap transaction in Taiwan because the foreign-exchange control and the money market have yet to be developed. After July 1987 under the new regulations, spot and forward markets became available for major foreign currencies, such as the U.S. dollar, Japanese yen, deutsche mark, French franc, British pound, Hong Kong dollar, and Singapore dollar.[73] However, the forward market was de facto suspended by the designated banks for more than two years' time due to the heavy trading of foreign exchange and the expectation of the appreciation of New Taiwan dollar. Some say the absence of a foreign-exchange forward market may have created unavoidable foreign-exchange losses. However, it is contended that unless the exchange rates can be stabilized, the reopening of the forward market can only provide another casino gamble for speculators.

The following institutions engaged in foreign-exchange operations: appointed foreign-exchange banks, the Foreign-Exchange Trading Center, and the Central Bank of China.

Appointed Foreign-Exchange Banks. Under the banking law, appointed banks are eligible to engage in foreign-exchange operations under the authorization of the Central Bank. Up to the end of 1980, there were thirty-three appointed banks in Taiwan, of which twelve were local banks and the rest foreign.

The Foreign-Exchange Trading Center. The Foreign-Exchange Trading Center was set up to facilitate the transactions between the appointed banks and the Central Bank. Five major commercial banks—Bank of Taiwan, the International Commercial Bank of China, the First Commercial Bank, Chang Hua Commercial Bank, and the Hua Nan Commercial

Bank—organized the Center when the foreign-exchange market began to operate in 1979. These five commercial banks also set the foreign-exchange rates at the beginning of each trading day with the ceiling not exceeding 2.25 percent of the buying and selling rates of the previous business day. Since 15 July 1987, the central spot rate of the NT dollar against the U.S. dollar has been established by the five major authorized foreign-exchange banks on the basis of the weighted average rate of interbank transactions in U.S. dollars on the previous day without the ceiling of 2.25 percent limitation.

The Central Bank of China. The Central Bank plays the role of adjusting the market demand and supply—selling and buying foreign exchange to avoid sudden fluctuations in foreign exchange. The intervention of the Central Bank in the foreign-exchange operation is important to keep a stabilized exchange-rate system and to affect the exports and imports directly.

The operations of the financial institutions in Taiwan are policy-oriented and the market forces have yet to play a more significant role. Since the Cathy Crisis, the government has begun to liberalize the financial system to give more leeway for market forces and to establish a sound money market. However, the money market in Taiwan is relatively small and underdeveloped, thus legalizing the small-scale banking activities of the black market is vital to the further development of the sound money market. Due to the foreign-exchange controls, the financial institutions have played a limited role in fostering economic growth. As the foreign-exchange reserve fluctuates, the appreciation of the NT dollar continues, and the capital account of the nation begins to enjoy a greater surplus than ever before, it is expected that, accompanied by the liberalization of exchange controls, the financial institutions of Taiwan will play an ever-increasing role in fostering economic growth.

NOTES

1. U.S. Department of State, Bureau of Public Affairs, *Background Note: Taiwan* (Washington, D.C.: Government Printing Office, September 1983).

2. See Mo-huan Hsing, "Taiwan Industrialization and Trade Policies," in *Industry and Trade in Some Developing Countries, The Philippines, and Taiwan* (London: Oxford University Press/OECD, 1971), pp. 149–51.

3. Gustav Ranis, "Industrial Development," in *Economic Growth and Structure Change in Taiwan: the Postwar Experience of the Republic of China*, ed. by Walter Galenson (Ithaca: Cornell University Press, 1979).

4. As noted earlier in Chapter 1, Taiwan experienced an annual 500 percent inflation rate during 1946–49. In the first half of 1949, the inflation rate was 5,000 percent!

5. Shirley W. Y. Kuo, *The Taiwan Economy in Transition* (Boulder: Westview Press, 1983), pp. 288–89.

6. Shirley W. Kuo and John C. Fei, "Causes and Roles of Export Expansion in the Republic of China," in *Foreign Trade and Investment, Economic Growth in the Newly Industrializing Asian Countries*, ed. by Walter Galenson (Madison: University of Wisconsin Press, 1985), pp. 48–49.

7. *Taiwan Statistical Data Book, 1989* (Taipei: Council for Economic Planning and Development, 1989), Table 3-2b.

8. Average annual inflation rate of 8 percent was recorded during 1953–62. Ibid., Table 9-1.

9. Ranis, "Industrial Development," p. 214.

10. The land reform program was conducted in three stages: farm rent reduction, public land lease-to-own, and land-to-the-tiller. For more detail, see Erik Thorbecke, "Agricultural Development," in *Economic Growth and Structure Change in Taiwan*, ed. by Galenson, pp. 200–5.

11. The essential elements of the reforms are as follows: (1) A thorough review of earlier control measures, with a view to liberalization; (2) preferential treatment for private enterprise in the areas of taxes, foreign exchange, and finance; (3) reform of the tax system and administration to foster capital formation; (4) reform of foreign exchange and the international trade system in order to establish a unitary exchange rate and liberalization of trade control within the limits imposed by required payments; and (5) a broadening of measures to encourage exports, improvement of procedures governing settlement of foreign exchange earned by exports, and an increase in the number of contracts with foreign business organizations.

12. NT$ = New Taiwan dollar.

13. Kuo and Fei, "Causes and Roles," p. 49.

14. *Taiwan Statistical Data Book, 1989*, Table 1-1b.

15. Foreign direct investment is the major stream of capital inflow. The role and impact of foreign direct investment in Taiwan will be discussed in detail in the next section.

16. *Taiwan Statistical Data Book, 1989*, Table 10-8.

17. Ranis, "Industrial Development," p. 256.

18. Ibid., pp. 226–51.

19. Kuo, *Taiwan in Transition*, pp. 200–4.

20. Yuan-li Wu, *Becoming An Industrialized Nation, R.O.C.'s Development on Taiwan* (New York: Praeger, 1985), p. 22.

21. The well-known Ten Great Projects Program included the North-South Freeway, Yaoyuan International Airport, railroad electricity, nuclear power plants, Hualien Seaport, Taichung Harbor, an integrated steel mill, a petrochemical refining plant, Suao Harbor, and Kaohsiung Shipyard.

22. From 1953 to 1989, the lowest economic growth rates were recorded in 1974 at 1.1 percent and 3.3 percent in 1982. This experimental test proved that an outward-oriented economy is vulnerable to external shocks.

23. The economic growth rates in 1983 and 1984 were 7.9 and 10.9 respectively.

24. *Statistics on Overseas Chinese and Foreign Investment, Technical Cooperation, Outward Investment, Outward Technical Cooperation, the Republic of China* (Taipei: Investment Commission, Ministry of Economic Affairs, May 1990), Tables 14 and 15.

25. For example, when the Netherlands announced the sale of two submarines to Taiwan, Communist China cut off diplomatic relations with the Dutch government.

However, in 1983, KLM, the Dutch airline, decided to fly to Taipei in spite of Communist China's threats. Dutch trade with Taiwan (total US$486 million in 1982) was cited as a decisive factor in the decision of KLM. (Sol W. Sanders, "Washington and Beijing call a Truce on Taiwan," *Business Week*, 18 July 1983, p. 71.)

26. OECD, *Financial Statistics*, Part 1: *Financial Statistics Monthly* (Paris: OECD).

27. As estimated by officials, half of the investments before 1962 were financed by U.S. aid. Shirley W. Y. Kuo, Gustav Ranis, and John C. H. Fei, *The Taiwan Success Story: Rapid Growth with Improved Distribution in the Republic of China, 1952–79* (Boulder: Westview Press, 1981), p. 29.

28. Samuel P. S. Ho, *Economic Development of Taiwan, 1860–1970* (New Haven: Yale University Press, 1978), p. 224.

29. Mo-huan Hsing, "Taiwan Industrialization," p. 217.

30. Gustav Ranis, "Industrial Development," p. 246.

31. *Free China Journal*, 28 July 1985, p. 4.

32. *Free China Journal*, November 1986, p. 4.

33. Dennis Fred Simon, "The Hsin-chu Science Industry Park," in *Contemporary Republic of China, The Taiwan Experience, 1950–80*, ed. by James C. Hsiung et al. (New York: Praeger, 1981), p. 205.

34. Other industries, such as machinery and instruments accounted for US$815 million, metal products accounted for US$815 million, the textile industry accounted for US$215 million, and the construction industry accounted for US$145 million. (*Statistics on Overseas Chinese and Foreign Investment*, June 1986.)

35. Kunio Yoshihara, *Foreign Investment and Domestic Response: A Study of Singapore's Industrialization* (Singapore: Eastern Universities Press, 1976), pp. 105–6.

36. Executive Yuan (the cabinet), Republic of China, *The Report of the Executive Yuan Tax Reform Commission*, Part III, Special Research Topic, Vol. I (Taipei: Executive Yuan, June 1970), p. 100; see also Jordan C. Schreiber, *U.S. Corporate Investment in Taiwan* (New York: Dunellen Publishing, 1970), p. 67. Schreiber's research, however, indicated that the reasons for investing in Taiwan are attractive market (14), minimal risk (19), low-cost labor (7), political and economic stability (6), and government attitude and business climate (5).

37. James Riedel, "The Nature and Determination of Export-Oriented Direct Foreign Investment in a Developing Country: A Case Study of Taiwan," *Weltwirtschaftliches Archiv* 3 (1976), p. 522.

38. Gustav Ranis and Chi Schive, "Direct Foreign Investment in Taiwan," in *Foreign Trade and Investment, Economic Growth in the Newly Industrializing Asian Countries*, ed. by Walter Galenson (Madison: University of Wisconsin Press, 1985).

39. Vivian Carlip, William Overstreet, and Dwight Linder, eds., *Economic Handbook of the World* (New York: McGraw-Hill, 1982), p. 135.

40. *Free China Journal*, 12 November 1986, p. 4.

41. Kuo, Ranis, and Fei, *Taiwan Success Story*, p. 30.

42. OECD, *Investing in Developing Countries: OECD/DAC Member Countries' Policies and Facilities with Regard to Foreign Direct Investment in Developing Countries*, 5th rev. ed. (Paris: OECD, 1982), p. 7.

43. Ranis and Schive, "Direct Foreign Investment," Table 2.3.

44. Ranis, "Industrial Development," p. 251.

45. Ranis and Schive, "Direct Foreign Investment," Table 2.5

46. Ranis, "Industrial Development," p. 251.

47. Ibid., Table 2.4.

48. Agricultural employment accounted for 50 percent of the labor force in 1964, and then declined to 12.9 percent in 1989. In contrast, employment in industrial and service sectors grew rapidly from 21.3 percent and 29.2 percent, respectively, in 1964 to 42.2 percent and 44.9 percent in 1989. (*Taiwan Statistical Data Book, 1990*, Taipei, Council for Economic Planning, 1990, Tables 2–9b, p. 16.)

49. Ranis, "Industrial Development," p. 251.

50. Chi Schive, "The Purchasing by Foreign Investors in the Domestic Market: And Its Linkage to Secondary Export Substitution," in *Taiwan's Foreign Trade Conference* (in Chinese), (Taipei: Economic Institution, Academic Scinica, August 1981).

51. Ranis and Schive, "Direct Foreign Investment," p. 126. However, it is arguable that the sewing machine does not require high technology and that there were plenty of domestic supplies.

52. Schive, "Purchase of Foreign Investors."

53. *Free China Journal*, 8 September 1985, p. 4. Another issue which both parties could not agree upon was the export ratio. After mid-1986 when the government terminated all export ratio requirements of foreign investors and stopped applying the local content rule, Toyota again proposed a US$21.9 million investment in an existing truck plant, Kuo Zui, and a US$1.2 billion investment for manufacturing body parts and other components. The project was approved by the government. (*Far Eastern Economic Review*, 27 August 1986).

54. The following examples are excerpted from Business International Asia, *World Sourcing Sites in Asia, Manufacturing Costs and Conditions in Hong Kong, Korea, Singapore, and Taiwan* (Hong Kong: Business International Asia/Pacific, November 1979). The approximate exchange rate was NT$40 per dollar.

55. The source of this section of the chapter is mainly derived from Central Bank of China, *Financial Institutions in Taiwan, the Republic of China* (Taipei: Central Bank of China, February 1984).

56. Jian-pao Yuan, "Taiwan's Banks," *Taiwan Economics and Finance Journal* (in Chinese) (Economic Research Department, Bank of Taiwan), 21, no. 5 (May 20, 1985).

57. In 1986, the government allowed foreign banks which had been set up more than five years to open second branch offices in Taiwan. Citibank of the United States and the Hollandsche Bank of the Netherlands were the first two banks to open their branch offices in the port city of Kaohsiung in southern Taiwan. This was the first step of the government to expand the scope of operation for the foreign banks. Other steps under consideration are to extend the acceptance of deposits for more than six months and to provide better access to the loans of the New Taiwan dollar. ("Taiwan Financial Outlook," *Business Asia*, 27 June 1986).

58. The so-called Cathy Crisis was the largest scandal in the financial sectors in Taiwan. Two government ministers resigned and the executive of the board of the Cathy Cooperative was convicted on charges of fraud. The crisis also caused the collapse of dozens of small businesses and at least US$500 million in bad debt on the part of foreign banks. The scandal involved such malpractice as postdated checks, borrowing under an employee's name without permission, and keeping fraudulent accounts. ("Taiwan, Banking on Change," *Economist*, 12 July 1986).

59. The commercial paper is defined by the regulation as promissory notes issued by well-known business firms for the purpose of raising short-term funds.

60. *Financial Statistics Monthly, Taiwan District, The Republic of China* (Taipei: Economic Research Department, Central Bank of China, 1989).

61. These insurance companies are the Federal Insurance Company of the CHUBB

Group, the American Family Life Insurance Company, and the AETNA Insurance Company. (*Free China Journal*, 1 December 1986 and 12 January 1987, p. 4; "Three Already Approved, Limit Lifted on Quota of U.S. Insurance Firm Branch in Taiwan," *Free China Journal*, 4 March 1987.)

62. Part of the following introductory materials in excerpted from Ronald H. C. Ho, President of the International Commercial Bank of China, "The Financial System in Taiwan, Republic of China, Its Function and Operation" (Taipei: October 1981).

63. In practice, the current reserve requirements are: (1) checking deposit, 29 percent; (2) demand deposit, 27 percent; (3) savings deposit, 20 percent; and (4) time deposit, 12 percent. The latest changes were made on 1 April 1990. (*Financial Statistics Monthly, Taiwan District, The Republic of China*, July 1985, Table 12.)

64. Another data source from the Central Bank indicated that the black market provided more than 36 percent of the funding for private enterprises. See Hu-wang Chang, *The Financial Industry in Taiwan, Practices and Cases Analysis* (in Chinese) (Taipei: Hai Ten, June 1984), Table 4.

65. The savings rate as the percentage of GNP in Taiwan has been over 30 percent since 1971. (*Taiwan Statistical Data Book, 1989*, Table 3-11.)

66. *Free China Journal*, 29 September, p. 4.

67. The export-promotion loans carry an interest rate lower than official lending rate. Recently, the government decided to stop subsidizing the interest-rate differential, due to the rising cost of funding and the exporters being more profitable than bankers. (*Central Daily News*, in Chinese, 6 January 1987, p. 4.)

68. The export insurance covered both political and commercial risks for the export's receivables and commercial bank's credit risks. Now, a line of export insurance that covers the loss of machinery and equipment exports caused by the currency fluctuation of the NT dollar between 3 and 20 percent is available. (*Free China Journal*, 10 November 1986, p. 4.)

69. Seven-year loans featured an annual interest rate of 6 percent, whereas the one-year loans carried an annual interest rate of 9.5 percent.

70. The reasons for adopting a deficit budget lie mainly in the cutback in revenue, tariff cuts, lower and new value-added taxes, increase in the income tax deductible items, and the dismantling of state-run monopolies.

71. *Free China Journal*, 10 November 1986, p. 4.

72. It is estimated that the exchange rates of the NT dollar are dominated by the U.S. dollar (80–85 percent) despite the floating-exchange-rate system applied. ("U.S. Revaluation Pressure on Korea and Taiwan May Succeed—Modestly," *Business Asia*, 18 August 1986.) The floating exchange rates also are being criticized because the Central Bank only allowed a 0.5 percent fluctuation range on either side of the day's opening rate and because of the heavy intervention by the Central Bank. ("Taiwan [New] Dollar," *1984 World Currency Handbook*, ed. by Philip P. Conwitt [Brooklyn: International Currency Analysis, 1985], p. 725.)

73. American Institute in Taiwan, *Foreign Economic Trends and Their Implications for the United States* (Washington, D.C.: U.S. Department of Commerce, International Trade Administration, January 1986), p. 17.

3

Special Circumstances
Affecting Taiwan

Since the 1970s foreign direct investment has been the major source of capital inflow to Taiwan, and encouragement of foreign direct investment has played a key role in attracting foreign capital and technology into Taiwan. In the 1960s, technology know-how accompanied the inflows of foreign direct investment, providing a sound basis for Taiwan's industrial development, and subsequent export expansion. In light of capital short-ages and the small domestic market, the government adopted a series of incentive measures and lower entry standards to attract foreign investors. In the 1970s, the domestic situation was stabilized and the economy performed well, also making the investment climate more attractive to foreign investors. In the 1980s, due to worldwide recession, growing foreign protectionism, and competition from less-developed countries, export-oriented policies were being questioned by some. Nevertheless, the amount of foreign direct investments has been rising and technology transfer has become a major concern of the authorities. Although the incentive measures have not changed basically, the criteria for reviewing foreign direct investment applications have broadened from traditional labor-intensive industries to include high-tech industries.

Another important factor which affects international capital flows is foreign-exchange controls. The foreign-exchange controls have played an important role in preventing capital flight and other speculative capital flows, thereby supporting domestic public confidence and encouraging domestic public savings for domestic investment needs. In recent years, due to the accumulated surplus in the nation's current account, as the result of a long-term trade surplus, and the needs to stimulate the nation's export expansion, more overseas outward investment has been urged by the government. Thus, in addition to the strategy of economic development, the foreign-exchange controls on capital inflows and outflows have become a critical issue for the authorities to cope with domestic and international economic changes.

This chapter will review the measures of encouraging foreign direct investment and foreign-exchange control. Meanwhile, in light of the Communist regime on Mainland China and its persisting threats to isolate Taiwan politically and economically, more complications are arising and affecting the operations of Taiwanese policy formation and its regulatory framework. An overview of the threats from Mainland China also will be helpful in understanding the policies and legal schemes.

ENCOURAGEMENT OF STRONG FOREIGN PRIVATE DIRECT INVESTMENTS

Overview

Foreign direct investment has been cordially welcomed in Taiwan. The Act for investment by Foreign Nationals and the Act for Investment by Overseas Chinese, as amended in July 1986, stipulate that the scope of foreign direct investment includes: (1) investments in productive or manufacturing enterprises which are needed domestically; (2) investments in science industries which are needed domestically; (3) investments in enterprises which have an export market; (4) investments in enterprises which are conducive to important industries, mining, or communication enterprises; (5) investments in enterprises which engage in scientific and technical research and development; and (6) investments in enterprises which are conducive to the domestic economic and social development.

The Industrial Development and Investment Center of the Ministry of Economic Affairs (IDIC) provides a list of industries which are desired in Taiwan. Other bylaws, including Categories and Criteria for Special Encouragement of Important Productive Enterprises, Categories and Criteria of Productive Enterprises Eligible for Encouragement, and Applicable Scope of the Strategic Industries, also provide detailed guidelines for foreign investors. However, according to the official interpretation, investments in enterprises which are not in these guidelines are not necessarily excluded in Taiwan.[1] For instance, Western fast-food chain stores were allowed to operate in Taiwan even before the amendment of the statutes to cover the service industry.[2]

On 26 May 1989, under the policy guide of internationalization and liberalization, the Statutes for Investment by Foreign Nationals and Overseas Chinese were revised to adopt a so-called negative list legislation, that is, except in industries prohibited or restricted by the Statutes, any foreign investment is allowed. This amendment reflects that the export-oriented policy has shifted to an export- and import-oriented policy and that inward and outward investment are given the same weight in the future economic development. Under the 1989 amendment, the following kinds of industries are classified as prohibited: those against public security or public policy, high-pollution-creating industries, a monopolized industry which is guaranteed by law, and foreign investment which is prohibited under statutes other than this act. Foreign investments in this prohibited category of industries is forbidden. The following kinds of industries are classified as restricted: public utilities, insurance and banking industries, news and publishing industries, as well as any industry which the foreign investment is restricted by statutes other than this act. Under the new rules, individual foreign investments are usually approved automatically, except for those connected with the aforementioned industries. This policy change, together with the relaxation of foreign-exchange controls, has provided freer entrance to foreign investors.

On 11 July 1990, the Ministry of Economic Affairs promulgated the negative list according to the delegated legislation of the act. The list includes seventy-six prohibited industries and fifty-five industries which are restricted. The prohibited list covers the agriculture sector and polluting, defense, refining, construction, transportation, and broadcasting industries. The restricted industries include mining, communication equipment, aviation, banking, insurance, security, newspaper publication, and health technology industries and travel and shipment sales agencies. Under the list, foreign nationals and overseas Chinese have equal footing to compete with the domestic investors.

The term "investment" as referred to in the Statutes is of the following kind: (1) cash in the form of foreign exchange which is remitted or brought in; (2) imports against self-provided foreign exchange of machinery, equipment, raw materials for self-use, or commodities under permissible import categories for sale to raise funds for plant erection or working capital; (3) technical know-how or patent rights; and (4) those portions of invested principle, net profit, interest, or any other income from investment which have been approved for exchange settlement. Investment profits refer to investors transferring the surplus of their investments including the retained earnings and the reinvestment stocks of the investing corporation, but not including the appreciation of the land and profits gained from land sales. Under the regulations governing the use of patent rights and technical know-how as equity investment, the term "technical know-how" refers to a newly developed technology having economic value, required by the invested enterprises and not having been previously adopted in the country. Patent rights or technical know-how which can be used for production or for the manufacture of raw materials not presently producible or manufacturable in Taiwan, or which can be used for improving the quality of existing products or for cost reduction are eligible to be capitalized as equity investment. The following restrictions are imposed, however: (1) the amount of capitalized patent rights shall not be in excess of 20 percent of the paid-in capital stocks of the invested enterprises; and (2) the amount of capitalized technical know-how shall not be in excess of 15 percent of the paid-in capital stocks of the invested enterprises. The investor who has capitalized such technical know-how shall, at the same time, make additional capital contributions in cash or in kind of an equal amount or more.

Other types of investment which are defined by the Statutes include: (1) establishing a new enterprise or expanding an existing enterprise through the increase of capital by undertaking capital investment individually, in association with other investors, or jointly with the Chinese government, Chinese nationals or judicial persons, or foreign nationals or judicial persons; (2) purchasing stock or bonds of existing enterprises or extending loans of cash, machinery, equipment, or other raw materials thereto; and (3) furnishing technical know-how or patent rights as capital stocks.

From the overview of the legal framework, it is evident that the policies have emphasized foreign direct investment. Although foreign investors can purchase stock and bonds of existing enterprises, in practice, the cases of foreign investors purchasing equity shares are rare due to the underdeveloped stock market and foreign-exchange controls. Until as recently as 1985, foreign investors could be allowed to purchase stock of existing enterprises directly only on a case-by-case authorization basis.[3] However, there are new funds which have operated since 1984 which provide other channels for foreign investors to invest in the domestic stock market indirectly.[4]

Strictly speaking, the only restriction on foreign direct investments is the prior-approval requirement. Investors are required to submit investment applications along with their investment plan and relevant documents to the Investment Commission (IC) of the Ministry of Economic Affairs for approval. Although the government has become more selective about which investments are deemed helpful for restructuring industries, new opportunities are gradually opening to foreign investors. The Categories and Criteria of Productive Enterprises Eligible for Encouragement, Criteria for Encouragement of Establishment or Expansion of Industrial and Mining Enterprises, and the Applicable Scope of the Strategic Industries all provide guidelines for the discretion of the government. Furthermore, under the Ten-year Economic Development Plan for Taiwan, Republic of China (1980–89), the basic policies set for the manufacturing sectors are: (1) stepping up development of the machinery, electronic, and information industries and other strategic technology-intensive industries, with high added value and a relatively low energy coefficient, so as to improve the industrial structure; (2) accelerating the introduction of advanced technology and stepping up research in industrial and applied science, in order to stimulate development of a broad technological base and technological innovation while raising domestic technological standards; (3) actively promoting the use of computers and developing information-industry technology with a view toward raising production and management efficiency; (4) promoting coordination and technological interflows between military, public, and private enterprises so as to attain greater self-sufficiency in defense production and encourage integrated development; and (5) promoting the improvement of production equipment in order to attain more efficient use of energy by industry.

The Categories and Criteria of Productive Enterprises Eligible for Encouragement, as amended on 16 November 1986, set forth some general criteria and specific criteria for certain industries. Some general criteria, such as scale of production, automation, location, machine operations, computer controls, etc., apply to certain industries. For instance, in order to be eligible for encouragement, investments in the production of automatic vending machines and money exchange machines are confined to those which are controlled by computers. The general criteria vary from one industry to another. Generally speaking, any investment which is to bring in new technology or design, to achieve economic scale of production, or to have the effect of labor or energy conservation will be eligible for encouragement. Two kinds of specific criteria—export ratio and local content requirements—often are the investor's greatest cause for concern.[5] Under the current statutes, the export ratio requirement only applies to the seafood cultivation industry, seeds and seed growing industry, and handicraft industry, due to the saturated domestic market. The local content requirements cover some textile, machinery, electronic and electrical, as well as automobile industries where the quality and quantity of the local supplies are adequate, thereby linking the domestic industries and foreign direct investments.

A foreign investor may invest in the industries which are not eligible for encouragement under the statutes and thus do not enjoy the privileges provided by the statutes. For instance, Proctor & Gamble Company and Colgate Palmolive Company decided to invest in the production of toothpaste, soap, and other household productions in Taiwan.[6]

A complication arises under the Japanese investment cases. In 1978, the Investment Commission ruled out any new Japanese expansion investment projects in color TV set assemblies, because the Japanese used the investments as a strategy to circumvent trade barriers and caused a burden on the exports of local products.[7]

Two kinds of locations apply different rules from others. Under the Establishment and Management of Export Processing Zone Act, the investors who invested in the export processing zones are required to export all the products unless a special permission to sell the product into domestic market is given by the authority.[8] The Establishment and Management of Hsinchu Science Park Zone Act provided that only technology-intensive industries be eligible to operate in the Park and also focused on international market competition.[9] Other specific requirements, that will not be treated here, also apply to these industries set up in the export processing zones as well as in the science-based industrial park.

Some policy implications stem from the operation of the legal frameworks of the Statute for Encouragement of Investment. Since the restructuring of domestic industries has been urged to cope with the changing economic situations domestically and internationally, the government, on the one hand, has shifted the policy emphasis from labor-intensive industries to technology-intensive industries. On the other hand, the openness of domestic market for foreign goods and investments is necessary to introduce competition into domestic industries and to head off the rising protectionism in the United States. In 1987, the Statute of Encouragement for Investment was passed by the Legislative Yuan (branch of government) to enlarge the scope of industries which are eligible for encouragement. The new law provides that all investors (foreign and domestic) who invest in manufacturing industries in Taiwan will be eligible for encouragement as compared to previous stipulations which specified the industries which were eligible for encouragement.[10] The new amendments combined with the partial openness of service industries[11] and the narrowing down of export ratio and local content requirements indicates the policy is shifting from export-promotion to export- and import-promotion strategy.

Because the Encouragement of Investment was due to expire by the end of 1990, the Executive Yuan sent a new draft of Industry Upgrade

Promotion Act to the Legislative Yuan in April 1990. The new Act, which was passed in December 1990, shifts the policies from the ideology of encouraging investment in specific industries to all the industries. This recent development, combined with the negative list legislation regarding foreign investment, has provided a favorable climate of national treatment and equal protection to foreign investors.

Overall, the government has played a key role in policy formation and other transitions thereby leading the way for strong economic development of a highly industrialized country.

Fiscal Incentives

The widely used fiscal incentives include tax exemption, tax deduction, and accelerated depreciation.[12] In Taiwan, the Statute for Encouragement of Investment was promulgated on 10 October 1960 and has been amended repeatedly to meet economic needs as well as to accelerate economic development. The latest amendment was made on 26 January 1987. Since the late 1970s, fiscal incentives have been given specifically to capital- or technology-intensive enterprises important to the development of the heavy petrochemical and defense industries. The encouragements have emphasized technical renovation, research and development, quality inspection, pollution control, energy savings, and improvement of industrial health and safety. In addition, the so-called "strategy industries" which include precision and automated machinery, transportation equipment, information and computer software, microcomputer and peripheral equipment, and numerical communication and related electronic industries are highly encouraged.[13] The 1987 amendment focuses on the encouragement of establishing capital-venture companies to cope with the needs of the information industry.

The fiscal incentives provided under the Statutes are as follows:[14]

1. A newly established productive enterprise[15] in the encouragement categories is entitled to enjoy either a five-year income tax holiday or accelerated depreciation of the fixed assets. An enterprise in the capital- or technology-intensive category may, at its option, defer the application of tax exemption by one to four years to be decided within two years after start-up. This stipulation allowing the capital- or technology-intensive industries to enjoy the benefit of tax exemption takes into consideration that these enterprises at start-up stage normally are expected to run with little profits due to the capital needed and research and development costs.

2. When increasing capital for expanded production, an encouraged productive enterprise is entitled to a four-year income tax holiday or accelerated depreciation and deferment of its tax holiday benefits the same as those accordable to the original investment.

3. A five-year income tax exemption and delayed application of tax holiday benefits also are accordable to the following enterprises: those that explore, exploit, and process natural resources abroad and subsequently ship the products back to Taiwan; those that produce and process the government-specified agricultural or industrial material and subsequently ship the products back to Taiwan; and those that transfer the government-specified technologies back to Taiwan.

4. The profit-seeking enterprise income tax and surtax on productive enterprises, on big trading companies, and on venture-capital investment enterprises according to certain criteria are limited to 25 percent of their taxable income, reduced further to 22 percent for specified capital- or technology-intensive enterprises.[16]

5. Cost of research and development programs may be charged to the current year's operation expenses. Where the amount of annual R&D expenses exceeds the highest amount of R&D expenses over the preceding five years, only 20 percent of the exceeding amount may be deducted but not to exceed 50 percent of taxable income. However, the insufficient amount of the deduction may be offset in the ensuing five years.

6. Accelerated depreciation is allowed for machinery and equipment purchased by enterprises specifically for the purpose of energy conservation, waste treatment, or pollution prevention.

7. Additional accelerated depreciation is allowed for new equipment acquired to replace old equipment.

8. Payments to a foreign company for technical services in the construction of a plant for an important productive enterprise in Taiwan are exempted from taxation.

9. Where a productive enterprise reinvests its undistributed earnings for the addition or replacement of machinery and equipment or for transportation facilities as referred to in the Statute for the Encouragement of Investment, the registered stock newly issued to its stockholders shall not be subject to taxation in the current year. However, subsequent sales or transfers of such stock are liable for tax assessment.

10. For a productive enterprise, the amount of earnings retainable is limited to the equivalent of its paid-up capital, while a strategic industry is limited to an amount not exceeding twice its paid-up capital. However, retained earnings in excess of the above limits is permissible provided an additional 10 percent business income tax is paid for the exceeding earnings to be retained.

More tax incentives are offered for these foreign direct investments located in the science-based park and export processing zones as follows:

1. Industrial, mining, and other productive enterprises which meet the encouragement criteria may import authorized machinery and equipment duty free.

2. Import duty on machinery and equipment not available in Taiwan may be paid in installments.

3. Import duty exemption and installment payment of import duties also may be allowed for importation of parts, components, and materials used in manufacturing, production machinery, and equipment.

4. Instruments, machinery, and equipment may be brought in duty free for approved R&D programs.

5. A 100 percent export-oriented productive enterprise which benefits the country's economic development or employs advanced technology is entitled to a five-year deferment of duty on imported machinery and equipment.

6. Import duties, harbor dues, and commodity taxes paid or payable on imported raw materials for manufacturing exportable products may be refunded or bounded.

There are two bylaws which stipulate the details of the extent of deduction or exemption from taxes: (1) Measures Governing the Application of Tax Reduction for Investment in Procurement of Machinery and Equipment by Private Productive Enterprises and (2) Enforcement Rules Governing the Payment in Installments of and Exemption from Duties Leviable on Machinery and Equipment Imported by Productive Enterprises. An exceptional case of tax exemption and deferment applies to the companies which invest in the construction of international trade buildings for lease pursuant to the plan for the establishment of the World Trade Center by the government. This indicates that the government is encouraging private enterprises to participate in the construction of public goods.

It is argued that the fiscal incentives are somewhat inefficient and ineffective. These incentives are ineffective because every country could have offered a similar and competing scheme. And these incentives are reducing the host country's revenue (a great cost to the host country),[17] and the investors are not necessarily benefiting under these schemes due to the home country's tax system and legal requirements. Thus, a more general economic policy better emphasizing access to the investment market might be more effective and efficient.[18] As the survey noted in Chapter 2, the tax incentives are not the most important reasons for the foreign investors to invest in Taiwan. However, since the Statute for Encouragement of Investment applies to both domestic and foreign investors, the fiscal incentives have helped the government in forming economic policies and are significant to some investors for comparing the investment conditions offered by other nations. Another important function of these fiscal incentives may lie in their encouragement of research and development as well as of pollution controls which are critical issues for the Taiwan economic development.

Financial Incentives

Often-used fiscal incentives include grants, loans, and loan guarantees.[19] In Taiwan, because the operations of the financial system are predominated by publicly owned banks, the government also participates in investment projects via bank investments. For instance, the Bank of Communications is one of the investors of the United Optic Fiber Communication, a Sino-U.S. joint venture, to produce fiber optics.[20] Recently, the state-run bank has been engaged in the formation of a venture-capital company to provide indirect financial assistance to the high-technology industries.[21]

One of the financial incentives offered by the government is the full repatriation of invested capital one year after the commencement of the business operations of the investing enterprise. Foreign investors are allowed to repatriate capital gains which have been derived from: (1) the sale of company shares; (2) capital revenues; (3) premiums; (4) net appraisal surpluses; (5) disposal of assets; and (6) the fair market value of assets of merged companies in excess of liabilities and payments for shares. Foreign investors are required to submit relevant documents to the authority in charge of foreign exchange for approval of exchange settlements. This provides a higher mobility of capital for foreign investors to utilize their capital.

To encourage the so-called "strategic industries," foreign investors who invest in the strategic industries are allowed to borrow from the Bank of Communications. TRW, an electronics components company, for instance, in 1984 obtained a five-year loan of NT$60 million with 7.635 percent annual interest. These medium- and long-term subsidized loans are available for investment in the strategic machinery and information industries. The TRW loan was used to finance its investment in electronic calculators and switch-mode power supplies.[22]

The Bank of Communications and the China Development Corporation serve as development banks to handle long-term financing of strategic and basic industries. A development fund established under the Executive Yuan can be used for investing or extending credit to technology-intensive and important productive enterprises. It also may be used as venture capital for financing projects to promote a technology transfer. For instance, the Development Fund Committee decided to invest NT$2.65 billion in the Taiwan Semiconductor Manufacturing Company in order to lead the development of the very large semiconductor integration industry.[23] A special fund under the Central Bank also is available for supporting large development projects and for financing private enterprises to expand productive capacity and to upgrade the quality of products and productivity.[24]

One new field for financing investment in Taiwan is the venture-capital company which provides financial loans to qualified investors. Under the Project for Improving the Environment and Promoting Investment, as passed by the Executive Yuan on 15 April 1982, the provision pertaining to venture capital for strategic industries is an important step in fostering economic restructure. As noted in the previous chapter, commercial bank lending in Taiwan is not available if the borrower cannot provide collateral. For these technology-intensive enterprises, borrowing from Taiwan banks is particularly unfeasible due to the lack of business experience, R&D expenditures, and untested products at the start-up stage.[25] Since 1984, the government has encouraged the establishment of the venture-capital company to provide financial aid to technology-intensive industries. Currently there are three venture-capital companies in Taiwan: Multiventure Investment, Sino Scan Venture Fund, and Han Tech Venture Capital Investment Corporation. Another three venture-capital companies have been approved by the Ministry of Finance: Asiatec Venture Capital Company, Taiwan International Venture Investment Corporation, and Stenberg & Lyman Health Care Ventures. Among these venture-capital companies, the Han Tech Venture Capital Investment Corporation is the one with official support. The Bank of Communications has played a major role in setting up the venture-capital company. The company invested US$10 million abroad mainly to lure these would-be investors to set up operations in Taiwan.[26] And, because investment in the venture-capital companies is specifically encouraged by the government, foreign investors are attracted by the incentives provided in the statutes. Thus, the function of the venture-capital companies is not only to provide financial aid to the investors but also to provide an investment opportunity to attract more foreign capital inflow.

Another type of financial incentive is the loan guarantee. Under the Law Governing the Foreign Loans Guaranteed by the Government to Foster Economic and Social Development, as amended on 6 June 1983, the borrowers are limited to government agencies, public enterprises, privately owned financial institutions, and privately owned enterprises which are important to the nation's economy. The Treasury will guarantee the loans not exceeding US$9.5 billion, if the loans are approved by the authorities. Since the loan guarantees are predominantly for the public enterprises or government agencies to undertake infrastructure construction or basic commodity production, they are not so significant in attracting foreign investors.

The financial system in Taiwan has not yet fully developed. And, since 1981, domestic savings have exceeded domestic investment needs.[27] However, bank lending is policy oriented and thus venture capital is only available to some high-technology industries. As a result, the idle money in the banking industry is aggregated and has become the target for criticism. Thus, either to enlarge the scope of borrowing the venture capital or to eliminate the collateral requirements of the bank lending will be a most important subject to encourage investments.

Other Incentives

Other incentives which are important to foreign investors may not necessarily be fiscal or financial ones. A stabilized economic and social environment in addition to a well-developed infrastructure are basic to luring the inflows of foreign direct investment. The successful industrial and trade policies have brought the nation to an industrialization basis. As mentioned in Chapter 2, the influx of foreign capital in recent years has been further attracted by the rapid economic growth in Taiwan. The foreign direct investment also shifted from import substitution in the 1960s to export substitution types in the 1970s, and again to export expansion and import expansion types in the 1980s. The rising demand of the domestic market and the well-developed infrastructure for import and export production are crucial to the decision of foreign investors to invest in Taiwan.

Secondly, labor availability is Taiwan's most valuable asset. Education in Taiwan is mandatory through ninth grade and 95 percent of the work force is educated up to this level. Since the late 1970s, the government has emphasized vocational and occupational training[28] to cope with the industrial needs. During 1976–81, the demand for the labor force was growing faster than the supply and the average annual rate in monthly wages in manufacturing was 18.9 percent compared to 4.5 percent annual growth rate of productivity. From 1982 to 1985 the average annual growth rate of productivity was 3.3 percent, and a 12 percent wage increase was reported in 1986. Thus, a slowdown in the growth of labor supply and continued heavy upward pressure on wages has been a threat to the export-oriented economy due to the increasing labor costs in Taiwan. Rising wages have pushed the traditional labor-intensive industries, such as textiles, to re-structure their operation of manufacturing via computerization and auto-mation. The labor force has gradually shifted from unskilled to more skillful capabilities through education and vocational training to earn a better living. The average unemployment rate was 2.3 percent in 1980–87. By the end of 1988, the unemployment rate fell to 1.48 percent and a labor shortage was recorded. Some sectors, especially labor-intensive indus-tries, such as construction, have introduced foreign labor to cope with the high wages and labor shortage. Thus, foreign direct investment in a labor-intensive industry no longer enjoys a low wages advantage. However, to those capital- and technology-intensive industries, a well-educated and disciplined work force will continue to be one of the attractive factors for luring the inflows of foreign direct investment into Taiwan.

Another advantage to foreign investment is the establishment of industrial districts, export processing zones, and a science-based industrial park. These industrial sites provide public roads, tap water, a draining system, an electricity supply, communication facilities, a sewage treatment plant, street lights, and a service center for foreign investors. In export processing zones and science-based industrial parks, more facilities are readily available, such as a customs branch office, a tax collection office, several banks, a post office, a business office of the communications administration, a service station of the Taiwan Power Company, an airline business office, and service station of the public employment center. Procedures including the imports and exports, settlement of foreign exchange, customs inspection, and investment application and implementation all can be conducted within the zones and the park.[29] Under the Statute of Encouragement for Investment, all the industrial sites can be procured through private negotiation. When an entrepreneur is in need of land for establishment of a new plant, the government will gladly lease or sell the land in the industrial sites to the enterprises. The government also provides assistance to the investors in leasing or procuring suitable designated industrial land which is located outside the industrial district, export processing zones, or science-based industrial park. The services and infrastructure provided by the government not only offer foreign investors a better investment climate but also help to balance the urban and rural development.

One article in the draft of the Industry Upgrade Promotion Act provided that the investor could build up or rent an industrial harbor for his own use. This provision was caused by the so-called Formosa Plastic Company shock. In December 1989 the Formosa Plastic Company, the largest chemical petroleum enterprise in Taiwan, decided to invest in Mainland China to build up a petroleum refining plant, thus causing the government concern economically and politically. The company had planned to build a petroleum refining plant in Taiwan. However, due to the antipollution sentiment of the public and the high cost of buying an industrial site, the plan had not become a reality after more than three years of negotiations. Under the new act, the government will build a harbor for the convenience of shipment from the company's petroleum refining plant in order to keep the company from moving to Mainland China.

The Statute for Investment by Foreign Nationals and the Statute for Investment by Overseas Chinese provide a full wall of protection against government appropriation or requisition. Under the statutes, no foreign direct investment will be expropriated for twenty years after commencement of business provided that 45 percent or more of the total capital is foreign owned. If the foreign participation is less than 45 percent, the enterprise can be expropriated with compensation only on the grounds of national defense needs.[30] There is no limitation on foreign equity and the recent amendment of the statutes has lifted the requirement that a 45 percent or more foreign-owned company shall give the employees first right of refusal when issuing shares for a capital increase.[31] In the past, only one company, NSE Far East Corporation, a subsidiary of the National Distillers and Chemical Corporation of the United States, has been asked to divest its equity shares to its employees and local investors when issuing new shares for capital increase. The company sold the total value of US$24 million stocks to Chinese investors and became a 50 percent Chinese-owned company in 1976.[32]

In order to attract more foreign direct investment, the government has adopted a series of measures to foster the protection of intellectual property and to promote fair trade practices. The government realized that the counterfeiting problem has become a disincentive to foreign direct investment and technology transfer.[33] In January 1985, the government revised the Trade Mark Law raising the maximum jail term for counterfeiting to five years. An amendment on 28 June 1985 to the Taiwanese Copyright Law provides more protection to computer software, photographs, videotape recordings, etc., and also imposes a stiff penalty against counterfeiters.[34] The Patent Law, which was amended in 1986, extends the protection of patent rights to cover chemical components and pharmaceutical products.[35] Another new piece of legislation, the Fair Trade Law, will prohibit the counterfeiting of another's commodity name, brand, package, or other elements which could cause confusion for the public. Further, the law prohibits the use or counterfeiting of trademarks which are not registered in Taiwan.[36]

These incentives, other than fiscal and financial ones, play a significant role in attracting foreign direct investments. As other nations are offering similar monetary incentives to attract foreign investment, neither fiscal nor financial incentives could have a decisive impact on the inflows of foreign direct investment. Instead, a decision to encourage foreign direct investment must be based on economic benefit as a whole in order to fully realize the comparative advantage. For instance, the government was able to attract Flow Industries, which produces water-jet cutting equipment, by leasing a new plant to the American firm in the Hsinchu Science-based Industrial Park and participating in the finance of 49 percent of the equity, among other fiscal incentives.[37]

Currently in Taiwan, all the incentive measures used by the government are emphasizing the development of high technology. In light of losing its low-wage advantage and in order to compete with other developing countries, it is evident that the nation may no longer rely on foreign direct investment to bring in more capital, but should encourage technology transfers instead. More precisely, today the policies are aimed at encouraging strong foreign high-technology investment.

PREVENTION OF CAPITAL LEAKAGE WITH STRICT FOREIGN-EXCHANGE CONTROLS

The regulations in the areas of foreign-exchange administration and operations provide comprehensive foreign-exchange controls in Taiwan. Due to the painful experience learned on the Mainland, the government has adopted a conservative and cautious attitude toward the management of financial sectors and foreign-exchange markets. This policy has paid off in the past thirty years by restoring public confidence and stabilizing exchange rates, thereby offering a basis for economic development. As stated in Article 1 of the Statute for Foreign Exchange Regulation, the purpose of the foreign-exchange controls is to attain a balance in international payments, thus achieving financial stability.

Overview

Under the Statute for Foreign Exchange Regulation, as amended on 15 July 1987, the authorities responsible for matters related to foreign exchange include the Ministry of Finance, which is in charge of foreign-exchange administration, and the Central Bank, which in turn is in charge of foreign-exchange operations. The term "foreign-exchange administration" referred to in the Statute includes: (1) the handling and supervision of foreign borrowing and lending of government agencies or public enterprises; (2) the guaranteeing and management of external debt; (3) the authorization for outward foreign-exchange settlements, borrowing, and imports of government agencies; and (4) imposition and collection of fines levied in accordance with the provisions of the Statute. The "foreign-exchange operations" are: (1) to manage the country's foreign exchange and prepare estimates of foreign-exchange receipts and payments; (2) to designate and supervise appointed banks engaged in foreign-exchange business; (3) to maintain orderly conditions in the foreign-exchange market; (4) to screen applications and grant approval to private inward and outward remittances; (5) to supervise foreign currency loans and guarantees made by appointed banks on behalf of private enterprises; (6) to buy and sell foreign currency notes and negotiable instruments; and (7) to handle other matters related to foreign-exchange operations. Thus, the Central Bank plays a key role in the operations of foreign-exchange controls and the Ministry of Finance only provides some administrative assistance.

The scope of foreign exchange which was subject to foreign-exchange controls included gold, silver, foreign currencies, securities, and other negotiable instruments denominated in foreign currencies. On 14 May 1986, the foreign-exchange regulations were revised to exclude gold and silver from the scope of foreign-exchange controls[38] in order to ease the influx of foreign-exchange reserves aggregated by the trade surplus. Despite the deregulation of gold trading, the import of gold has been impeded by the value-added tax.[39]

The 1987 amendment further lifted restrictions on foreign exchange. The amendment's profound influence on foreign-exchange controls is reflected as follows: (1) Individuals and firms are allowed to hold foreign exchange without any reason to report; (2) the current-account transactions are fully liberalized without limitation; (3) capital-account transactions are substantially liberalized with the limitation of US$5 million outward remittance and US$1 million inward remittance (however, any amount of remittance over the maximum limitation is allowed with prior approval of the authority, and beginning 15 March 1991, both maximum limitations are set at $3 million); and (4) the forward market is opened and the exchange rates are decided by five major government-appointed banks. However, as noted supra, the forward market has not operated in fact due to the fluctuation of the NT dollar against foreign currencies.

Since Taiwan's financial system is predominated by state-run banks and by restrictive regulations on capital outflows in Taiwan, foreign lending by local banks is thus subject to the scrutiny of the Ministry of Finance and its policy-oriented goals. In other words, the foreign-exchange controls in Taiwan are focused on nonbanking activities. Most of the foreign-exchange control operations are designed to appointed banks. Under the Regulations Governing Appointed Banks for Operation of a Foreign Exchange Business, in order to operate a foreign-exchange business, a bank may apply to the Central Bank for designation as an appointed bank. An appointed bank is authorized to engage in the following foreign-exchange businesses: (1) inward and outward remittances; (2) issuing and advising of letters of credit; (3) purchase of export bills; (4) foreign currency deposits and foreign-exchange proceeds deposits; (5) foreign currency loans; (6) guarantees for payment in foreign currency; (7) import

Figure 3.1
Foreign-Exchange Regulations Explanatory Chart

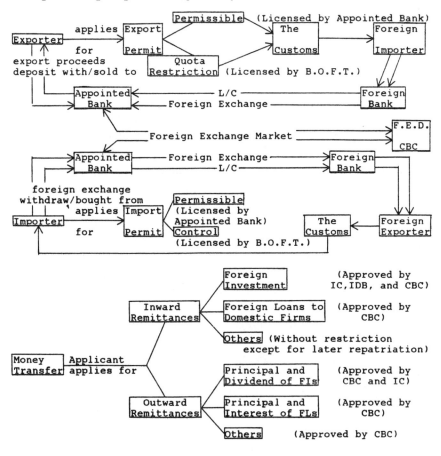

B.O.F.T.: Board of Foreign Trade, Ministry of Economic Affairs
F.E.D., CBC: Foreign Exchange Department, The Central Bank of China
IC: Investment Commission, Ministry of Economic Affairs
IDB: Industrial Development Bureau, Ministry of Economic Affairs
FIs: foreign investments
FLs: foreign loans to domestic firms

and export credit investigations; and (8) other foreign-exchange businesses specifically designated by the Central Bank.

As a general rule, the public was not allowed to hold foreign currency
unless otherwise provided by the law. With the 1987 amendment, the
public is allowed to hold foreign exchange; however, the expectation of

appreciation of the NT dollar has changed the situation only a little. Foreign exchanges are required to sell to or buy from the Central Bank or its appointed banks. The controls on foreign exchange are commonly seen in both inward and outward capital flows. (See Figure 3.1.)

Controls on Capital Inflows

Foreign bank lending to the government agencies or public enterprises is subject to the scrutiny of the Ministry of Finance and is guaranteed by the Treasury. Remittances of foreign capital for direct investment are subject to the approval of the Ministry of Economic Affairs. These two major long-term capital inflows are operating under the supervision of the Central Bank, the Ministry of Finance, and the Ministry of Economic Affairs.

One of the major capital inflows is export proceeds. Under the Statute of Foreign Exchange Regulation, export to reexport proceeds shall be deposited with appointed banks in a foreign-exchange-proceeds deposit account and may be sold either in the foreign-exchange market or through appointed banks or the Central Bank.[40] Before 18 August 1986, all exporters were required to apply for preapproval from the Central Bank or appointed banks for foreign-exchange acceptance before the transaction is made. Under the current rules, except for payments longer than 365 days which are considered as accounts receivable, a foreign-exchange declaration system has been set up, that is, an aftermath monitor, to cut red tape and speed transactions.[41] Under this new system, the exporters are only required to file the declaration form stating the amount of export proceeds in the form of foreign exchange and the settlement date with the customs office. The customs office only accepts these declarations with export permits. The Central Bank will audit the declaration form and customs form periodically to prevent false declarations or a failure to declare export proceeds. Those who make false declarations or fail to make declarations will be penalized a fine equal to twice the amount of the foreign exchange involved plus confiscation of the foreign exchange.

Another inflow of capital is portfolio investment. Under the Regulations Governing Securities Investment by Overseas Chinese & Foreign Investors & Procedures for Remittance, as promulgated on 26 May 1983, foreign investors can invest in the Taiwan stock market only through the purchase of beneficiary certificates issued by a securities investment trust enterprise within the country and sold by agents outside the country. A preapproval procedure is required for issuing beneficiary certificates and the Securities and Exchange Commission shall address the Ministry of Finance to obtain the consent of the Central Bank. The first fund managed by the International Investment Trust Company was set up in 1983 as Taiwan (R.O.C.) Fund with US$121 million and was underwritten by Vicker da Costa and Credit Suisse Boston. Another three new funds started operations in 1986. The Formosa Fund was issued by Kwang Hwa Securities Investment and Trust and its foreign partners Interallianz Bank Zurich, Hoare Govett Asia, Federated International Management, and MIM (Asia Pacific) in March 1986. The Taipei Fund was funded in May 1986; its domestic issuer was the National Investment Trust, and the foreign partners were Prudential-Bache Securities U.K., F. T. Management Asia, and Bankers Trust Foreign Investment Corporation. However, these two new funds and the Taiwan (R.O.C.) Fund are listed only on the London exchange market and are not traded publicly. The secondary market for these three funds is limited and traded only between private brokers for long-term investment. The issue of the Taiwan Fund by China Development, Merrill Lynch, Fidelity International, and Bangkok Bank has been listed and traded on the American Stock Exchange since 16 December 1986.[42] Since 1986, beneficiary certificates of the investment fund have been raised in the domestic market also. According to the Overseas Chinese and the Foreigner Securities Investment Project, there are three steps to opening the Taiwan stock market for offshore investment: (1) Allow foreign investors to invest indirectly in securities only through the purchase of beneficiary certificates; (2) permit foreign professional investment institutions to invest directly in securities; and (3) allow foreign investors, including individuals and institutions, to invest directly in securities. According to the Securities and Exchange Act as amended in January 1988, foreign investors are allowed to participate in securities transaction through investment in local securities firms and the management of these firms. No timetable has been established for the opening of the stock market to foreign investors.[43]

The foreign-exchange controls are sweeping for almost all the income derived from abroad. Under the foreign-exchange regulations, the following foreign exchanges are required to deposit into the foreign-exchange deposit account or to surrender to the appointed banks or the Central Bank: (1) income derived from services, shipping, and insurance; (2) inward remittances; (3) income arising from investment abroad which is approved by the government for Chinese nationals who have their domicile or residence in the Republic; (4) principal, interest, net profit, and royalties accruing from foreign investment by domestic enterprises approved by the government; and (5) other income in foreign exchange. Some significant regulations which provide a tight scheme for exchange controls on inward remittance have been subsequently introduced.

On 26 June 1987, the Statutes for Foreign Exchange Regulation was amended and put into force to cope with the changing economic situations domestically and internationally. The Executive Yuan is authorized under the law to suspend the application of Articles 6-1, 7, 13, and 14, which govern the aforesaid control measures unless there is a long-term trade surplus, aggravation of foreign-exchange reserves, and fluctuation in international economics. According to this authorization, the Executive Yuan has suspended most of the foreign-exchange control de facto. Under the Regulation Governing the Civilian Inward Remittance, the receiver of the inward remittance is only required to file an application form with the appointed bank. And the receivers or depositors of the following exchange earnings are eligible to sell out the foreign exchanges without prior approval: (1) foreign-exchange earnings of export proceeds or service fees; or (2) for an individual domiciled in the territory of the Republic who is over twenty years old with an identification card, foreign exchange totaling no more than US$3 million or its equivalent during a one-year period. Under the Regulation Governing the Civilian Inward Remittance, an individual is eligible to remit the following foreign-exchange earnings without prior approval: (1) payment of imported commodity or invisible fees paid by domestic registered companies, firms, or groups; or (2) domestic registered companies, firms, or groups and the individual domiciled in the territory of the Republic who is over twenty years old with an identification card may remit no more than US$3 million or its equivalent during a one-year period.

The new legislation represents the trend of the foreign-exchange administration. Because of the influx of foreign exchanges during the period of 1987–89, the outward remittances are encouraged by the government compared to the years of restricting capital outflows for domestic needs. However, since early 1990, the influx of foreign exchanges has slowed and the depreciation of New Taiwan dollars is expected by the public, and the government is reconsidering whether the policy of foreign-exchange control should be further liberalized. The question remains intact. And the new revision of the Statutes for Foreign Exchange Regulation has been suspended.

Under the Regulations Governing the Screening of Foreign Loans to Industrial and Mining Enterprises, as promulgated on 20 December 1972, inward remittances of foreign loans were subjected to the approval of the Central Bank. The foreign loans were limited to the following uses and cannot be reloaned to any other party: (1) to purchase machinery and equipment or raw materials abroad with detailed dates of repayment of the loan, import permits, and other relevant documents; and (2) to convert into New Taiwan dollars for domestic use with prior approval from the Central Bank. The foreign loans shall be for terms of no less than one year and the remittances of interest and lending charges shall not exceed the maximum amount of interest and charges allowed for foreign loans as prescribed by the Central Bank at the time the remittance is made. The appointed banks may reloan borrowed capital funds to domestic productive enterprises for importation of machinery and equipment in the original foreign currency. In the case of reloaning for importation of raw material, the period to be allowed for payment of the loan in foreign exchange shall not exceed six months for each loan. The investment and trust companies may be allowed to reloan the borrowed foreign capital for importation of machinery and equipment only.

To handle insurance denominated in foreign currency, Chinese insurance companies are required to establish a special account in the foreign currency concerned with an appointed bank. Foreign-exchange earnings derived from operating insurance businesses by Chinese insurance companies must be deposited in a special account and any expenses incurred from insurance denominated in foreign currency shall be drawn from that account. When a domestic insurance company underwrites an insurance policy denominated in a foreign currency, the insurance premium shall be collected in the New Taiwan dollar if the domiciles of the policy applicant and the insured or the beneficiary are within the territory of the Republic except for the marine insurance of exports. Also, the reinsurance premium and payments are conducted through a special New Taiwan dollar account opened by foreign insurance companies with an appointed bank. Thus, the premium, claims, and expenses all will be paid or received from this special account. For the balance of either a foreign currency account or a New Taiwan dollar account, an exchange settlement may be made to convert the foreign currency into the New Taiwan dollar or vice versa by the appointed bank.[44]

The Regulations Governing the Screening of Foreign Exchange Receipts and Expenditures of Chinese Shipping Companies, as amended on 2 February 1979, provides that all Chinese shipping companies are required to remit their foreign currency receipts, including charter fees, within six months from the day such receipts are reported to the Central Bank. And the companies are required to collect the receipts in the New Taiwan dollar when the payment is made in Taiwan. When the companies obtain foreign currency loans from appointed banks to meet their operational needs, the total amount of such loans shall not exceed the total amount of the operational receipts reported in the last six months by the companies. However, there is no restriction on the amount which the companies can borrow abroad for shipbuilding purposes with prior approval from the Central Bank.

Another source of foreign-exchange inflows is the freight and fares received by shipping companies and airlines. Foreign shipping companies which undertake the shipment of import and export commodities or passengers to or from Taiwan are required to collect the freight and passenger fares in the New Taiwan dollar. When a foreign shipping company generates no or insufficient receipts to defray its expenditures in Taiwan from a voyage to and from there, the expenditures or deficits shall be remitted by the foreign shipping company within three months of the ship's arrival at or departure from a port in Taiwan.[45] In the case of airline freights and fares, a Chinese airline is required to declare its foreign currency income and remit the foreign exchange in its foreign-exchange-proceeds deposit account with an appointed bank within six months from the day of declaration. A prior approval from the Central Bank is required in borrowing foreign currency funds from domestic or foreign banks for the purpose of purchasing aircraft or matching its operational needs. A foreign airline should apply to the Central Bank for registration. For the fares and freight received by the foreign airline, the airline, after deducting expenditures, may apply for the settlement of exchange or request to convert the foreign currency note into foreign exchange. If the foreign airline has no operational income in the Republic or its income is not sufficient to meet the expenditures thereof, all the expenditures or deficits shall be deducted from the operation income of the next month or remitted in the same amount of foreign exchange within the three-month period immediately following the end of each month.[46]

Among these foreign-exchange controls on inward capital flows, the following impacts of control measures can be seen in the regulations: (1) Authorization requirements are widely used in all of the regulations involved, thereby assuring the inflows of capital are not offsetting the domestic monetary policies; (2) the uses of foreign funds are limited to productive purposes, such as importation of machinery, equipment, or raw materials, thereby making the best use of foreign capital and preventing the foreign debt from being unmanageable; (3) in most cases, the foreign-exchange holders are required to remit their foreign exchange within a certain period of time, thereby allowing the Central Bank to control its foreign-exchange reserves more effectively; (4) the design of foreign-exchange deposit accounts gives more leeway for private enterprises to use their foreign exchange without official intervention, thereby fostering the foreign-exchange holders' flexibility to manage the working capital and speeding up international transactions; and (5) the surrender requirement also applies to individual remittances, thereby preventing any possible leakage and making the control measures more effective.

Due to the painful experience of capital shortage and capital flight in the 1950s and early 1960s, the government is more cautious about capital outflows than capital inflows. In the past, any form of capital inflows into Taiwan has been welcomed if the foreign exchange was surrendered to the Central Bank. From early 1986 to January 1987, the New Taiwan dollar appreciated against the U.S. dollar more than 12 percent.[47] The inflows of short-term speculative capital have caused the concern of the authorities. At least one legal loophole has troubled the authorities in dealing with capital inflows—the foreign exchange brought into the country by travelers, since no regulation governs the amount of foreign exchange an individual traveler can carry into Taiwan. The amount of capital inflows via this channel are substantial and has worsened the pressure on the New Taiwan dollar appreciation.[48] Since July 1987, the inward and outward remittances have been liberalized and the government has gradually shifted to relying on market functioning to solve the problem.

Controls on Capital Outflows

Official restrictions on capital outflows have played a significant role in Taiwan's economic development. As with the case of restricting capital outflows, prior-approval requirements are commonly used in most of the regulations. There are even more restrictive measures with respect to the controls on capital outflows.

Before the 1980s, outward investments from Taiwan were negligible.[49] On 12 June 1964, the Regulations Governing the Screening and Handling of Outward Investment and Outward Technical Cooperation Projects was promulgated and has been amended to cope with the changing domestic and international economic situations. The latest amendment was made on 27 March 1989. Under the rules, the term "outward investment" refers to the following domestic company's outward investments: (1) investment furnished by a single domestic company or by several domestic companies jointly or in association with a foreign government, a judicial person, or an individual for establishing a new enterprise or expanding an existing enterprise through an increase of capital or the purchase of shares issued by a foreign company; or (2) establishing or expanding the overseas branch offices, plants, or other business offices. Thus, the regulation governs direct investment and portfolio investment abroad by domestic companies in Taiwan, and individual outward investment is not allowed. In early 1986, the government allowed five appointed banks to operate foreign outward investments in foreign government bond and treasury bills as well as bonds and certificates of deposit issued by leading international banks with maturities from six months to five years for their customers in order to curb the cumulating foreign-exchange reserves.[50] Because the New Taiwan dollar is appreciating in value, the public is reluctant to invest abroad.[51] However, this was the first time that the public had been allowed to invest abroad indirectly, and some investors who put their money in a certificate of deposit in Japanese yen earned in interest an amount up to 20 times the total due to the appreciation of the Japanese yen.[52]

According to the regulation, outward investments are confined to one of the following conditions and are limited to these industries which are beneficial to the nation's economic development: (1) to help domestic industries to acquire needed raw materials; (2) to promote the increased export, or safeguard the export market, of the nation's products; (3) to induce the inflow of key technical know-how needed in Taiwan; (4) to be conducive to the exportation of technology and, thus, to an increase in foreign-exchange earnings; (5) to promote international economic cooperation; (6) to adjust the structure of domestic industries; and (7) to invest in venture-capital investment companies abroad for indirect technology transfers into Taiwan. However, an outward direct investment or technical cooperation is not subjected to the aforesaid restrictions, if the case is deemed necessary by the government under policy consideration and has been approved by the government. In addition, all outward investments must be screened and handled by the Investment Commission of the Ministry of Economic Affairs. The regulation, in particular, empowers the Investment Commission with discretion to meet its policy goals.

There are other restrictions on outward investments. Should the investors invest capital stock in the form of outward remittances of foreign exchange, more than NT$20 million paid-up capital and less than 30 percent of debt/capital ratio are required. Other follow-up procedures such as proof of the establishment and capital increase of the invested enterprise, time limits on the completion of the investment project, approval for the transfer of reinvesting capital, etc., are required to prevent any unjustified capital outflow.

Furthermore, any one of the following foreign-exchange incomes shall be remitted back to Taiwan: (1) the capital paid on an already-implemented outward investment project after the approval thereof has been revoked; (2) paid-in capital recovered from the foreign government, judicial person or individual to whom the company has transferred its invested capital; (3) the net profit realized from an outward investment; (4) other earnings realized from an outward investment; (5) compensation received when the local government requisitions or expropriates the invested enterprise; and (6) other income realized in accordance with provisions of local law that is allowed to be repatriated to Taiwan in the form of foreign exchange. Thus, the regulation not only covers outgoing direct investment but also governs outward portfolio investment from Taiwan. The regulation also governs the outward investment from investment to disinvestment, thus it is effective in preventing speculative long-term capital outflows but also in impeding the profitability of the idle domestic currency. To curb the influx of foreign-exchange reserves and domestic money supply since early 1986, attention has been paid to liberalizing and encouraging direct or indirect outward investment by the public.

A second source of capital outflows is the payment of imported commodities and related expenditures incurred. Under the Statute for Foreign Exchange Regulation, as amended on 14 May 1986, importers are required to declare foreign exchange for import payment through an appointed bank when applying for a letter of credit, accepting a bill of exchange, or paying for imported goods. A prior-approved exchange settlement no longer is required. As with import earnings, the Central Bank audits the transactions periodically. Alternatively, importers are allowed to pay the cost and expenditures of imports by withdrawing the foreign exchange from the special foreign-exchange deposit account without a foreign-exchange settlement.[53]

In addition to the export payments, the following payments abroad are subject to exchange control and the Ministry of Finance shall formulate such regulations in consultation with the Central Bank:[54] (1) payment of expenditures on services by shipping, insurance, and other industries; (2) expenditures required for travel abroad for study, inspection tours, medical treatment, visiting close relatives, employment, and business trips; (3) expenses for family maintenance abroad by nationals or foreigners serving in governmental organizations and private enterprises within the country; (4) the principal, interest, and net profit accruing from investments in the country by foreigners and overseas Chinese; (5) the principal, interest, and guarantee fees of foreign loans made with the approval of the government; (6) the payment of royalties to foreigners or overseas Chinese resulting from their technical cooperation with domestic enterprises; (7) the investment or lending abroad with the approval of the government; and (8) other necessary expenditures approved by the government. These regulations, partly coordinated with the aforesaid outward investment controls, have effectively prevented most speculative capital outflows from Taiwan. A review of some significant regulations is given subsequently.

The payments of expenditures on services by shipping, insurance, and other industries are treated in the Regulations Governing the Screening of Foreign Exchange Receipts and Expenditures of Chinese Shipping Companies as amended on 2 February 1979. The Chinese shipping companies should prepare a detailed list of the expenditures within six months from the date on which the expenditures were incurred with the name of the ship, the voyage number, the items and amount of the expenditures. This detailed list together with the relevant invoice and documents is required to apply for foreign-exchange settlement or to offset the foreign-exchange earnings of the companies. The amount of foreign-exchange settlement or offset every year shall be no more than the amount of operational receipts. The companies may apply for settlement of foreign exchange for the payment of principal and interest due or offset with their currency receipts if the loan has been approved by the Central Bank. The insurance companies, as noted above, are required to deposit foreign-exchange earnings in a special account and any payment for business expenses must be drawn from the account. Should the special account not be sufficient to cover the expenditures, the insurance companies may apply for a foreign-exchange settlement by submitting the relevant documents to the Central Bank. A foreign insurance company is required to open a special New Taiwan dollar account with an appointed bank for depositing the reinsurance premium paid.[55] An application for a settlement of foreign exchange should be filed by the Chinese coinsurer on a quarterly basis under a specific procedure.[56]

Since a foreign shipping company which handles the shipment of import and export commodities or passenger business to or from Taiwan is required to collect the freight and passenger fares in the New Taiwan dollar, the agents of foreign shipping companies should apply for a foreign-exchange settlement for the balance of the receipts and expenditures within three months of the arrival or departure of the vessel. In an exceptional case in which a foreign shipping company is undertaking the shipment of imported bulk goods, the agent of the company is required to obtain prior approval from the Board of Foreign Trade of the Ministry of Economic Affairs for the purpose of a foreign-exchange settlement.[57]

For the airline industry, a Chinese airline may apply to the Central Bank for a foreign-exchange settlement of various foreign currency expenses within six months from the day the expenses are incurred or by offsetting the expenses from its foreign-exchange earnings. A foreign airline may apply for the settlement of foreign exchange or request to convert the foreign currency notes received into the form of foreign exchange on a monthly basis within three months immediately after the end of each month. A detailed list of receipts, including passenger fares and cargo freight as well as expenditures, is required for auditing purposes when applying for a foreign-exchange settlement.[58]

One kind of foreign-exchange settlement is for expenditures related to travel abroad for study, inspection tours, medical treatment, visiting close relatives, employment, and business trips. The applications for a foreign-exchange settlement for these purposes are governed by the Regulations Governing Applications for Foreign Exchange for Trip Expenses by Persons Going Abroad, as amended on 21 February 1979. Persons going abroad may apply for the settlement of foreign exchange under the following categories: (1) pocket money; (2) per diem expenses; and (3) others. Persons who are eligible to apply for pocket money include: (1) Chinese nationals going abroad to visit or live with relatives or for overseas employment, assignments, study, etc.; (2) overseas Chinese employed by public or private institutions in Taiwan and the returned overseas Chinese who have resided in Taiwan for more than six months; (3) aliens employed by public or private institutions in the Republic with the approval of the government authorities concerned or the general managers of the Taiwan foreign company branches who have resided in Taiwan for more than six months and have been dispatched by their employers for trips abroad;[59] (4) overseas Chinese and foreign students in Taiwan who return to their countries of residence for reasons of graduation, suspension, or withdrawal from an academic institution; (5) Chinese who hold official passports or diplomatic passports; and (6) the managers and submanagers of the Taiwan foreign company branches who are dispatched abroad for business reasons with a formal letter from the branch offices. There are limits on the amount of foreign-exchange settlement—no more than US$1,500 per person in a three-month period of time.

The following persons may apply for settlement of foreign exchange for per diem expenses: (1) Chinese nationals going abroad for international conferences, inspections, business negotiations, medical treatment, or sales promotion visits (including news assignments); (2) Chinese nationals going abroad for training, studying, supervising production, installing machinery, or purchasing; (3) family members accompanying the elected members or employees of the central government with permission and holding an official passport but without trip expenses allocated from the Ministry of Finance; and (4) Chinese going abroad as tourists. The amount of foreign exchange settlement for per diem expenses is prescribed by the authorities at US$2,200 per person for each month with a maximum amount of three months. For tourists under twelve years old, half of the amount can be applied for.

The third category of foreign-exchange settlement for persons who are going abroad is limited to the following personnel: (1) emigrants; and (2) crew members going abroad to take over a new ship or aircraft. There is a US$2,000 limit for each emigrant and a US$600 for each crew member. To apply for any one of the aforesaid foreign-exchange settlements, a passport and exit permit are required to substantiate the need for a foreign-exchange settlement.

Chinese or alien personnel employed by public and private enterprises and civil organizations registered under pertinent laws with the approval of the competent authorities in charge may apply for a foreign-exchange settlement for outward remittances of up to 60 percent of their income in salary and allowances (including overtime pay) as needed for family maintenance abroad. The travel expenses for these personnel coming to Taiwan also can be covered with the application for a foreign-exchange settlement. The application shall be filed every month or every three months. Failure to file the application within a two-month time limit will result in foregoing privilege of applying for foreign exchange, and no application will thus be accepted. Should the overseas Chinese or alien employees be exempted from income tax, or where their income tax is paid by their employers by agreement, the amount of the foreign-exchange settlement may be increased by 20 percent. The income tax payable by overseas Chinese or alien employees shall be withheld by the employers on the day the foreign-exchange settlement is made. The employer also is responsible for making a declaration of employment to the Central Bank listing the time, numbers, and the port of entry of the overseas Chinese or alien employees together with approval of employment documents issued by the competent authorities in charge.[60]

Another supplementary regulation governs the outward investment operation. Under the Regulations Governing Application for Settlement of Foreign Exchange for the Use of the Operational Expenses of Agencies in Foreign Countries Established by Domestic Enterprises, as amended on 5 November 1980, a Chinese enterprise which has obtained approval for establishing an agency abroad may apply for the foreign-exchange settlement to be used as operational expenses of the agency established in foreign countries. The operational expenses include establishment expenses and regular operational expenses. The establishment expenses are the actual costs subject to be duly certified by a public notary of the place where the agency is located. The regular operational expenses depend on the number of employees involved and the area in which the agency is located.[61]

As noted above, incomes, including the principal, interest, and profits accruing from investments in the country by foreigners and overseas Chinese, are allowed to remit back to home countries one year after the commencement of the invested business. The repatriations of the foreign capital also are safeguarded by the Statute for Investment by Foreign Nationals and the Statute for Investment by Overseas Chinese. Similarly, payments of royalties to foreigners or overseas Chinese resulting from the technical cooperation with domestic enterprises may be applied for through a foreign-exchange settlement to the extent of the amount approved under the technical cooperation agreement.[62]

There are regulations governing the procedures of small amounts and comparatively large numbers of foreign-exchange settlements. To simplify the procedure of foreign-exchange settlements of this character, the Central Bank has authorized the appointed banks themselves to handle foreignexchange settlements not exceeding US$100 for payment of admission fees, application fees, registration fees, handling charges, inspection charges, certification fees, test fees, and screening fees.[63] The appointed banks are also being authorized to handle foreign-exchange settlements not exceeding US$200 for payments for trademark fees, patent fees, and imported sample fees. These small foreign-exchange settlement amounts, however, are confined to certain uses, and the applicants are required to prove the payments are for the applicable purpose. Under the Regulations Governing Small Amount Remittance, as amended on 11 July 1986, Chinese nationals over twenty years old are allowed to remit no more than US$5,000 each year abroad for unspecified purposes. The applicants are only required to file the application form and present an effective identification. The public has widely taken advantage of these regulations to remit money abroad for various purposes, sometimes only to secure the money abroad by holding foreign currencies.[64]

In Taiwan, the foreign-exchange controls on outward capital flows are more restrictive as compared to the restrictions on capital inflows. Although there are common uses of authorization requirements, time limits, and purpose specifications, quantity restrictions are more frequently used in outward control regulations. In contrast, the quantity restrictions are only loosely regulated in the case of capital inflows. The most evident case is that of the incoming traveler who is allowed to bring in foreign exchange without limitation on the amount whereas the outgoing traveler can carry no more than 62.5 grams of gold jewelry, 625 grams of silver jewelry, and foreign currencies with a total not exceeding the equivalent of US$1,000.[65] The structure of foreign-exchange schemes, including outward and inward restrictions, reflects the traditional thinking of the developing countries to accumulate scarce capital for domestic uses, particularly the foreign direct investments which enjoy a relatively free mobility of capital. In Taiwan, the fact that importers and exporters are given more leeway to use their foreign-exchange earnings via the foreign-exchange deposit account also indicates the policy implications of an export-oriented economy. The operations of exchange controls are heavily dependent upon coordination between the Central Bank and the appointed banks; this is part of the reason why the foreign banks in Taiwan are not allowed to accept the New Taiwan dollar deposits and operate investment and trust businesses for those money flows that are invisible and difficult to regulate.[66] One of the purposes of the foreign-exchange controls is to maintain an orderly foreign-exchange market, thereby stabilizing the financial system. Any sudden increase in capital inflows or outflows is not desirable because it would surely offset the domestic monetary policies particularly for the case of Taiwan with a small and not fully developed money market.

As stated above, the 1991 amendment revised the amount of foreign exchange which one can remit inward or outward. The aforesaid restrictions do not apply if all the payments or proceeds of an individual or a company are under the annual amount of US$3 million. Although it is arguable that this is only partial liberalization of foreign-exchange control, the de facto liberalization of exchange control is an actuality to the public.

One sector of banking activities is not subject to foreign-exchange controls in Taiwan—offshore banking. The Offshore Banking Act was promulgated in December 1984. The purpose of establishing the offshore banking center is to create a world financial center, thereby facilitating the internationalization of the nation's economy. The offshore banking activities as provided in the Act include: (1) accepting foreign-exchange deposits from individuals, legal entities, or government agencies outside the country; (2) accepting foreign-exchange deposits from financial institutions; (3) raising funds on the international financial market; (4) managing funds on the international market; (5) engaging in foreign currency trade and remittance; (6) making loans to individuals, legal entities, government agencies, or financial institutions; and (7) booking and managing foreign currency loans. The offshore banking branches are not allowed to handle remittances or conversions between foreign currencies and the New Taiwan dollar unless approved by the Central Bank. In the final analysis, the impact of offshore banking operations on the domestic financial system is limited and isolated.

Complications Arising from Mainland China

In Taiwan, foreign-exchange controls stem from the need for stabilized exchange rates and a reliable financial system to provide the background for economic development. A complication thus arises from the threat of Mainland Communist China. Before 1949, the sabotage measures used by the Communists to disrupt the nation's financial system, thereby diminishing public confidence in the national currency in the Mainland, was said to be attributable to the ensuing hyperinflation and economic destruction. The nationalist government learned the lesson from the painful experiences of the Mainland and has been cautious in implementing foreign-exchange controls and foreign-exchange reserves.

Historically, the 1950s and 1960s were periods of reconstruction from World War II and the immense military threat from Communist China. Capital shortages and potential capital flight were a serious problem for Taiwan's economic development. As noted before, estimates indicate that before 1960, 90 percent of domestic investments came from the United States. In 1965, when the United States terminated aid to Taiwan, the insufficiency of domestic savings and capital formations was evident and the attention was therefore shifted to the encouragement of foreign direct investments. The decade of the 1970s was an eventful one. In November 1971, Taiwan withdrew from the United Nations when the United Nations accepted Communist China as the sole legitimate government to represent China. In September 1972, Japan followed other nations' decisions to terminate diplomatic relations with Taiwan, even though it was the Republic of China which signed the peace treaty with Japan after World War II. A series of actions taken by other nations have isolated Taiwan from the international community, and the reliance on the United States as a long-term and faithful friend has become deeper. Unfortunately, the United States closed its embassy in Taipei in 1978 and established diplomatic ties with Communist China. The shock was startling and caused the delay of the 1978 elections in Taiwan. A decree was issued by the president on 16 December 1978 to deal with the changing situation. In early 1980, Taiwan was ousted from the IMF and the World Bank despite the fact that the Republic of China was one of the initial members of the organization. Thus, the special drawing rights and development loans have no longer been available to Taiwan. In April 1986, the Asian Development Bank changed the official name of Taiwan as the Republic of China to China Taipei and accepted Communist China as the sole name of People's Republic of China. Taiwan boycotted the Bank's annual meeting and the issue remains unresolved.[67]

By reviewing Taiwan's history, it is not difficult to understand why the authorities in Taiwan have been cautious and conservative toward the liberalization of foreign-exchange controls. In the 1950s and 1960s, public confidence in the nation's currency was ruled out by low incomes, construction needs, and substantial military expenditures to fight against possible invasions of Communist China. The problems involved then were not only capital shortages but also capital flight which could have endangered the stabilization of the financial system and worsened the creditworthiness of international loans. Foreign-exchange controls were crucial in restoring public confidence and establishing orderly exchange rates. Most important, as these exchange control measures prevented capital flight effectively on the one hand, the exchange controls successfully adjusted the needs of domestic capital by channeling the scarce national foreign exchange to industrial development on the other hand. By 1965 the United States terminated its official aid to Taiwan, the government has become more concerned with using foreign exchange to purchase raw materials, machinery, equipment for economic development.

In the 1970s, Taiwan experienced two OPEC crises, and the political isolation was worsened. To cope with the changing situation and to restore public confidence, the government adopted a series of measures to curb the inflation in 1974. In 1978, the second OPEC crisis accompanied with the shock of the severance of diplomatic ties with the United States touched off another economic crisis in Taiwan. During the 1970s, capital flight and investments decreased again and became tough issues for the authorities' consideration in the wake of one external shock after the other.

In the early 1980s, when the Taiwan economy began to pick up development, the impacts of withdrawal from the IMF and the World Bank were rather minimized because of strong economic performance and public confidence. Since the early 1980s, the nation has accumulated foreign-exchange reserves that have been far more than adequate.[68] Due to the rapid growth in the past thirty years, creditworthiness is no longer the nation's urgent concern and the gross external debts are negligible compared to the strong export surplus.[69] However, due to the small outward economy domestically and the political strains internationally, there is little doubt that a secure foreign-exchange reserve and cautious foreign-exchange management is not only necessary but critical to the nation's economic development.

A new challenge to Taiwan is that Communist China has posed the so-called "open-door" policy which is designed to attract more foreign direct investment and to foster external trade with others, especially

Western nations, since 1979. The rich resources, low wages, and a huge domestic market are tempting to foreign investors and the international environment has become more hospitable toward Communist China. The implications of this development are clear that, in the short term, foreign investors will shift their investments to the Mainland, and, for the long run, that Communist China will be a viable competitor in the international market. To cope with the changing events, Taiwan has shifted investment policy to encourage more sophisticated production and industrial restructuring. More foreign direct investments and technical cooperation are needed to achieve the policy goals. Therefore, internationalization and liberalization of the domestic economy to meet the needs of foreign trade expansion and enhance substantial relationships with other nations have resulted in the reform of the financial system and the partial liberalization of foreign-exchange controls.

On 15 July 1987, the government lifted martial law. On 1 May 1991, on his inauguration, President Lee announced that the so-called "temporary provisions of the Constitution," which had been promulgated forty-two years earlier to cope with the unusual situation caused by Communist China, were to be terminated within one year. More statutes and regulations are under review to cope with the changing situation between the two sides of the Taiwan strait. However, how to keep the balance of development needs and limited involvement with the Mainland to avoid economic dependence will be important in formulating any policy changes.

The impressive economic achievements in Taiwan have brought more foreign commercial and economic ties to Taiwan with other nations. In the Asia Development Bank, for instance, Taiwan was one of the original founders and has been a net contributor rather than a borrower of the fund. Thus, there are more reasons to maintain a seat in the Bank for Taiwan than to exclude Taiwan as a member. It is argued that the necessity of defending against the imminent Communist China threat is losing its ground, in light of the economic reforms on the Mainland. However, because the trustworthiness of Communist China remains uncertain[70] and because of the reluctance to reform the poorly performing socialist system, it is hardly a persuasive argument to convince the nationalist government to be fully unconcerned with the threat of Communist China, at least for the time being. In the near future, the liberalization of foreign exchange controls will progress slowly with particular heed paid to national security. After all, Communist China has repeated that it never precluded the possibility of using force against Taiwan.[71]

NOTES

1. Ministry of Economic Affairs, *Investment Opportunities in Taiwan, the Republic of China* (Taipei: IDIC, October 1981).

2. Both Article 5 of the Statute for Investment by Foreign Nationals and the Statute for Investment by Overseas Chinese were amended in June 1986 to include the service industry into the investment scope. McDonald's opened its first restaurant in early 1984. Maria Shao, "U.S. Food Chains Sprout in Taiwan, as Affluence Creates New Appetites," *Asian Wall Street Journal*, 9 September 1985.

3. As noted before, the Nissan investment project was the first one which allowed an investor to purchase stock of a local car maker directly.

4. These funds are the Taiwan (R.O.C.) Fund, the Formosa Fund, the Taipei Fund, and the Taiwan Fund. The only openly traded fund is the Taiwan Fund which is listed on the American Stock Exchange. A more detailed description of these funds' operations will be given later in this chapter.

5. The previous export ratio requirement was one of the reasons for the cancellation of the Toyota deal in 1983. In 1986, the export ratio caused the United States concern, and it invoked Section 301 of the Fair Trade Law to investigate whether there was any unfair trade practice involved, when Toyota returned. (Robert E. Norton, "Trade War: A New Track, The Administration Objects to Taiwan's Plan to Export Cars," *Fortune*, 26 May 1986, p. 94.) Since then the export ratio requirement has been called off in the Toyota case. (*Free China Journal*, 11 August 1986, p. 1.)

6. Maria Shao, "U.S. Steps Up Pressures on Taipei to Lift Curb on Trade and Investment," *Asian Wall Street Journal*, 14 October 1985.

7. Business International Asia, *World Sourcing Sites in Asia, Manufacturing Costs and Conditions in Hong Kong, Korea, Singapore, and Taiwan*, A Business International Asia Research Report (Hong Kong: Business International Asia/Pacific, November 1979).

8. The government is undergoing a revision of the law to allow the manufacturers in the export processing zones and science-based industrial park to distribute up to 50 percent of their products directly into domestic markets. (*Free China Journal*, 26 January 1987, p. 4.)

9. The enterprises in the Park are not allowed to sell their products in the domestic market unless the products are not otherwise producible in Taiwan. However, the government is considering the possibility of allowing the subsidiaries of the foreign companies to sell the parent companies' products in the domestic market with a view to attracting more foreign high-technology investments and to easing the financial difficulties for those industries during the start-up stage. (*Central Daily News*, in Chinese, 4 January 1987.)

10. *Free China Journal*, 26 January 1987, p. 4.

11. In 1989, the outputs of the service industry reached 51.5 percent of the GNP and contributed to the 9.9 percent of the economic development (as compared to the 5.3 percent of the industrial sectors). As stated in the Tenth Economic Construction Medium Plan (1990–1993) of the Republic of China, one of the basic policies of the government toward the service industry is to further lift the restrictions on foreign investment to attract modern business management ideas and technology.

12. OECD, *International Investment and Multinational Enterprises, Investment In-*

centives and Disincentives and the International Investment Process (Paris: OECD, 1983).

13. Council for Economic Planning and Development, *Ten-Year Economic Plan* (Taipei: Council for Economic Planning, 1980).

14. Ministry of Economic Affairs, *Legal Consideration for Investment in Taiwan, Republic of China* (Taipei: IDIC, 1985).

15. The term "productive enterprise" is referred to in the statute as any one of the following types of operations which produce goods and render services and which is organized as a company limited by share in accordance with current law.

16. The 1987 amendment reduced the 22 percent taxable income to 20 percent of the taxable income, and the big trading companies are now able to enjoy the same treatment as those companies designated as high-tech.

17. The corporation income tax exempted by the government has been estimated to cost US$1–2 billion. (*Business Asia*, 19 January 1987).

18. K. Billerbeck and Y. Yasugi, *Private Direct Foreign Investment in Developing Countries: Policy Issues for Host and Home Governments and for International Institutions*, World Bank Staff Working Paper, No. 348 (Washington, D.C.: World Bank, July 1979), pp. 17–18.

19. OECD, *Investment Incentives and Disincentives*.

20. *Industry of Free China*, February 1986, p. 29.

21. *Central Daily News* (in Chinese), 13 January 1987, p. 3.

22. "Financial Outlook: Taiwan," *Business Asia*, 27 January 1986.

23. *Central Daily News* (in Chinese), 12 November 1986, p. 2.

24. IDIC, *Legal Consideration for Investment in Taiwan*.

25. George E. Charles, *Developing Venture Capital in the Republic of China, An American Banker's Viewpoint* (Taipei: IDIC, June 1984).

26. "Simplified Red Tape Lures Increased Venture Capital," *Free China Journal*, 8 September 1986, p. 2.

27. From 1981 to 1986, domestic savings exceeded gross domestic capital formation by more than NT$900 million (*Taiwan Statistical Data Book, 1986*, Taipei: Council for Economic Planning and Development, 1986) and since domestic interest rates are relatively lower than world financial market rates, the foreign firms are more interested in borrowing from local financial institutions.

28. *Ten-Year Economic Development Plan*, 1980–89.

29. Ministry of Economic Affairs, *A Brief Introduction to the Industrial Estates in Taiwan, the Republic of China* (Taipei: IDIC, June 1985).

30. Article 15 of the Statute for Investment by Foreign Nationals and Article 16 of the Statute for Investment by Overseas Chinese; both statutes have been amended as of 26 May 1989.

31. "Investment Law Changes, Trim Forex Restrictions, Widen Scope in Taiwan," *Business Asia*, 9 June 1986, pp. 180–81.

32. Business International, *World Sourcing Sites in Asia*.

33. Steve Shin-ting Tsai, "The Development of R.O.C.-U.S. Economic Ties," *Industry of Free China* 61, no. 4, (April 1984).

34. "Taiwan's New Copyright Law: A Great Leap Forward, but Many Hurdles Remain," *Business International*, 19 July 1985, pp. 225–26.

35. *Business Asia*, 19 January 1987; *Central Daily News* (in Chinese), 13 December 1986, p. 2.

36. The Fair Trade Law was passed by the Executive Yuan in 1986 and was passed and enacted by the Legislative Yuan in February 1991. See "Taiwan's Fair Trade Law Now under Deliberation Breaks New Ground," *Business Asia*, 6 October 1986, p. 333, for comments on the draft.

37. Earl H. Fry, *The Politics of International Investment* (New York: McGraw-Hill, 1983), p. 152.

38. The government lifted the ban on the import and trade of gold and silver, but the export of gold and silver is still subjected to control. Exports of gold are required to obtain a prior approval from the Ministry of Finance and the exports of other precious metals are subject to the prior approval of the Ministry of Economic Affairs under the new rules.

39. The 5 percent value-added tax in Taiwan was imposed in April 1986 and the gold traders are required to pay the value-added tax. ("Dealers Say Tax Is Killing Gold Trade, Despite New Rules," *Free China Journal*, 23 August 1986).

40. Before 20 December 1978, all the export or reexport proceeds were required to be sold to the appointed banks or the Central Bank.

41. "Taiwan Liberalizes Forex System," *Business Asia*, 1 September 1986, p. 276.

42. "Taiwan Funds," *Far Eastern Economic Review*, 8 January 1987, p. 99.

43. One report indicated that foreign individual investors may invest in the Taiwan stock market directly by setting up New Taiwan dollar deposits with multinational bank branches in Taiwan. (Philip Bowing, "Individual Can Play Too," *Far Eastern Economic Review*, 26 March 1987, p. 75.)

44. Regulations Governing the Application of Settlement of Foreign Exchange by Insurance Companies, as amended on 26 July 1979.

45. Regulations Governing the Screening of Application for Foreign Exchange for Freight by Agents of Shipping Companies, as amended on 2 February 1979.

46. Regulations Governing the Settlement of Foreign Exchange for Fares/Freight by Airlines, as promulgated on 17 September 1980.

47. Julia Leung, "Taiwan under Fire for Regulating the Rise in Its Currency, Government Intervention Sparks Speculation, Fear of Inflation, Quick Fix for Trade Friction?" *Asian Wall Street Journal*, 12 January 1987, p. 1.

48. The amount of capital inflows through this channel was estimated by the officials concerned to be as high as US$400 million during 1986. (*Central Daily News*, in Chinese, 28 December 1986, p. 2.)

49. Before the 1980s, average outward investment from Taiwan accounted less than US$4 million annually according to official statistics. In 1980–85, the amounts of approved direct investment abroad were as follows: US$42.12 million in 1980, US$10.76 million in 1981, US$11.63 million in 1982, US$10.56 million in 1983, US$39.26 million in 1984, and US$41.17 million in 1985. (*Statistics on Overseas Chinese and Foreign Investment, Technical Cooperation, Outward Investment, Outward Technical Cooperation, the Republic of China* (Taipei: Investment Commission, Ministry of Economic Affairs, various issues.)

50. By the end of 1986, the foreign-exchange reserves reached US$46 billion in Taiwan according to the Central Bank statistics. ("Slowly, Slowly, Taiwan Reforms Forex Controls," *Business Asia*, 25 August 1986.)

51. In order to make more effective use of foreign-exchange reserves, the Central Bank provided refinancing for overseas investments by local enterprises. Top priority investment projects include the acquisition of foreign mineral deposits, the opening of offshore financial affiliates, the gaining of footholds in major markets, and the acquisition of equity interests in high-tech enterprises. (*Industry of Free China*, April 1990, p. 42.)

52. Ibid.

53. The appointed banks in Taiwan are authorized to issue import licenses. To balance the trade deficit with Japan, some measures are used to restrict the imports from Japan, such as the ban on the importation of Japanese automobiles since the late 1970s. In Taiwan, the restrictions on the importation of commodities are classified as prohibited, controlled, and permissible.

54. Article 13, the Statute for Foreign Exchange Regulation, as amended on 18 May 1986.

55. Before the end of 1986, there was no foreign insurance company operating an insurance business in Taiwan. However, the foreign insurance companies are allowed to underwrite reinsurance.

56. Within six months of the end of each quarter, the Chinese coinsurer shall, first, on behalf of the foreign insurance company, apply to the Central Reinsurance Corporation by submitting the bills of the reinsurance premium in consecutive serial numbers and the detailed statement for issuance of a "licensing memo" for the application of foreign-exchange settlement of reinsurance premium receipts. Within one month of the issuance of such "licensing memo," the application for settlement of foreign exchange shall be submitted to the Foreign-Exchange Department of the Central Bank, and an application over the prescribed one-month period shall not be accepted. (Regulations Governing the Application of Settlement of Foreign Exchange by Insurance Companies, as amended on 26 July 1979.)

57. Regulations Governing the Screening of Applications for Foreign Exchange for Freight by Agents of the Shipping Companies, as promulgated on 2 February 1979.

58. Regulations Governing the Settlement of Foreign Exchange for Fares/Freight by Airlines, as promulgated on 17 September 1980.

59. When dispatched abroad by their employer, employees are required to submit a letter of approval of employment issued by the government authorities in charge to apply for the settlement of foreign exchange for per diem expenses.

60. Regulations Governing Application by Overseas Chinese and Aliens Employed for Work in Taiwan for Foreign Exchange to Cover Family Subsistence and Travel Expenses, as amended on 26 December 1975.

61. The criteria of foreign-exchange allowance for the said regular operational expenses are as follows: (1) for the agency which has three or more staff members and is set up in Europe, North America, Japan, or the Middle East, the amount of foreign-exchange allowance each month shall be no more than US$9,000, and shall be no more than US$6,000 if the agency is set up in South America, Southeast Asia, or Africa; (2) for the agency with two staff members, the amount of foreign-exchange allowance each month is limited to US$6,600 and US$4,800 respectively according to the different areas; and (3) for the agency with only one staff member, the amount of foreign-exchange allowance each month is limited to US$3,600 and US$3,000 respectively, again depending on the area where located.

62. The Statute for Foreign Exchange Regulation, Article 13 and the Statute for Technical Cooperation, Article 13.

63. Authorization to Handle Settlement of Foreign Exchange in Small Amount for Other Remittances, as amended on 18 November 1974.

64. In addition to this loophole, it is conceded that the exporters and importers are being allowed to use a falsified voice to evade controls. However, the amount of capital outflows via illegal channels is difficult to evaluate.

65. Passengers who have carried more than US$1,000 into Taiwan are allowed to

carry the same amount of foreign currency out of the country, provided they declared the amount of foreign currency to the customs office at the time of entry.

66. However, the government began allowing foreign banks in Taiwan to accept the New Taiwan dollar savings deposits in 1987.

67. James Glad, "The ADB Slackens Its New Commitments, Last-Resort Lender," *Far Eastern Economic Review*, 15 May 1986, p. 64.

68. The foreign-exchange reserve reached US$46 billion by the end of 1986 according to the Central Bank statistics.

69. The gross external debts totaled US$6–7 billion up to the end of 1986 and the trade surpluses were estimated to be US$15.6 billion. ("Statistical Data, R.O.C. on Taiwan," *Free China Journal*, 9 March 1987, p. 4.)

70. On 16 January 1987, the sudden resignation of the Communist Party's General Secretary, Hu Yaobang, once again demonstrated the Communists' unstable policy guides and again created uncertainty and confusion as to both foreign and domestic policies. ("Hu's Dismissal Signals an Orthodox Backlash, Reforms in Jeopardy," *Far Eastern Economic Review*, 29 January 1987.)

71. "An Interview with Hu Yaobang, Peking Lashes Out at Washington-Taipei Link," *Far Eastern Economic Review*, 24 July 1986.

4

Current Developments and Partial Liberalization in Taiwan

During the four-year period from 1982 to 1985,[1] Taiwan's economic growth fluctuated due to the worldwide recession. An average annual growth rate of 6.0 percent in real terms of industrial products was reported with falling fixed investment by industries.[2] Nevertheless, the gross product of the so-called strategic industries contributed to the gross manufacturing product which rose from 21.4 percent (NT$150.46 billion) in 1981 to 22.8 percent (NT$213.66 billion) in 1984. The performance of industrial output indicates that encouragement of development in strategic industries has been paying off (although not enormously, and the growth of domestic investment has been weaker as a whole).[3]

With respect to foreign direct investment in 1989, the leading three sectors of investment attracting industries other than service and trade industries are as follows: electronic and electric products accounting for US$391 million, chemical industries accounting for US$519 million, and machinery equipment and instruments accounting for US$175 million. The total amounts of investment in trade and service industries are US$222 million and 312 million respectively.[4] During 1989, the total amount of foreign direct investment increased over 100 percent (US$2,418 million) compared to 1988. This large increase in the total amount of foreign direct investment and the major sectors invested in by the overseas investors again indicates that the encouragement of strategic industries and the establishment of a favorable investment climate have been effective. And the service industries are no longer to be regarded as forbidden land to foreigners, thus becoming another major sector for foreign investors.

However, in 1986, the Chrysler Corporation of the United States decided to pull out of a joint venture with the Taiwan carmaker, Yue Loong Motor Company, and Nissan Company, due to the appreciation of the New Taiwan dollar and the Japanese yen, making costs too high to compete on the international market.[5] Thus, the cost of currency appreciation has become another issue to be dealt with in the negotiations of foreign direct investment. Other issues involving foreign investment include the openness of the stock market and outward investments by Chinese (Taiwan) nationals. Some regulations, such as the Statute for Encouragement of Investment by Foreign Nationals, the Statute for Encouragement of Investment by Overseas Chinese, and the Securities and Exchange Act are revised to provide a more liberal climate for foreign and overseas Chinese investment.

Another current development with respect to international capital flows is the liberalization of financial market operations and exchange controls. In 1988, the gross national savings were 37.5 percent of GNP and domestic investments were 16.27 percent of GNP.[6] How to convert domestic savings into domestic investment has become a serious concern of the authorities. Meanwhile, the influx of foreign-exchange reserves due to the export boom and speculative capital inflows induced by the expectation of the New Taiwan dollar appreciation in 1986 pushed the foreign-exchange reserves to a record level of US$76 billion by the end of 1989. Pressures on the appreciation of the New Taiwan dollars have consistently increased. Some critics have been arguing for more liberal exchange controls and banking operations. To use the foreign-exchange reserves more effectively to reduce exchange risks and stimulate domestic investments via liberalizing the foreign-exchange controls has been widely debated.

This chapter will review the current developments in Taiwan with respect to foreign investment and banking operations as well as foreign-exchange controls. Although some of the new regulations and policies are debatable, the trend of the developments represents a new era of economic development.

FOREIGN INVESTMENT RECONSIDERATIONS

Foreign Direct Investment

Under the Ninth Medium-term Economic Development Plan, the basic policy toward foreign direct investment is to "review and update existing tax and financial measures to encourage investment; continue to improve the domestic environment for investment; promote the liberalization of investment; and raise incentives to investment by domestic and foreign entrepreneurs." The supporting measures to promote foreign direct investment include: (1) allowing free entry by private investors into industries other than those affecting national defense, public security, environmental sanitation, and ecological conservation, so as to encourage the flows of capital into industry; (2) revising laws and regulations governing investment, simplifying administrative procedures, strengthening investment services and measures of encouragement, and raising incentives to private investments; (3) adopting a "negative list" approach to gradually phase out the existing case-by-case screening procedures for foreign investment, promoting liberalization and internationalization of investment, and above all, emphasizing the introduction of high-level precision industry and high-tech information industries; (4) studying and relaxing restrictions on overseas investment by the Republic's nationals; (5) amending the Labor Standards Law to safeguard the interests of both labor and business concerns; and (6) reviewing the current state of industrial estate utilization, adequately planning for the future development of such estates, and assisting private enterprises to acquire land for industrial use. However, the Tenth Medium-term Economic Development Plan has focused on only two points regarding foreign direct investment: simplify the administrative process and update tax laws to encourage civilian investment as well as to review and update the negative list of foreign investment to enlarge the scope of industries which are eligible for foreign investors. Thus, it is evident that a more liberal policy to deal with foreign direct investment has been undertaken.

On 16 January 1987, the Legislative Yuan passed the amendment of the Statute of Encouragement for Investment. The main points of the amendment include: (1) approved foreign direct investments organized as a company limited by shares according to the Corporation Law and those engaged in the productive enterprise can enjoy the privileges stipulated by the statute, that is, a five-year tax holiday for new establishment, a four-year tax holiday for reinvestment, a one- to four-year tax deferment, accelerated depreciation, etc.; (2) the foreign branch offices reinvesting their undistributed earnings may be exempted from income tax; (3) corporations which invest in a venture-capital company or an important productive enterprise are not subject to the Corporation Law which restricts the gross amount of transinvestment to 40 percent of paid-in capital of the investing company; (4) when a company organized under the Corporation Law invests in a venture-capital company, 80 percent of the earnings are exempted from income tax; (5) when an enterprise or individual invests in high-technology-intensive industries, 30 percent of the investing amount is deductible from annual taxable income; (6) reducing the land property tax of the land sale and exempting the conduct taxes leviable on the factory in order to encourage the productive enterprises to move in government-designated industrial sites; and (7) international trading companies and international tourist hotels are listed as encouraged productive enterprises.[7]

The amendments are still aiming at selective high-technology development following the current economic development policies. Nevertheless, the approach to the policy goals is rather different from current statutes. Under the current statute, only the investors who invest in one of the productive enterprises listed in the categories of encouragement are eligible to enjoy the privilege of various incentives offered by the government. The new revisions will provide wide-ranging incentives to all productive enterprises with additional benefits to the high-technology industries. This policy approach shift can be seen from two perspectives: First, the development of export-oriented industries is no longer the nation's highest concern, instead an export-expansion and import-substitution policy has been advocated in recent years to meet the rising domestic demand and balance the trade abroad. Thus, any productive enterprise which can foster the economic development either by selling domestically or exporting abroad is encouraged equally. Second, the government is willing to trust the enterprises to invest at their own option under the comparative advantage rule. Due to rising local wages, as compared to other developing countries, the investors will choose to invest in more sophisticated product production or in automated factories in order to compete on the domestic and foreign markets.

A draft of the Statute for the Promotion of Industrial Upgrading was promulgated on 29 December 1990. The new bill provides a generally applied tax exemption to all the productive enterprises. This signals that the policy has shifted from selective encouragement to a more commonly applied basis.

As aforementioned, the fiscal incentives offered by the government are considered by some to be inefficient and insufficient. A possible long-run trend toward treatment of investment is the gradual phasing out of the fiscal incentives. Because the cost of fiscal incentives is high,[8] the Statute for the Promotion of Industrial Upgrading will expand the scope of encouraging enterprises and the long-term trend is to lower the tax rate for all productive enterprises by replacing the current tax exemption for specific industries.

Other measures for liberalizing foreign direct investment include:

(1) continuing the expansion of the categories of enterprises in which foreign investors are eligible to invest. The Ministry of Economic Affairs has provided a "negative list" to replace the current case-by-case approved system on 11 July 1990. The new list provides freer entry for foreign investors through the following measures: (1) List the industries that are not available for foreign ownership; other investment projects should be effected automatically. (2) Lift the restrictions on the remittance of invested capital within one year after the commencement of an investment project,[9] thereby enhancing capital mobility. (3) Allow the invested enterprises to engage in such operations as the selling and buying agency of the parent company.[10] (4) Include the profits of land sales as part of the invested capital which is eligible for remittance.[11] (5) Dismantle state-run enterprises for private investment. For instance, the Broken Hill Proprietary Company of Australia will purchase the publicly owned Taiwan Metal Mining Corporation.[12] Other state-run enterprises, such as the China Shipping Company, the China Petrochemical Development Corporation, Taiwan Machinery Manufacturing, and the China Steel Corporation are under evaluation for a possible opening to private investors. Three publicly owned enterprises—the Taiwan Power Company, the China Petroleum Company, and the Taiwan Sugar Company—may invite more public equity participation.[13] The gas stations have been the first ones opened for private investment.[14] Recently, the government has finished the process of selling the publicly owned stock of three commercial banks. However, the sale was not successful because the stock market price of these stocks fell below the distributing price. (6) Extend the credit line to the enterprises which aim to explore international markets, secure raw materials, or transfer technology under an approved plan. The credit offered will allow the enterprise to borrow three times of the paid-in capital.[15] (6) Phase out performance requirements, that is, export ratio requirements. For instance, the government decided to call off the performance requirements in all automobile investment projects[16] after the United States objected to the Toyota deal by invoking Section 301 of the Trade Agreement Act.[17]

These current developments and measures signal the relaxation of foreign direct investment restrictions and the gradual openings of the domestic market for the foreign investors. Most significantly, the negative list provides more investment opportunities for foreign direct investment and cuts red tape. The elimination of the time restrictions on the remittance of investment capital further guarantee a freer flow of capital. Although potential speculation does exist, the ample foreign-exchange reserves can minimize any adverse impacts. Thus, another incentive offered by the government to the foreign investors will be a driving free-market force with profit-seeking momentum.

Another facet of foreign direct investment is the outward direct investment by the Chinese nationals in Taiwan. Although the outward direct investment has been encouraged by the government since 1985, implemented measures are not yet fully satisfying for the public. Under the Tenth Medium-term Economic Development Plan, one of the supporting measures is to encourage the outward investment by the domestic enterprises to explore industrial materials, to expand international market, and to diversify trade market. The following measures have been posed for further consideration:[18] (1) eliminating the restrictions on the amount of paid-in capital (to no less than NT$20 million) and the debt/capital ratio to no more than 300 percent; (2) lifting Article 13 of the Company Law which restricts the amount of new investment in other businesses to 40 percent of the paid-in capital; (3) deducting a portion of the outward investment amount from the investors' annual taxable income from the investors' annual taxable income; (4) shortening the procedure of the outward investment applications; (5) providing financial services for the investors by setting up foreign branches of the domestic banks; (6) establishing an agency to fulfill the operations of assessing outward direct investment; and (7) relaxing foreign-exchange controls on outward direct investment.

Due to the traditional conservative attitude toward outward capital flows and the lack of diplomatic relations with host countries, the performance of outward direct investment has lagged behind the economic development needs. In 1989, the amount of approved outward direct investment totaled US$56.9 million, of which 80.77 percent (US$46.0 million) went to the United States, US$5.8 million went to Thailand, and US$1.8 million went to Indonesia.[19] As the economy has matured and policy has changed, the outward investment has increased substantially since 1987. In 1989, the total amount of approved outward direct investment was US$930.98 million, the largest amount to date, of which 62.38 percent (US$508.73 million) went to the United States, US$174.48 million went to Malaysia, and US$300.37 million went to other Asian countries.[20] Thus, the United States and Southeast Asian countries are the most attractive places to domestic investors because of the political stability in the former and the cheap labor force in the latter.

It is argued that the outward direct investment should diversify to Southeast Asia and other developing countries where the Taiwanese firms have comparative advantage to manufacture and compete. Nevertheless, the government has encouraged the local firms to invest in the United

States with a view to help the imbalance of trade surpluses and to acquire high technology. The measures used by the government include: (1) encouraging medium and large enterprises to establish technology bases in the United States and distribute high-technology products to the international market; (2) transferring the traditional labor-intensive industries to the United States and making shelter arrangements with Mexican manufacturers; (3) purchasing into the existing bank network in the United States to expand the international banking and provide market information to Taiwanese investors abroad; (4) encouraging local law firms, public accountant offices, and market survey corporations to set up branch offices in the United States; (5) offering overseas investment insurance to cover the investment activities in the region of the United States, Canada, and the Mexican-U.S. border; and (6) negotiating tax agreements with the United States to avoid possible double taxation.[21] As the nation's foreign exchange reserves reached a record high, more outward direct investment restriction cuts are feasible in the near future with a special emphasis on the U.S. market to eliminate the conflicts arising under the trade imbalance and to head off rising protectionism. Meanwhile, since exports to European countries have been regarded as a way to diversify trade partners, outward investment in the European Community (EC) also is encouraged to meet the possible challenge of the integration of European market.

Foreign Portfolio Investment

Inward foreign portfolio investment has been another channel for foreign investors to invest in Taiwan. Since Nissan bought minority stock shares of the local car maker to implement the investment project in 1985, foreign investors have shown their interest in purchasing stocks of local firms. However, up to date, foreign investors are only allowed to invest on the Taiwan stock market indirectly—through the issuance of beneficiary certificates by the specific overseas fund operations, unless a special authorization has been granted to implement the investment projects.[22] In 1986, there were three multinational securities investment and trust companies investing US$75 million on the Taiwan stock market.[23] Another US$75 million was remitted to the China Investment and Trust Company by the end of December 1986 for purchasing stocks at the appropriate time.[24] It is argued that the Taiwan stock market should not allow foreign capital to flood in due to the following reasons: (1) the idle money is still far more than investment needs dictate, leaving no need to bring in the foreign capital; (2) the Taiwan stock market is not well developed and the malpractice of some brokerages could frustrate the foreign investors forever, making it a rather important task to establish a sound capital market rather than to invite the foreign participation right away;[25] (3) the New Taiwan dollar is appreciating against the U.S. dollar, thus, the potential speculation on the Taiwan stock market by foreign investors to earn the foreign-exchange profits may exceed the investment motivation; (4) greater foreign capital inflows will worsen the already too-high foreign-exchange reserves, thereby pushing the New Taiwan dollar to an unacceptable high level; and (5) because the foreign ownership requirement has not been stipulated by the government, the risk of foreign control is inevitable.[26]

The government has adopted a more liberal view toward inward foreign portfolio investment. The policymakers believe that the openness of the Taiwan stock market will introduce new management technology, new investment ideas, and more competition which all are needed to establish a sound capital market. Furthermore, internationalization of the Taiwan stock market will be an important step in fostering the internationalization of the domestic economy. The Securities and Exchange Act, which was amended on 29 January 1988, allows foreign investors (including overseas Chinese) to invest in securities investment and trust companies. Also, an existing foreign securities and trust company is eligible to set up its branch office in Taiwan to engage in stock market activities. The amendments allow the securities investment and trust company to be listed on the Taiwan stock market and to purchase stocks on its own behalf with a stiff penalty against inside traders.[27]

Some arguments for the openness of the Taiwan stock market can be justified on the following grounds: (1) though domestic investors are hesitant to invest in the underdeveloped stock market and despite previous experiences of suffering losses, foreign investors are willing to invest on the Taiwan stock market because of the consistent domestic market growth providing promising returns, and the inflows of foreign capital can provide lessons of investment rather than speculation to domestic investors; (2) the scale of the Taiwan stock market can be enlarged via the participation of foreign investors; (3) the local securities investment and trust companies can learn the most advanced capital consultant services from the foreign firms; (4) more foreign capital inflows to the stock market will foster public confidence and stimulate the local enterprises to list on the stock market as a means of achieving multinational operation; (5) the openness of the Taiwan stock market will give the nation a better international image and help the nation to deal with multilateral negotiations on the issues of trade and finance; and (6) in the case of international portfolio investments, most of the investors are seeking no more than a 5 percent share of the stocks of a specific company to diversify risks in contrast to foreign direct investment,[28] thus foreign control of a domestic economy is not likely to happen simply via opening the stock market to foreign investors.

The new amendment of the Securities and Exchange Act provides more channels for foreign investors to invest in Taiwan indirectly. Furthermore, the openness of the securities investment and trust company as one of the sectors for foreign investment will attract more foreign direct investment inflows. Since with regard to the portfolio investment, foreign investors are free to withdraw from the fund or trade on a secondary market, the openness of inward portfolio investment can be seen as another step toward the liberalization of foreign-exchange controls.

With respect to outward portfolio investment by the national Chinese in Taiwan, some current developments are to be noted. In 1986, the amount of outward portfolio investment via the operation of overseas trust and investment funds reached US$246 million. The overseas trust and investment funds have been set up by five appointed, state-owned banks. The banks accept the deposits from the public and have been only allowed to invest in foreign government bonds, treasury bills, foreign banking securities (bonds and certificated deposits), and some of the corporate bonds (with outstanding performance corporations) with maturities of 6 months to 3 years. It has been criticized that the foreign government bonds, treasury bills, banking securities and corporate bonds all carry an interest of 6 percent (more or less) while the New Taiwan dollar has appreciated over 12 percent against the U.S. dollar; thus the profits of investing abroad, particularly in the United States, have been offset by the exchange losses.[29] To encourage the public to invest in the overseas stock markets, the Ministry of Economic Affairs has decided to allow the public to purchase the stock of foreign companies through the issuance of beneficiary certificates by the securities investment and trust companies.[30] The move in line with the openness of the securities investment and trust companies to foreign investment will break through the monopoly of the overseas investment and trust funds which have been operated by five state-owned banks. Because the foreign banks will be allowed to invest in the securities investment and trust companies after the amendments of the Securities and Exchange Law have been completed, the outward portfolio investments will be fostered by introducing more competition and foreign securities.

Some policy implications can be seen from these recent developments: (1) The government will no longer depend on inward foreign direct investments as the only way to attract foreign capital and a more liberal attitude toward inward foreign portfolio investments can reach the same goal—encourage capital inflows with freer capital movement; (2) although the government also encourages the public and enterprises to invest abroad, the climate for inward foreign investment is still better than outward foreign investment due to the foreign-exchange control regulations remaining the traditional means of restricting capital outflow and the appreciation of NT dollar has made the returns of investment more difficult to articulate; and (3) export expansion and import substitution have emerged with a view to liberalize and internationalize the Taiwan economy, and the formation of multinational enterprises will be next on the agenda with a view to setting up overseas branches as the best way to circumvent trade barriers and secure the supply of raw materials.[31]

In line with the liberalization of foreign-exchange controls, the Central Bank is considering an amendment of the Statute of Foreign Exchange Regulation thereby allowing foreign investors who invest in high-technology enterprises to offset the expenditures from foreign-exchange earnings and report the balance to the Central Bank periodically. The amendment will give more leeway to foreign investors in using and holding foreign-exchange earnings and thus alleviate the influx of the nation's foreign-exchange reserves.[32] In fact, in addition to the negative lists which help to open more sectors to foreign investments, other meaningful liberalization will directly or indirectly confront the foreign-exchange control problems. And the high mobility of capital will be another incentive to foreign direct investment and also to the establishment of multinational enterprises.

To develop a small-scale stock market like Taiwan's,[33] the government believes that more foreign capital inflows will foster the prosperity of the stock market and enhance the confidence of the public. As a result, foreign investors will be able to invest on the Taiwan stock market in the long run. At present, the openness of securities investment and trust companies will provide more ways for foreign investors to invest indirectly. Because the brokerage system has been well developed in most of the advanced countries, there is little doubt that more inflows of foreign portfolio investment will flood Taiwan in the near future.

Whether the current outward portfolio investment via overseas investment and trust funds will be changed substantially after more securities investment and trust companies are set up remains to be seen. Partly because the outward portfolio investments are difficult to trace and the potential inevitable speculation does exist, the government has been cautious toward the openness of outward portfolio investment without foreign-exchange controls. Again, due to the small and outward Taiwan economy, any potential destabilizing factor, such as inflation or a military threat across the Taiwan strait, could cause unrecoverable damage to the Taiwan economy.

PARTIAL LIBERALIZATION OF FINANCIAL OPERATIONS

Background Note

An analysis of current developments in the financial situations of Taiwan will provide the background for understanding the changes in the policies and regulations most recently promulgated. First, due to the depreciation of the U.S. dollar and the rising value of the Japanese yen as well as of the European currencies, Taiwan's 1986 and 1987 trade surpluses hit record highs of US$15 billion and US$18 billion respectively. As observed by a Western writer, "a mercantilist policy of pushing exports while retarding imports can have only one immediate result: foreign exchange reserves pour in."[34] The foreign-exchange reserves more than tripled between 1986 and 1989, going from US$22.5 billion in December 1985 to US$73 billion in December 1989, with a peak of US$76 billion in December 1987. The influx of foreign-exchange reserves created potential pressures of inflation because of the increasing domestic money supply.[35] In July 1990, the inflation rate was 4.8 percent, the highest in the past three years and the government has been cautious toward the inflationary pressure.

In order to offset the adverse impact of the increasing money supply, the government has adopted restrictive monetary policy and sterilized operations. The following policy instruments are being used to stabilize the financial system and consumer prices: (1) Strictly control the bank's reserve requirements to a high level.[36] (2) Issue government bonds for public construction purposes. (The government issued US$300 million and US$540 million in construction bonds in March and November 1986 respectively.)[37] (3) Raise the interest rates of short-, medium-, and long-term loans to a record high since 1980 in order to cool down the overheated economy. (4) Lead the formation of private fixed capital with strong government investment in infrastructure development projects.[38] (5) Encourage outward foreign direct and portfolio investment. (6) Issue savings certificates with higher interest rates to attract idle money held by the public.[39] (7) Use selective credit controls to encourage the manufacturers to purchase machinery and equipment via provisions of medium- and long-term loans. (The interest rates offered to the strategic industries for medium- and long-term loans have been lowered to 5.25–5.5 percent annually to encourage the production of strategic products and the purchase of pollution-control equipment and machinery.[40] The Bank of Communications also has expanded the credits to cover the importation of raw materials, precision machinery, tools, and technology. The annual interest rate has been fixed at 6 percent or less and the loans can be extended to 10 years.[41] (8) Offer tax incentives by reducing corporation tax up to 15 percent to encourage the issuance of stocks.[42] (9) Allow the public to invest in the publicly owned enterprises through the issuance of stock on the stock market to tap idle money and help the privatization of public enterprises. (10) Cut the import tariffs consistently to encourage imports, particularly on those items with which domestic products are able to compete. (The upper-end tariffs have been cut to 57.5 percent compared to 120 percent in the past.)[43] (11) Realign foreign-exchange rates to reduce the increasing domestic money supply. (Up to July 1990, the New Taiwan dollar had appreciated over 45 percent against the U.S. dollar since the G-5 meeting on 22 September 1985.) (12) Assign three commercial banks to hold high levels of foreign-exchange reserves. (For instance, in 1986, the three designated banks, The First Commercial Bank, Hwa Nan Commercial Bank, and Chang Hwa Commercial Bank, held US$1 billion in foreign-exchange reserves to alleviate the burden of the Central Bank. Due to the huge exchange losses of these commercial banks, the Central Bank has lowered the foreign-exchange reserve level to US$500 million).[44] (13) Issue corporate bonds through publicly owned companies to absorb excessive money supplies. For instance, the Taiwan Power Company had issued a total of NT$10 billion in corporate bonds to match operation needs.[45] Thus, the government has used many means to sterilize the foreign exchange earned in trade surplus.

Among the measures used by the government, the foreign-exchange-rate alignment policy has been a controversial one. The pros and cons of the New Taiwan dollar appreciation have been widely debated. The adverse impacts of the New Taiwan dollar appreciation are posed as follows: (1) Export competition will be reduced because of the higher prices on the international market; (2) foreign direct investment, particularly those foreigners who are interested in the export-oriented industries, will be hampered because the appreciation of the New Taiwan dollar will cause products to lose their competitive edge as compared to products made under other developing countries' currencies;[46] (3) the Central Bank and other banks which hold a large amount of U.S. dollars are suffering huge losses due to the currency fluctuation (in 1986, the Taiwan banking industries, including the Central Bank, suffered foreign-exchange losses estimated to have reached NT$40 billion);[47] and (4) the expectation of appreciation has encouraged speculative capital inflows and distorted export growth. The amount of speculative capital inflows is estimated at around US$4–8 million.[48] The exporters have been forced to export as soon as possible and have converted the foreign exchange earned into the New Taiwan dollar without delay. During 1986–89, this practice pushed the growth of exports far better than imports and added another pressure on the inflationary effect.

Those who advocate that the New Taiwan dollar should be appreciated further against the U.S. dollar argue that: (1) The New Taiwan dollar has been undervalued for more than ten years to encourage exports and that the consumers will benefit from cheaper imported goods as a result of appreciation; (2) the New Taiwan dollar appreciation also reduces the cost of imported raw and intermediate materials for exports, thus the cost of exports will not be elevated so drastically as others had expected; (3) 99 percent of the domestic energy supplies in Taiwan are bought from abroad, so the high New Taiwan dollar will offset part of the adverse impacts of rising oil prices or other energy supplies (thus the industries will be the largest beneficiary of the New Taiwan dollar appreciation); (4) the New Taiwan dollar appreciation will encourage manufacturers to purchase more machinery and equipment abroad to upgrade their production lines and improve pollution-control systems which in turn is helpful to the badly needed restructuring of industries;[49] and (5) the New Taiwan dollar appreciation has helped the liberalization of foreign-exchange controls and the internationalization of domestic financial systems by providing more leverage for the public to invest abroad without adversely affecting the confidence problem.

The government has been implementing a slow but steady appreciation policy. The debate over the issue whether the government should allow the New Taiwan dollar to appreciate against the U.S. dollar all at once or to continue with the current appreciation policy in order to better serve the Taiwan economy will be discussed in the final section of this chapter.

The Partial Liberalization of Financial Operations

Under the Ninth Medium-term Economic Development Plan for Taiwan (1986–89), the financial measures to support economic development include: (1) strengthening the role of the Development Fund and all specialized banks in investment and financing (this is in line with the aforementioned selective credit controls to encourage domestic fixed investments thereby upgrading industrial structure and rising industrial productivity); (2) continuing the promotion of international banking, strengthening ties with international financial institutions; (3) making timely adjustments of the Central Bank's rediscount rate and deposit and loan rates of the banking industry in line with the market demand and supply of the capital market and accelerating the liberalization of interest rate adjustments in full scale; (4) deregulating the export-import foreign-exchange collections and payments, and gradually easing foreign-exchange controls; and (5) easing the restrictions on bank financing of buildings and home purchases as well as promoting the sound development of building construction.[50] Furthermore, the Central Bank announced in 1987 that the policy of the Central Bank with respect to foreign-exchange controls is to liberalize the restrictions with heed paid to the stabilization of the financial system.[51]

Several changes have taken place and more liberalizations of the foreign-exchange control system and bank operations are expected with a view to channeling the huge foreign-exchange reserves into industrial development. The following measures are under consideration and further amendment of the existing regulations are needed to give more leeway for market forces with respect to financial operations.

The Relaxation of Foreign-Exchange Controls

The Central Bank has promulgated regulations governing invisible transactions within thirty days.[52] The new regulations will include the following business transactions: (1) import expenditures except for commodity costs, including insurance premiums, cargo freight, and others; (2) payments and expenditures incurred from business transactions or services offered by shipping, insurance, and other industries; and (3) expenses needed for family maintenance abroad by Chinese nationals or foreigners serving in governmental organizations and private enterprises within the country. The new regulations will allow the enterprises or individuals who need to settle the aforesaid foreign exchanges to remit the amount actually incurred or limited without prior approval. The Central Bank will audit the foreign-exchange settlements periodically. With respect to the inward remittance, the Central Bank will screen only the total sum of remittance over US$1 million of the export proceeds, income of shipping, insurance, and other industries, as well as income derived from the outward direct investments. Other income over US$10,000 remitted from abroad also will be subject to the Central Bank's screening. The appointed bank will handle those inward remittances which are not subject to the scrutiny of the Central Bank.

The Central Bank also raised the limits on the amount of foreign exchange which the public can acquire for the purpose of traveling abroad, operating foreign branch offices, dispatching personnel expenditures, or for the living expenses of students abroad to US$5 million.[53] In addition to allowing the public to invest in foreign stock markets indirectly via overseas investment and trust funds, the Central Bank also lowered the capital adequacy requirements for domestic enterprises' outward direct investments, that is, only a NT$10 million paid-in capital and less than 300 percent debt ratio are required.[54] Under a survey conducted by the Council of Economic Planning and Development, the manufacturers are expecting the Central Bank to allow the enterprises and individuals to hold part of their foreign-exchange earnings without surrendering to the Central Bank or its appointed banks and further to lift the capital adequacy requirements for outward investments by domestic enterprises.[55] The Ministry of Finance has amended the tax structure of the value-added tax which exempts the gold trader from paying value-added taxes in order to implement the policy goal of freeing gold from foreign-exchange controls.[56]

The Liberalization of Interest Rates

Since the Central Bank partially relaxed the controls on interest rates, the discount rate of negotiable instruments, transferable certificated deposits, and financial securities has been decided by individual banks. The range of interest rates for bank lending was enlarged. The Central Bank sets the ceiling for demand deposits, savings deposits, and time deposits to simplify the interest controls.[57] On 17 July 1989, the liberalization of interest-rate controls has been undertaken by amending the banking law which authorized the Central Bank to regulate various interest rates.[58] The new amendment has lifted the control of the Central Bank on deciding interest rates.

Since the current financial situation in Taiwan is one where domestic savings have exceeded domestic investment over 20 percent of the GNP, the official interest rates of bank lending therefore had been consistently lowered in order to encourage investment, on the one hand. On the other hand, due to the fear of inflation caused by the increasing domestic supply, it is necessary to raise the interest rates on bank deposits in order to attract more savings thereby offsetting part of the inflationary pressure. Thus, the government-issued construction bonds and savings certificates feature a higher interest rate than commercial bank deposits. The issuance of these construction bonds and savings certificates had been welcomed by the public, and the hot sales reflect the public demand for higher returns. Beginning with April 1988, to curb the rising stock and real estate prices, the government tightened the money supply by issuing treasury bills and raising the reserve level of the banks, thus pushing the interest rates to a high level. (The current commercial interest rates are over 10 percent annually.) Under the current situation, the liberalization of interest rates is expected to have the impact of enhancing competition among the banks, thereby providing more channels for attracting idle money held by the public and for encouraging the renovation of the management in the banking industry.[59]

Another move in line with the liberalization of interest rates is the internationalization of the banking industry. The government has announced that domestic banks with outstanding records in offshore banking operations will be encouraged to establish foreign branch offices in other countries.[60] The foreign branch offices of the domestic financial institutions can extend loans and credits to foreign borrowers according to the host country's regulations and business needs. Under the previous practice, domestic banking law required a financial report endorsed by a public accountant in the case of bank lending over NT$30 million, which has been a barrier in offering bank loans to foreign customers in host countries.[61] In 1986, financial institutions invested US$20 million abroad and the relaxation of bank overseas lending together with the lifting of fixed interest will open another channel for the international investment of the banking industry. Thus, the interest rates offered by the banks in the future will not only compete on the domestic market but also on foreign markets.

Relaxing the Restrictions on Foreign Bank Operations

The opening of the domestic financial market to the United States has become a hot issue in the trade negotiation agenda between the United States and Taiwan. Under the previous banking law, foreign banks were not allowed to set up trust and savings departments in Taiwan; thus foreign institutions were confronted with the capital availability problem in offering loans or extending credits to the domestic borrowers. In 1986, there was a policy change to allow foreign banks to take savings deposits and to offer seven- to twenty-year loans to the domestic borrowers, and there is no limitation on the amount of the loans, in other words, equal treatment as for the local banks, without having to set up a savings department to handle these deposits and loans. On 22 March 1990, the Executive Yuan approved the revised regulations governing the foreign bank operation under the banking law which was amended on 17 July 1989. The revised regulations included the following points liberalizing foreign bank operations in Taiwan: (1) A bank among the world's 500 largest banks with a representative office in Taiwan for one year is eligible to set up a branch in Taiwan; (2) the foreign banks are allowed to open savings and trust departments to underwrite and trade in securities on behalf of their customers; and (3) the foreign banks are allowed to accept NT dollar deposits up to 15 times the amount of their paid-in capital, instead of the previous 12.5 times. The new measure will channel more domestic currency into foreign banks, and a possible capital outflow via multinational bank operations is inevitable. However, the government is confident that the liberalization of foreign bank operations will enlarge the domestic financial market and provide a more competitive environment for domestic banks, thus a freer flow of capital to supporting economic development is foreseeable.

The Privatization of the Banking Industry

Among fifty-six banks in Taiwan, forty of the banks are privately owned foreign institutions. It is arguable that the privatization of the banking industry has been undertaken by allowing the foreign banks to operate in a whole range of the local bank's business, that is, to set up second branch offices in Taiwan, accept the New Taiwan dollar savings deposits, extend long-term loans, operate trust and investment transactions, etc.

Basically, the banking industry in Taiwan is operating on a specialized basis—each bank has its own specific role in a specific sector of the economy. For instance, the Bank of Communication plays the role of a development bank to provide medium- and long-term loans for enterprises in improving productivity. By offering venture capital or equity participation in the high-technology industries, the bank also helps the government to develop strategic industries. Thus, the privatization of the banking industry is not to change the role of the publicly owned policy-oriented banks but to foster the growth of publicly owned commercial banks and new small-scale banks to cope with the rising competition of the foreign banks and to eliminate the illegal money market, thereby creating a sound money market and protecting the interests of the public. On 12 April 1990, the Executive Yuan approved the regulations proposed by the Ministry of Finance to set the standard for the establishment of new commercial banks under the 1989 banking law, and thus lifted the forty years' ban on the establishment of new banks. Under the new regulations, the organizers of a new commercial bank are required to raise 80 percent of their paid-in capital and a minimum of NT$2 billion paid-in capital is required before filing the application with the Ministry of Finance. The opening of new financial institutions could allow private individuals to operate small-scale banking services for the public. Under the plan, a special license will be offered which will allow those newcomers to provide consumer loans, mortgages, and leasing. Operation funds will be limited to securities, bank loans, and self-owned capital.[62] The new measure is expected to provide a more responsive lending policy to cope with the public needs and to siphon more idle money into the small and medium enterprises which often lack the essential creditworthiness of the commercial bank standards.

Strengthening the Stock Market

One of the efforts to strengthen the stock market is to encourage financial institutions to purchase stocks on the stock market to foster individual investment and public confidence because the banks are owned by the government. Investment in stock is a relatively new phenomenon of the banking activities in Taiwan. Previously, stock investments by the banks had been restricted by the banking law which stipulated that only the savings banks were eligible to invest in the stock market without the prior approval of the authorities. The new revision of bank law explicitly allows the banks to engage in stock transactions. In August 1986, the Ministry of Finance authorized the five state-run banks to purchase the total sum of NT$50 million stock and the other privately owned financial institutions also followed the move to buy in an equal amount of stock. This was the first time that public banks went into the stock market with a view to stop the declining stock prices.[63]

The stock market enjoyed a heyday from 1988 to early 1990, and the monthly weighted stock index of the Taiwan Stock Exchange reached its highest point of 11983 in February 1990. The total trading value in 1989 was over NT$25 billion and there were 181 listed companies with capital amounting to NT$439,230 million. The scale of the Taiwan stock market has been enlarged substantially. However, the speculative capital inflows and outflows, small scale of the market with limited listed companies, malpractice of inside trading, unperfected competition in the stock finance, and the disclosure requirement not being entirely fulfilled by the listed companies all are said to be factors in a potential crisis of the Taiwan stock trading. To cool down the overheated trading, the government has encouraged the domestic companies to issue stocks in order to expand the stock market and to increase the stock supply. The government also continues to promote the issuance of public shares in publicly owned enterprises as a means of expanding the securities market and strengthening the competitive ability of these enterprises.

Since February 1990, the stock prices have declined over 50 percent up to July 1990, and the government put the labor pension fund into the stock market to stimulate the market operation. Some critics argue that the measures used by the government are against the free-market functioning. However, the Taiwan stock market is vulnerable and how to restore public confidence and market order will be the most urgent agenda for the government to deal with.

Establishing a Money Market

The Taiwan money market is only fifteen years old as of 1991. There are three bill finance companies, subsidiaries of three state-owned banks, which are engaged in open market operations. Since the operation of an open market "requires a sufficiently deep market in high-quality securities," the open market operation has been more significant in advanced developed countries as a policy tool to control the money supply.[64] The money market in Taiwan is predominated by commercial paper which is guaranteed by a financial institution or backed by a bank's line of credit. Due to the lack of a credit rating system and because the secondary market is limited, the underdeveloped money market is said to be a barrier to channeling the money into industrial development. The lack of a sound money market also caused the difficulties in determining the market interest rates.

To improve the existing money market, the Ministry of Finance has introduced the following measures to enhance open market operations: (1) increasing the amount of treasury bill issuances as a high quality security to adjust the money supply and demand on the market; (2) encouraging the use and negotiation of commercial paper based on legal transactions; (3) encouraging the banks to engage in money-market transactions; (4) establishing the financing channels for the bill finance companies to meet the demand of short-term capitals; (5) improving and simplifying the transactions of commercial paper and negotiable instruments; (6) establishing a credit rating system[65] to safeguard the interests of the lender and establish public confidence; and (7) enhancing the intermediary function of the Center for Inter-Bank Borrowing in order to facilitate short-term capital adjustment.[66]

Establishing the Deposit Insurance System

In 1986, the Central Deposit Insurance Act was enacted and the Central Deposit Insurance Company was erected to handle the deposit insurance of the banking industry. After the Cathy Crisis broke out in 1985, shocking the financial system, the authorities became more cautious toward financial reports of the system. The Central Deposit Insurance Company has developed a rating system which is similar to the Uniform Inter-agencies Bank Rating System of the United States to evaluate the performance of the banks and detect a troubled bank in advance. The following elements are emphasized in the rating system: (1) asset quality; (2) total amount of assets and liabilities; (3) total amount of loans and deposits; (4) the possible losses, including overdue loans and bad debts; and (5) other operations indexes. The banks will be evaluated under five categories to show the performance of the banks. A Financial Examination Committee which includes the members of the Central Bank, the Ministry of Finance, and the Central Deposit Insurance Company will issue warnings, improvement notices, and suspensions of the insurance right to a bank if the bank has been found with a low rating under the rating system.[67] The establishments of the Central Deposit Insurance Company and the rating system are expected to provide a stabilized financial system, particularly after the lessons of a failing bank.

Currency Diversification

Before February 1979, the New Taiwan dollar was pegged against the U.S. dollar. In order to stabilize the exchange rate, the Central Bank held and managed the total amount of foreign-exchange reserves, mostly in the U.S. dollar, and no appointed bank or other enterprise was allowed to hold foreign exchange. After the floating-exchange-rate system was introduced in February 1979, the appointed banks and enterprises were allowed to hold part of the foreign exchange earned with limited uses or amounts. The appointed bank held foreign-exchange funds limited to the amount stemming from the needs resulting from the domestic foreign-exchange transactions with a view to preventing arbitrage or speculative forward exchange operations.[68] The foreign-exchange deposits of the manufacturers (or exporters and importers) are confined to specific uses as follows: (1) for making payments abroad through an appointed bank; (2) for selling to the foreign exchange market through an appointed bank or surrendering to the Central Bank or an appointed bank; and (3) for transferring to the same depositor's account from one appointed bank to the other. All the transactions must be made through an appointed bank and no cash withdrawals are allowed.[69]

Although after 1984 the Central Bank allowed the appointed banks to keep a portion of their foreign exchange exceeding the domestic foreign-exchange transaction needs, the article which restricted the foreign-exchange transactions abroad by the appointed banks—no arbitrage or speculative forward exchange transaction—remains untouched. Furthermore, under the Regulations Governing Buying and Selling Foreign Exchange by Appointed Banks, as amended on 13 June 1980, the foreign-exchange rates of the foreign currencies (other than the U.S. dollar) are calculated on the basis of the U.S. dollar spot rate vis-à-vis the opening and closing rate on the international market for each of the foreign currencies as well as on the basis of taking market trends into consideration. Thus, the U.S. dollar as the percentage of the total foreign-exchange reserves has been estimated at 80–90 percent.[70] And three commercial banks were designated by the Central Bank to hold US$1 billion foreign exchange respectively. Due to the appreciation of the New Taiwan dollar against the U.S. dollar, the Central Bank and the three designated banks have suffered huge foreign-exchange losses. Thus, the Central Bank lowered the three designated banks' foreign-exchange reserve levels, and the three designated banks have requested the Central Bank to allow them to diversify their foreign currency holdings into other foreign currencies, thereby avoiding foreign-exchange risks.[71] In fact, the restrictions on the foreign-exchange operations have been eliminated de facto by interpreting the currency diversification operations as some sort of domestic foreign transaction needs. For instance, the Bank of Taiwan has gained NT$600 million by converting the holdings of the U.S. dollar into Japanese yen and deutsche mark.[72] However, this new foreign-exchange operation has not been encouraged by the Central Bank and the uncovered exchange risk will be taken on by individual banks.

Strengthening International Coordination

In addition to the operation of offshore financial centers, the government has encouraged coordination between local and foreign banks. Up to the end of 1986, the Export-Import Bank provided over US$140 million fixed-rate loans to refinance foreign buyers in purchasing machinery and equipment from Taiwan via the foreign banks. In 1986, fifty-four foreign banks carried refinance contracts with the Export-Import Bank.[73] Furthermore, to enhance the cooperation between domestic manufacturers and overseas Chinese in Southeast Asia, the government encourages the Export-Import Bank as well as the International Commercial Bank of China to set up branch offices in Southeast Asia, thereby providing more import loans and credits for the overseas Chinese to import goods from Taiwan.[74] The basic idea of the development of overseas financial institutions is to combine the foreign branches and the overseas Chinese industries to provide another channel for capital flows and help the growth of domestic industries.

Some common features of these measures undertaken by the government can be seen as follows: (1) The liberalization of the banking operations is based on the Foreign Exchange Control Regulations which limits capital inflows and outflows. Thus some amendments of the exchange control regulations are needed to implement the liberalization and internationalization of the banking industry. (2) The traditional banking operation in Taiwan has failed to cope with the currency appreciation situation, something the nation never confronted before. Some new operation strategies such as financial investment, foreign exchange hedging, and stock investment have been introduced. (3) More competition will be seen as the result of liberalizing interest rates and of relaxing the restrictions on foreign bank operations. Thus, a possible privatization of the banking industry will foster the banking industry to meet the demand of industrial development.

With respect to the foreign-exchange controls, the influx of foreign exchange and the success of partial liberalization which did not cause any capital flight will bring more confidence to the government to reevaluate the control regime. A further foreign-exchange control liberalization is feasible because the huge domestic money supply has caused the pressures of potential inflation. The government thus faces the choice of a more liberalized outlook or a further appreciation of the domestic currency. Furthermore, the high foreign-exchange reserve level has become a burden on trade negotiations between the United States and Taiwan. The government has announced that it will give more leeway for market forces, that is, less government intervention. Because the service sectors are already opening to foreign investors and because the strategic industries which need more capital than traditional labor-intensive industries are encouraged by the government, the capital market is likely to open widely to foreigners and freer (inward and outward) capital flows are possible. In contrast, the underdeveloped money market will remain unchanged because the money market maloperation may have shaken the stability of the financial system and caused the inflationary chaos. For the most part, national security concerns are the major barrier to the openness of the money market.[75]

REMAINING ISSUES

Some internationalization and liberalization have been the two policy goals of the government in portraying Taiwan's economic development in the future. Although some supporting measures have been used to implement the policy goal (and some measures are under consideration), there are issues remaining to be resolved. This section will examine some of the important policy issues which are closely related to the further development of the Taiwan economy with respect to foreign investment and foreign-exchange controls.

Technology Transfers

One of the most important issues for a country desiring to encourage foreign direct investment is the technology inflows embodied in the flows of capital goods or disembodied in the forms of industrial property. The variety of foreign direct investment, such as joint ventures, licensing agreements, turnkey agreements, and other contract agreements have provided more channels to induce technology transfers to developing countries according to a recent survey of the United Nations.[76] The current trend in Third World development has indicated that the importance of technology acquisition "as an engine of growth" has become the advantage of multinational enterprises' operations.[77] In Taiwan, one survey conducted by the Industrial Technology Research Department in the late 1970s indicated that the Taiwan economy was heavily dependent on foreign technology to support its development. The use of foreign brands, trademarks, and other items of technology cooperation has been widely accepted by the local firms as a viable means to exploring domestic and foreign markets.[78]

The establishment of the Hsinchu Science-based Industrial Park in the early 1980s was aimed at fostering technology cooperation between local and overseas firms with basic R&D provided by the National Ching Hwa University and Chiao Tung University.[79] Several programs have been undertaken by the government to foster science and technology development, such as the "Science and Technology Development Program," the "Program for Strengthening Education, Training, and Recruitment of High-Level Science and Technology Personnel," and the "Program for Defense Science and Technology." These programs are aimed to upgrade technology and cultivate science and technology personnel. The goals of these programs are to foster coordination between the development of the applied sciences (or technologies) and the defense sciences (or technologies) and transfer the new technology to private industries via the mutual effort of the government, academic research, and private enterprises.[80] For instance, to develop the basic input/output system for local personal computer manufacturing, the Electronics Research and Service Organization, a government-owned institution, developed ERSO BIOS and transferred them to the small manufacturers for a moderate fee.[81]

The Taiwan economy has developed rapidly and the bottleneck of the technology development is being questioned. In 1986, the government has set an ambitious plan to boost R&D programs through private enterprises and public research institutions to cope with economic development needs.[82] The Investment Commission of the Ministry of Economic Affairs has stiffened its attitude toward technology cooperation cases between local and foreign firms via screening the contract terms, and particular attention has been paid to the Japanese cooperation cases because past experience shows that the Japanese firms were more interested in expanding trade than transferring technology.[83] The Industrial Technology Research Institution has reached an agreement with the Ministry of the Economic Affairs to spend NT$3–4 billion on technology renovation of traditional industries. Furthermore, the Regulations Governing the R&D Expenditures for Productive Enterprises was promulgated in January 1986. Under this regulation, private enterprises should spend part of their earnings on R&D.[84] One fund will be raised to manage the money levied from the enterprises which failed to meet the requirements of the regulation. Some foreign investors have protested against such a plan of a compulsory levy of R&D fees because most of the multinational enterprises engage in their own R&D in the home countries.[85] The mandatory R&D expenditure distribution among the private enterprises may cause a disincentive to foreign investors. Nonetheless, the government has decided that technology breakthrough is vital to the nation's further economic development. The lesson of Japanese industrial development shows that effective "technology borrowing" is a key element of success rather than depending on the traditional labor-intensive industries.[86]

One phenomenon of outward investment worthy of note is the high-tech industries investment. The most important reason for going abroad is to acquire new technology and insure continuous contacts with a host nation's technology innovation. For instance, the United Microelectronic Company has set up subsidiaries in Silicon Valley to open a new door for technology transfer.[87] However, the new form of technology transfer by investing abroad can only solve the nation's technology needs to a certain degree.

Environmental Pollution

In recent years, the environmental pollution problem has become a public concern. Due to rapid economic growth in the past thirty years and the expansion of industrial sites, some problems have arisen while most enterprises failed to pay heed to pollution control and prevention. In addition to the air, water, and noise pollution, the problems of overcrowding and soil chemistry change have been the major concerns of the authorities with respect to pollution-control issues. The family planning project, population diversification, and a pet-control management system have been undertaken.[88]

Four major laws which govern the pollution caused by the industries have been promulgated or revised as a last resort to deal with industrial pollution: the Air Pollution Control Act, the Water Pollution Control Act, the Waste Treatment Act, and the Noise Control Act. Some preventive measures such as inspection and enforced controls on factories, watching stations for gradual pollutants, coal smoke detection stations, and sulfur dioxide detection stations have been set up.[89]

The government has offered more incentives to enterprises which establish a sound pollution control system. Under the Statute for the Encouragement of Investment, a productive enterprise which reinvests its uncontributed earnings for the purpose of replacing or renovating machinery and equipment in need of pollution-control devices will have its registered stocks, newly issued to and acquired by its stockholders, excluded from the shareholder's consolidated income or the income of the enterprise in the current year for taxation purposes. A productive enterprise, with the approval of the authorities in charge of the enterprise, which imports instruments and equipment exclusively for the prevention of public pollution will have the incurred import duties and dues exempted. Should a productive enterprise purchase machinery and equipment with special devices for pollution prevention, such machinery and equipment may be depreciated at an accelerated rate.

The pollution control cost has become another burden to foreign investors, although the cost may be varied because of the different industry involved.[90] One foreign direct investment case, the Du Pont Company's investment of a chemical plant to produce titanic dioxide in Taiwan,[91] has been a hotly debated issue due to the possible adverse impact on the ecology of a small town on the western coast. To cool down public antagonism, the government requested that the Du Pont Company commit itself to pollution prevention and control before the commencement of the investment project.

The Du Pont Company has agreed to distribute part of its investing funds to facilitate pollution control and prevention.[92] Meanwhile, the government has instructed state-owned enterprises to spend NT$110 billion in the period of 1986–99 to boost their antipollution task.[93] And the government has announced that any foreign direct investment affecting environmental sanitation and ecological conservation will not be approved in the future.[94]

Under the Republic of China's Economic Plan for 1990, one of the policy goals is to strengthen environmental protection. In addition to updating the environmental protection legislation and plans, the following supporting measures have been adopted:[95] (1) Establish and strictly enforce pollution abatement guidelines, and improve the pollution-control facilities and operations of industrial and commercial enterprises and the livestock and agricultural industries; (2) suspend the import of scrap metal and expand the use of liquefied natural gas by Taiwan Power Company's thermal power plants; (3) accelerate the construction of noise barriers along highways, strictly implement the program to eradicate toxic emissions by motor vehicles, the open-air burning of refuse, and air pollution caused by construction work and industrial operation, and take steps to more effectively control noise pollution and improve air quality; (4) continue to introduce and develop new environmental-protection technology, and step up technical cooperation with other countries in pollution control; (5) provide effective incentives to encourage private environmental-protection industry; and (6) strengthen public education in the need and importance of environmental protection with emphasis on individual responsibility. Thus, the government has paid more and more heed to the problem of pollution control and foreign investors could have greater costs in scheduling an investment project.

Higher Wages

The large, well-educated labor force has been Taiwan's "most important and abundant resource."[96] The rapid industrial development has brought wages up through the 1960s and 1970s. By the end of the 1970s, labor supply was lagging behind the demand, thus rising wages were inevitable.[97] Meanwhile, the labor force has shifted from unskilled workers to semiskilled workers, thereby reflecting the rising demand for a higher-educated labor force as a result of the shifting industrial structure from traditional labor-intensive industries to more sophisticated capital- and technology-intensive industries.[98]

In the 1985 survey conducted by the Vocational Training bureau, among the total number of 41,440 workers completing vocational training in 1984, the textile industry accounted for 7,293 workers (17.6 percent) due to the investment in new equipment and automation facilities in order to cope with the shortage of the unskilled labor force and the strenuous competition on the international market.[99] In 1985, total employment in the export processing zones was 77,000, down from the peak of 86,000 in 1984 due to the automation of factories.[100] The trend indicates the diminishing comparative advantage of the low labor costs as compared to Korea and other developing countries in Southeast Asia.[101]

In addition to the rising wages, other benefits of the workers have been strengthened via the amendment of the Labor Standard Law. The law provides the basic protections to the workers, such as a minimum wage level, working hour restrictions, working conditions, etc. Furthermore, the Labor Insurance Act stipulates that the employers are mandated to pay 80 percent of the premium of the labor insurance for their workers.

After the government lifted martial law in July 1987, the Law of Labor Union was revised to allow labor unions to strike work under legal process. The Statute Governing Labor Disputes also has been amended to set up the rules of settling labor disputes. Thus, more invisible costs may have occurred in keeping the relationship of labor and employer running smoothly.

In light of the diminishing wage advantage, the government has encouraged the vocational training of workers and offered more vocational education to upgrade the productivity of the labor force. Thus, the productive labor force will replace the low-wage labor force to attract more foreign investors. However, the potential risk of losing the wage advantage is still an unresolved problem for the export-oriented industries and foreign investments.

Energy Shortages

Coal was the major supply for Taiwan's energy consumption in the 1950s. Due to the rapid industrial expansion in the 1960s and 1970s, the ratio of energy to demand growth contributed to the GNP was 1:4 for the decade of the 1970s. Thus domestic energy resource shortages have become a serious concern of the government, particularly after suffering two OPEC crises in the 1970s.[102] During the Six-Year Economic Development Plan (1975–81), the total energy supply increased 88.4 percent, with the domestic energy supply declining 5.4 percent. In 1975, the domestic energy supply accounted for 30 percent of the total energy demand, and in 1981, the domestic energy supply declined to 15.5 percent of the total energy needs. The high oil prices have been a burden to Taiwan's economic development. In 1981, the imported oil and related products reached a peak of US$5.1 billion, 24 percent of the import value and 12 percent of the GNP.[103] Thus, diversifying energy resources and avoiding the development of an energy-extensive industry have been emphasized by the government as policy guides.[104]

The slogan "to achieve a certain economic growth with a minimum consumption of energy" was posed to aim at energy conservation while achieving economic growth. The nation has worked hard to achieve a low energy elasticity in raising the GNP.[105] Some policies have reflected the government's concern over the energy issue as follows: (1) achieving high-technology-intensive industries and avoiding the expansion of energy-intensive industries; (2) extending the tax credit for investment in energy-efficient machinery and equipment to encourage greater energy efficiency; (3) encouraging industries with interrelated production processes to locate within the same industrial zone to increase energy utilization; and (4) encouraging investment in the development of foreign energy resources for use in Taiwan.[106]

Currently, Taiwan has three nuclear power plants in operation. The three nuclear power plants account for 43 percent of generating capacity and 50–60 percent of the actual supply.[107] The plan of building a fourth nuclear power plant has been delayed because a nuclear accident in one of the plants caused public concern over the safety problem.[108] Other energy sources, such as geothermal energy and wind energy, have been under experiment.[109] Meanwhile, the Taiwan Power Company has concluded a five-year agreement with Rocky Mountain Energy, a subsidiary of Union Pacific, to prospect jointly for uranium in Wyoming.[110] A coal mining agreement has been signed between Chung Hwa Overseas Mining Development Company and Indonesia's state coal company to explore coal mining for thirty years.[111] The Chinese Petroleum Corporation has expanded its oil search agreement with other nations, such as Papua New Guinea and the United Arab Emirates.[112] The company also reached an agreement with Kuwait to refine 20 to 30 thousand barrels of oil daily for Kuwait.[113] In April 1990, the corporation acquired a 16.67 percent share in the prospecting right to the natural gas deposit held by the Huffco Petroleum Company of the United States in the Snaga Block of Kalimantan, Indonesia.[114]

To search for steady energy supply sources has become an important task to the government because Taiwan's economy itself is so vulnerable to outside energy supplies. The payments on the energy supply abroad have been a burden on the nation's balance of payments, thus the energy shortages also constitute another reason to keep a high foreign-exchange reserve level.

Small and Medium Business Crises

Over 95 percent of Taiwanese enterprises are small and medium businesses, that is, with NT$40 million paid-in capital or less. These small and medium enterprises, mostly family owned, have contributed significantly to Taiwan's economic development during the past thirty years. Even today, the small and medium enterprises account for 92 percent of the total number of the enterprises and produce 55 percent of the GNP, 65–70 percent of the total export values, and employ 70 percent of the labor force.[115] Because they are small-scale operations, these enterprises have been able to shift from producing one product to another, particularly in these labor-intensive industries where large amounts of capital investment is not necessary. The ability to interchange their products from one to another has been a great advantage in capturing the international market trend. As observed by a Western writer, the small and medium enterprises are one of Taiwan's greatest assets and help the economy adapt quickly to economic changes.[116] The reporter stated an American lawyer's observation that "the other day I saw a company that went from ladies' dresses to laser." Another contribution of the small and medium enterprises to the Taiwan economy has been, it is said, the invisible brand names used (or the carrying of an American brand), thereby avoiding more criticism and protectionism abroad.[117]

Despite the advantage of the small and medium enterprises to the Taiwan economy, the government has sensed that the nation cannot build its own technology and industry without its own brand names in order to compete on the international market. The lack of a joint force from the small and medium enterprises has become a potential problem in the future economic development and capital flows. First, the openness of the domestic investment sectors to foreign investors, mostly multinational enterprises, will cause an immense threat to the survival of the small and medium enterprises. In addition, the trade liberalization trend as a means to cut back the influx of foreign exchange and head off protectionism abroad will be another crisis to the small and medium enterprises in competing with imported goods on the domestic market.

Another problem of these family-owned small and medium enterprises is the lack of a sound management system and R&D projects because of limited working capital. The lack of a sound management system in the small and medium enterprises and the traditional family-owned operations has been a barrier to the development of the stock market because most of these small and medium enterprises are not listed on the stock market for fear of overexposure and ownership change. The practice has impeded the development of a sound stock market and has been a barrier to the small and medium enterprises borrowing from the public. Furthermore, the banking industry also hesitates to extend loans to the small and medium enterprises because of the strict banking regulations and the credit rating system has yet to be established.[118] With respect to the R&D program, most of the small and medium enterprises cannot afford to pay the expenditures. The government has encouraged the small and medium enterprises to develop their own brands either by themselves or jointly with other firms. Furthermore, the government has engaged in some of the R&D programs and transferred them to the small and medium enterprises. In light of the shifting industrial structure from labor-intensive industries to capital- and technology-intensive industries and the openness of the domestic market for foreign investment and trade, the small and medium enterprises are facing a phase-out threat in the keenly competitive environment.

One problem of the small and medium enterprises is related to the exchange-rate change since the beginning of 1986. Because of the marginal profits and the limited working capital of the small and medium enterprises, the appreciation of the New Taiwan dollar has become an undue burden to these export-oriented small and medium enterprises. Because small and medium enterprises are not able to diversify their foreign market and currency holdings, the rising New Taiwan dollar has increased the manufacturing cost of the export products. To alleviate the adverse impacts of the New Taiwan dollar appreciation, the Central Bank has used a steady but slow appreciation strategy to give time for the small and medium enterprises to adjust to the new currency value.[119]

The current government policies to assist the small and medium enterprises in crises are as follows:[120] (1) assisting the establishment of a sound accounting system; providing business information, and encouraging the extension of credits by the banking industry; (2) considering the establishment of county- or city-level counselling service centers for small and medium enterprises, thereby reinforcing their operation and management; (3) providing medium- and long-term development credit; and (4) encouraging rationalization and automation of production as well as mergers under appropriate circumstances. A special fund has been set up to offer easier credit for the small and medium enterprises.[121]

Thus, the impacts of the small and medium enterprise crises on foreign investment and foreign-exchange controls can be seen as follows: (1) The government will pay close attention to avoiding the foreign control of domestic industries because foreign investors are better able to purchase small and medium enterprises than big enterprises;[122] (2) the Central Bank intervention on the foreign-exchange market will be inevitable to halt the New Taiwan dollar's appreciation while taking the small and medium enterprises' operation into consideration; (3) the capital market will continue to suffer development problems without the participation of the small and medium enterprises; and (4) the outward foreign direct investment will be impeded due to the capital adequacy of the small and medium enterprises under current restrictions.

Excessive Savings and Reserves

Domestic savings as a percentage of the GNP has exceeded 30 percent since the late 1970s. In recent years, these savings have exceeded domestic investment needs. In 1986, the influx of foreign exchange and the excessive savings together caused the concern of inflation because of the increasing money supply. Despite the government's sterilization operations, the M1b money supply grew 42.3 and 32.8 percent in 1987 and 1988 respectively.[123]

The 1989 inflation rate was 4.5 percent.[124] One economist pointed out that inflation will not become a problem for the Taiwan economy because past experience has indicated that inflation often is induced by the following factors, none of which are existing in Taiwan: (1) The government finances its budget deficit by issuing domestic currency over a long period of time whereby the domestic money supply exceeds the nation's reserves. Except during 1982, there was a budget surplus in Taiwan for a long time and the 1979 budget surplus reached a peak of NT$32.7 billion. (2) The financial institutions extend credits by making immense amounts of loans and cause the total sum of the loans to exceed the deposits. But there are too many deposits in Taiwan's financial system. For instance, the deposits of financial institutions exceeded loans over NT$1,571 billion in December 1989. (3) The prices of imported goods, such as raw materials, energy supplies, or consumer goods hiked and caused the domestic consumer price to rise as well. The two OPEC crises are typical cases. Currently, there is no expectation of an oil price hike and the price of agricultural products, raw materials, and metals are stable on the international market.[125] Another entrepreneur pointed out that because of the open economy and the export-oriented industries in Taiwan, domestic commodity prices will follow the international market price changes and the excessive money supply alone will not cause inflation. He argued that the exporters will shift to supply the domestic market if the domestic price is higher than international market price and vice versa. Thus, the domestic price will be changed only if the international market price changes because there is no shortage of domestic supply.[126]

Nonetheless, the government has been cautious toward excessive money supply, and the Central Bank has faced the choice between further liberalizing capital outflows or further strengthening the New Taiwan dollar due to the increase arising from the excessive money supply.[127]

Another adverse impact of the excessive money supply is the insufficient domestic fixed-capital formation. The domestic investment has lagged behind domestic savings in recent years, the gap as a ratio of the GNP was 15.5 percent in 1985 and 21.2 percent in 1986.[128] To stimulate the domestic fixed-capital investment, the government has consistently offered tax and tariff exemptions for importing machinery and equipment, as well as provided medium- and long-term loans for importation of raw materials, precision machinery, tools, and technology. Nevertheless, the willingness of enterprises to invest in capital goods is still weak.[129] This reflects the transition of the industrial structure from traditional labor-intensive industries to high-technology industries where the enterprises are reluctant to take the risk of producing high-technology products due to the unknown market and the large amount of capital involved. It is argued that the government should not only encourage the importation of capital goods, such as raw materials and machinery, but also encourage the imports of durable high-quality consumer goods in order to stimulate competition and create demand, and thus provide even more information and confidence to the enterprises to produce the products than before.[130] In recent years, the speculative money flows into the stock market to seek higher returns have complicated the problems.

The Ministry of Finance has asked the banks to use the following measures to tap more idle money for industrial development: (1) reinforcing lending to the commercial and industrial sectors; (2) offering consumer loans to the public; (3) providing more medium- and long-term loans to finance the infrastructure construction needs; and (4) channeling more credits and loans to small and medium enterprises. These measures are reported to narrow the gap between deposits and loans of the banking industries which reached over NT$1,100 billion up to November 1986.[131]

One phenomenon of the excessive money is the blind investment in the stock market and real estate. The rising prices of the stock market and real estate have encouraged more speculative operations, thus putting more pressures on potential inflation.[132] To encourage the public to invest in the stock through the more skillful investment and trust companies, the government has decided to allow three of the investment and trust companies to issue another total value of NT$6 billion beneficiary certificates to the domestic investors. In contrast, the issuance of beneficiary certificates to foreign investors abroad will be limited in order to avoid worsening the excessive money supply resulting from excessive domestic savings and foreign-exchange reserves.[133] This may be seen as the government temporarily retreating from the internationalization of the stock market.

Foreign-Exchange-Rate Realignment

Foreign-exchange-rate realignment has been the controversial issue for the government in recent years. Because of the undervaluation of the New Taiwan dollar and the currency talks with the United States, appreciation of the New Taiwan dollar has been expected since early 1986. The issue remaining is whether the government should allow the New Taiwan dollar to appreciate further against the U.S. dollar gradually or in one stroke. Since the foreign-exchange rates are decided by five appointed banks, they are not to exceed 2.25 percent above or below the central rate of the previous business day. Thus, over the year 1986, the New Taiwan dollar appreciated against the U.S. dollar no more than 5 cents per day.[134] Critics have pointed out that this policy of steady and slow appreciation has encouraged speculative operations and worsened the foreign-exchange reserves due to the inflows of speculative capital. Moreover, exporters have been encouraged to deliver their exporting goods and to convert their foreign-exchange earnings as soon as possible, thereby creating a fictitious export boom with a greater trade surplus, both of which have been the major source of the foreign-exchange inflows. The exporters eager to export in order to avoid the foreign-exchange risk have disrupted the export order. Furthermore, investment projects have been delayed because the investors were waiting for a better opportunity to import machinery and equipment at less cost. It is argued that the exporters would be able to absorb the one-time appreciation shock because the prices of imported raw and intermediate materials have helped to reduce the cost of exports. The gradual appreciation of the New Taiwan dollar implies strong intervention of the Central Bank thereby invoking the criticism of keeping low exchange rates to expand exports abroad from the trade partners.[135]

In contrast, those who support the government policy argue that the moderate appreciation of the New Taiwan dollar would provide more time for the small and medium enterprises to adjust their products with the higher New Taiwan dollar on the international market, an adjustment vital to the Taiwan economy.[136] The gradual appreciation of the New Taiwan dollar should provide the opportunity for the government to observe the domestic economy response which in turn would allow for a better policy to be formulated. The Taiwan economy has been heavily dependent on exports; a one-time appreciation would cause a detrimental impact on the export industries and on the economy as a whole. Furthermore, one of the functions of the Central Bank is to maintain an orderly foreign-exchange market. While other developing countries are using the managed floating-exchange-rate system, the intervention of the Central Bank does not offset the foreign-exchange market function as a whole; instead, the intervention provides an affordable foreign-exchange-rate system. The debate is eventually arising under two different government agencies, the Ministry of Economic Affairs and the Council for Economic Planning and Development.[137]

Although the Central Bank has insisted on its own policy route, more pleas requesting the Central Bank to define a bottom line for the New Taiwan dollar appreciation have been raised, especially as the New Taiwan dollar reached a record high in February 1987 and because of the frequent changes in foreign-exchange rate causing the adjustment difficulties of the industries.[138] The agreement for stabilizing the U.S. dollar reached by the six major industrial countries on 22 February 1987 temporarily stopped the debate.[139]

After the Sino-U.S. exchange-rate talk in April 1989, the Central Bank promulgated the new rules for exchange-rate determination. Under the new rules, the 2.25 percent ceiling for fixing the exchange rate is lifted and the exchange rates are decided by nine trading banks—five appointed banks and four foreign banks—in the morning of each trading day. However, the New Taiwan dollar has been stabilized after two years' appreciation and the Central Bank, the largest foreign reserve holder, has the decisive leverage on exchange-rate determination; thus, the new measure has only changed the pace of New Taiwan revaluation a little.

As the foreign-exchange reserves soared and the external trade surplus increased during 1986–89,[140] the government used some measures to liberalize and internationalize the Taiwan economy. Critics have argued that the relaxations of foreign-change controls are minor and insufficient to cope with current economic development. The major complaints have focused on the outward capital flow controls.[141] Indeed, further liberalization and internationalization of the Taiwan economy will be closely monitored, although there is a trend toward relaxation of the controls on capital movement, particularly the outward capital flows. Some cautious considerations are worthy of mention as follows: Once Taiwan begins to liberalize its exchange controls and to allow free outward capital flows, the beneficiaries' lobby will become a powerful lobby demanding more and more freedom. The risks of excess capital outflows can be seen as follows: (1) demolishing public confidence due to the drain of foreign-exchange reserves; (2) creating a capital shortage, if foreign direct investments begin to withdraw from Taiwan either due to an unstable political climate in Taiwan or pressures from home countries to provide more domestic jobs; (3) worsening the current-account deficits once the foreign trade surpluses decreased either because of maladjustment of the domestic industries or the growing protectionism abroad; (4) increasing serious capital flight if all of the capital flight constraints are broken down; and (5) offsetting domestic monetary policies and destabilizing the financial system as a whole thereby inducing inflation. Again, national security concerns will be a high priority consideration, above all the issues of Taiwan's great threat from Communist China. Thus, a limited liberalization, at least with effective surveillance, may better serve the nation's interests.

NOTES

1. This period was under the Four-Year Economic Development Plan for Taiwan, as ended in 1985.

2. During 1982–84, gross fixed investment by industries (at 1981 prices) fell 1.4 percent annually on average—0.02 percent in manufacturing, 3.3 percent in utilities, 3.3 percent in building construction, 17.1 percent in mining. (Council on Economic Planning and Development, *Ninth Medium-term Economic Development Plan for Taiwan, 1986–1989*, in Chinese, Taipei: Overall Planning Department, Economic Planning and Development, August 1986, p. 1.)

3. In 1986, due to the appreciation of the Japanese yen and low oil prices, exports increased over 27 percent and the fixed investment by private enterprises was estimated to rise 18.33 percent. However, bank deposits increased more than 30 percent, which far exceeds domestic investment needs. (*Central Daily News*, in Chinese, 8 December 1986, p. 7.)

4. *Industry of Free China*, September 1986, Table 41.

5. *Free China Journal*, 12 January 1987, p. 4.

6. *Central Daily News* (in Chinese), 1 February 1987, p. 7.

7. *Central Daily News*, 17 January 1987, p. 7.

8. It is estimated that the investment tax incentives cost the government some NT$20–25 billion annually. ("Taiwan Tax Reformers Will Have Another Try," *Business Asia*, 15 December 1986.)

9. *Central Daily News*, 17 January 1987, p. 1.

10. *Central Daily News*, 4 January 1987, p. 7.

11. *Central Daily News*, 22 August 1986, p. 7.

12. *Free China Journal*, 9 February 1987, p. 4.

13. *Central Daily News*, 22 December 1986, p. 1.

14. *Free China Journal*, 3 November 1986, p. 4.

15. *Central Daily News*, 11 November 1986, p. 1.

16. *Central Daily News*, 1 December 1986, p. 7.

17. Robert E. Norton, "Trade War: A New Track, The Administration Objects to Taiwan's Plan to Export Cars," *Fortune*, 26 May 1986, p. 94.

18. *Central Daily News*, 30 December 1986, p. 7.

19. *Central Daily News*, 16 January 1987, p. 7.

20. The aforesaid figures are according to official statistics. (*Statistics on Overseas*

Chinese and Foreign Investment, Technical Cooperation, Outward Investment, Outward Technical Cooperation, the Republic of China, Taipei: Investment Commission, Ministry of Economic Affairs, 31 December 1989.) The total amount of outward investments which were not reported to the Ministry of Economic Affairs could more than double the figures.

21. *Central Daily News*, 2 January 1987, p. 2.

22. Following the Nissan deal, the BTR Nylex Corporation of Australia bought the stocks of three local firms and the local firms became majority foreign-owned companies. The successful issuance of the Taiwan Fund is another example of showing the foreign investors' interest in buying from the Taiwan stock market. It was reported that the Taiwan Fund was six to eight times over-subscribed when it was listed on the American Stock Exchange. (Lourales Z. Lee, "Foreigners' Hunger for Taiwan Stock, Seen in Success of Newest Overseas Fund," *Asian Wall Street Journal*, 22 December 1986, p. 21.)

23. "Investment in Taiwan Hit 770.4 Million Last Year," *Asian Wall Street Journal*, 12 January 1987.

24. *Central Daily News*, 28 December 1986, p. 7.

25. *Central Daily News*, 27 January 1987, p. 2.

26. The foreign-ownership requirement which limits the foreign ratio of total stocks of a specific company will be implemented by the passage of the amendments of the Securities and Exchange Act. In the case of direct foreign investment in Taiwan, the government has not required any ratio of local participations.

27. "Taiwan Proposes Changes in Securities Law to Broaden Brokerages' Activities," *Asian Wall Street Journal*, 16 February 1987, p. 18.

28. See Chapter 1 for more comparisons.

29. Carl Goldstein, "Mountains of Green, Taipei Cannot Slow the Growth of Forex Reserves," *Far Eastern Economic Review*, 13 November 1986, p. 176.

30. *Central Daily News*, 4 February 1987, p. 7.

31. Ibid.

32. *Central Daily News*, 1 February 1987, p. 7.

33. The Taiwan stock market is relatively small with a total value of US$13.1 billion and the share of the overseas funds are US$156 million (1.1 percent). (*Central Daily News*, 30 November 1986, p. 7.)

34. Andrew Tanzer, "Taiwan Reaps the Rewards of Economic Virtue—but Virtue Can Become Fanaticism: the Trouble with Mercantilism," *Forbes*, 11 August 1986, p. 42.

35. In 1986, the domestic M1B money supply rose a monthly average of 40 percent and the M2 money supply grew a monthly average of 22 percent, thus contributing to the pressures of inflation. (Julia Leung, "Taiwan under Fire for Regulating the Rise in Its Currency, Government Intervention Sparks Speculation, Fear of Inflation, Quick Fix for Trade Fiction?," *Asian Wall Street Journal*, 12 January 1987, p. 1.)

36. The ten days' average of the banks' reserves has been raised to NT$5 billion. (*Central Daily News*, 9 June 1986, p. 7.)

37. *Industry of Free China*, December 1985, p. 25.

38. "Taiwan's 1986/87 Budget Boosts Spending and Deficit, Emphasizes Development," *Business Asia*, 14 April 1986, p. 115.

39. Critics pointed out that the issuance of savings certificates by will of the Central Bank encourages speculation and distorts the functions of the banks as financial inter-

mediaries. The Central Bank issued a total sum of NT$10 billion in savings certificates in November 1986. (*Central Daily News*, 22 November 1986, p. 7.)

40. *Central Daily News*, 8 December 1986, p. 7.

41. *Central Daily News*, 21 July 1986, p. 7.

42. The tax credit was introduced in 1984 for a period of three years and the current regulation has extended the three-year period to as long as the corporation's lifetime. (Larence Minard, "Taiwan's Stock Market Is Slowly Opening Up to Foreign Investors and Promises to Become One of Asia's Hottest Exchanges—but for Now It Remains Definitely Not for Widows and Orphans," *Forbes*, 4 June 1984, p. 58.)

43. P. T. Bangslerg, "Taiwan Pledges Further Cuts in Import Tariffs," *Journal of Commerce and Commercialism*, 12 February 1987, p. 44.

44. *Central Daily News*, 6 February 1987, p. 7.

45. *Central Daily News*, 23 October 1986, p. 7.

46. The Chrysler Corporation pulling out its investment from Taiwan is a typical example. During 1986 the New Taiwan dollar had appreciated 14.6 percent against the Hong Kong dollar and 10.82 percent against the Korean won.

47. Julia Leung, "Taiwan Banks Suffer Huge Foreign Exchange Losses," *Asian Wall Street Journal*, 12 January 1987, p. 17.

48. *Central Daily News*, 10 February 1987, p. 7.

49. For instance, Far Eastern Textile, the Chung Shing Textile Company, the Oemec Corporation, and the China Unique Garment Company have introduced computerized systems to upgrade their productivity. (*Free China Journal*, 1 December 1986, p. 4.)

50. "Ninth Medium-term Economic Development Plan for Taiwan, 1986–1989."

51. *Central Daily News*, 1 February 1987, p. 7.

52. *Central Daily News*, 14 February 1987, p. 7.

53. *Central Daily News*, 13 August 1986, p. 7.

54. *Central Daily News*, 2 February 1987, p. 7.

55. "Surging Reserves Prompting Taiwan to Reexamine Its Currency Controls," *Asian Wall Street Journal*, 2 February 1987, p. 17.

56. *Central Daily News*, 14 February 1987, p. 7.

57. Ching-ing Hou, "The Features and Issues of Interest Rate Liberalization at the Current Stage,"*Industry of Free China* (in Chinese), March 1986, p. 5.

58. Under Article 41 of the banking law, as amended on 17 July 1989, the government lifted the controls on interest-rate adjustments.

59. Hou, "Features and Issues."

60. *Industry of Free China*, April 1986, p. 27.

61. *Central Daily News*, 8 January 1987, p. 7.

62. *Central Daily News*, 22 September 1986, p. 2.

63. *Central Daily News*, 7 August 1986, p. 2.

64. Warren L. Coats, Jr., and Deena R. Khatkhate, "Money and Monetary Policy in Less-Developed Countries: Survey of Issues and Evidence," *Money and Monetary Policy in Less-Developed Countries: A Survey of Issues and Evidence*, ed. by Warren L. Coats, Jr., and Deena R. Khatkhate (Washington, D.C.: IMF; New York: Pergamon, 1980), p. 21.

65. The government decided to encourage the foreign investors to engage in the credit rating and investigation system, thereby introducing new technology and management of a credit rating system. (*Central Daily News*, 3 February 1986, p. 2.)

66. *Central Daily News*, 22 July 1986, p. 2.

67. *Central Daily News*, 28 August 1986, p. 2.

68. Attention by Appointed Banks in Buying and Selling Foreign Exchange Abroad and in Holding Foreign Exchange Funds for Business Operations, as Promulgated on 26 January 1979.

69. The Regulations Governing Foreign Exchange Proceeds Deposit, as amended on 27 March 1979.

70. One investigation report of Control Yuan indicated that over 85 percent of the foreign-exchange reserves are deposited in the U.S. dollar. (*Central Daily News*, 14 August 1986, p. 1.) Another report said that 88 percent of the foreign-exchange reserves were deposited in the U.S. dollar. (Carl Goldstein, "The Question That Gets You Thrown Out," *Euromoney*, February 1987, pp. 31–32.)

71. *Central Daily News*, 15 January 1987, p. 7.

72. *Economic Daily* (in Chinese), 29 July 1986, p. 2.

73. *Central Daily News*, 16 December 1986, p. 7.

74. *Central Daily News*, 10 June 1986, p. 7.

75. The government has shelved a proposal of the Economic Reform Committee in which the committee suggested that the government allow more bills and finance companies to operate on the money market. Currently, only three state-owned bill finance companies engage in the money-market operation. The prime minister has pointed out that the government has adopted a cautious attitude toward the money market. (*Central Daily News*, 24 July 1986, p. 7; Kuo-shu Liang, "Financial Reforms Recommended by the Economic Reform Committee, Republic of China," *Industry of Free China*, March 1986.)

76. *Transnational Corporations in World Development, Third Survey* (London: Graham & Trotman/United Nations, 1985), p. 119.

77. J. Davidson Frame, *International Business and Global Technology* (Lexington: Lexington Books/D. C. Heath, 1983), p. 96.

78. The survey also indicated that from 1952 to 1979, the number of private technology agreements approved by the government totaled 1,981 cases, of which 70.3 percent were from Japan, 19.3 percent were from the United States, and 18.7 percent were from European countries. (Dennis Fred Simon, "Technology Transfer to Taiwan," in *Contemporary Republic of China, The Taiwan Experience, 1950–1980*, ed. by James C. Hsiung et al. (New York: Praeger, 1981, p. 210.)

79. K. T. Li, "A Strategy for Technological Development," in *Contemporary Republic of China, The Taiwan Experience, 1950–1980*, ed. by Hsiung, pp. 200–5.

80. K. T. Li, "A Report on the Development of Science and Technology in the Republic of China, 1982–1986," *Industry of Free China*, June 1986.

81. William M. Raike, "Computing in Taiwan," *Byte*, December 1985, p. 297.

82. Under the Ten-year Science and Technology Plan (1986–95), the government will spend US$25–27 billion on R&D. ("Taiwan Technology Plan Sets Ambitious Targets, Relies on Private Sector," *Business Asia*, 22 September 1986.)

83. *Central Daily News*, 1 February 1987, p. 7; and Dennis Fred Simon, "Technology Transfer."

84. Under the regulations, it is mandated that a productive enterprise with NT$300–1,000 million annual business revenues should spend 0.5–1.5 percent of the income on R&D. The R&D expenditures of a productive enterprise with NT$1 billion or more annual business revenue should be 0.125–0.375 percent of the income. The R&D expenditures refer to the expense of new product research, improved management

technology, energy-saving research, pollution-control research, and marketing investigation.

85. *Central Daily News*, 29 December 1986, p. 7.

86. Terutomo Ozawa, "Japan," in *Multinational Enterprises, Economic Structure and International Competitiveness*, ed. by John H. Dunning (New York: John Wiley & Sons, 1985), p. 155.

87. Chi Schive, "Foreign Investment and Technology Transfer in Taiwan: Past Experience and Future Potentials," in *Conference on Economic Development Experience of Taiwan and Its New Role in an Emerging Asian Pacific Area*, Vol. II (Taipei: Institution of Economics, Academia Sinica, June 1988), pp. 345–85.

88. Li, "Strategy for Technological Development."

89. Executive Yuan, *Annual Report of Government Administration, Republic of China, 1982–1983*, ed. by Research, Development, and Evaluation Commission (Taipei: Executive Yuan, November 1984), pp. 267–68.

90. OECD, *International Investment and Multinational Enterprises: Incentives and Disincentives and the International Investment Process* (Paris: OECD, 1983).

91. The investment project as approved is the largest one in Taiwan, in which the Du Pont Company will invest a total amount of US$160 million.

92. *Free China Journal*, 23 February 1987, p. 4.

93. *Central Daily News*, 11 December 1986, p. 7.

94. *Central Daily News*, 6 July 1987, p. 7.

95. *The Republic of China's Economic Development for 1990—Macroeconomic Development Targets* (Taipei: Overall Planning Department, Council for Economic Planning and Development, Executive Yuan, 1990).

96. Kuo-shu Liang and Ching-ing Hou Liang, "Trade, Technology and the Risk of Protectionism: The Experience of the Republic of China," *Industry of Free China*, January 1984, p. 13.

97. Gustav Ranis, "Industrial Development," in *Economic Growth and Structural Change in Taiwan, The Postwar Experience of the Republic of China*, ed. by Walter Galenson (Ithaca, N.Y.: Cornell University Press, 1979).

98. Shirley W. Y. Kuo, "Labor Absorption and Full Employment," Chap. 4 in *The Taiwan Economy in Transition* (Boulder: Westview Press, 1983).

99. Interior Ministry, *Investigation Report of the Needs of Vocational Training* (in Chinese) (Taipei: Vocational Training Bureau, Interior Ministry, 1985).

100. Earl Wieman, "The Export Processing Zone System: Is What Foreign Investors Want," *Free China Journal*, 1 September 1985.

101. In 1985, the monthly average of manufacturing wages in Taiwan was US$325.34 as compared to the US$304.30 in South Korea. ("No Relief in Sight for Taiwan Wage Rates," *Business Asia*, 26 July 1985.) In September 1989, the monthly average of manufacturing wages in Taiwan were more than US$781.8 per month according to official statistics. (*Monthly Bulletin of Statistics of the Republic of China* 56, no. 14, Taipei: Directorate-General of Budget, Accounting and Statistics, Executive Yuan, November 1990.)

102. Patrick Smith, "Taiwan Rounds Off a Peak Performance," *Far Eastern Economic Review*, 11 March 1983, p. 12.

103. *Four-year Economic Development Plan for Taiwan, Republic of China, 1982–1985* (Taipei: Council for Economic Planning and Development, Executive Yuan, December 1981), p. 123; *Taiwan Statistical Data Book, 1986* (Taipei: Council for Economic Planning and Development, Executive Yuan, 1986).

104. "Ninth Medium-term Economic Development Plan for Taiwan, 1986–1989."

105. Kuo, *Taiwan Economy in Transition*, p. 132.

106. *Four-year Economic Development Plan for Taiwan, Republic of China, 1982–1985*.

107. Smith, "Taiwan Rounds Off."

108. One of the generators was shut down after a turbine broke, causing a fire on 7 July 1985. ("Nuclear Energy Accident Hinders on New Plant," *Free China Journal*, 29 September 1986.)

109. Li, "Strategy for Technological Development."

110. *Industry of Free China*, July 1986, p. 25.

111. Ibid., November 1985, p. 26.

112. Ibid., March 1986, p. 33.

113. Ibid., July 1986, p. 25.

114. Ibid., April 1990, p. 44.

115. *Central Daily News*, 6 February 1987, p. 7.

116. Tanzer, "Taiwan Reaps the Rewards."

117. A report indicated that the problem of using American brand names has been one reason why Taiwan wasn't targeted earlier for the currency talk. (Douglas R. Sease, "The Other Deficit: Dollar's Decline Fails to Have the Intended Effects of Narrowing the Trade Gap," *Wall Street Journal*, 7 January 1987, p. 18.)

118. Here is another flaw of the state-owned banking system. One of the banking regulations has set up a strict standard of writing off bad loans, and those who offered loans which turned out to be bad will be held liable with administrative penalties in the civil service grading system for minor mistakes and also with the risk of repaying the bad loans imposed. (Kuo-shu Liang, "Financial Reforms Recommended by the Economic Reform Committee, Republic of China," *Industry of Free China*, March 1986.)

119. *Central Daily News*, 11 February 1987, p. 7. The debate over the Central Bank's appreciation strategy will be discussed in detail at the end of the chapter.

120. "Ninth Medium-term Economic Development Plan for Taiwan, 1986–1989."

121. *Central Daily News*, 10 November 1987, p. 7.

122. For instance, the DEC Company of the United States purchased Hwa Kung Company with a high price of US$600–800 million. (*Central Daily News*, 5 December 1987, p. 7.)

123. In December 1989, the M1B money supply was 49.8 percent above the same period in 1988, and the money supply slid by 10 percent during 1990. (*Financial Statistics Monthly, Taiwan District, The Republic of China*, Taipei: Economic Research Department, the Central Bank of China, December 1990, Table 9.)

124. Julia Leung, "Taiwan under Fire for Regulating the Rise in Its Currency, Government Intervention Sparks Speculation, Fear of Inflation, Quick Fix for Trade Friction?" *Asian Wall Street Journal*, 12 January 1987, p. 1.

125. *Central Daily News*, 11 November 1987, p. 7.

126. *Central Daily News*, 29 November 1987, p. 7.

127. Leung, "Taiwan under Fire," p. 1.

128. *Central Daily News*, 4 February 1987, p. 7.

129. *Central Daily News*, 15 January 1987, p. 7. Although one report indicated that in the third quarter of 1986, the domestic fixed-capital investment reached 16.7 percent of the GNP, compared to the 37 percent of the gross national savings, this is still a low figure. (*Central Daily News*, 22 November 1986, p. 7.)

130. Chia-loong Wu, "Dissipating Foreign Exchange Reserves," *Central Daily News*, 22 and 23 December 1986, p. 7.

131. *Central Daily News*, 8 January 1987, p. 7.

132. You-thon Tang, "Interest Rates Fall, Idle Money Seeking Investment Opportunities, Blind Investment Shown on the Stock and Real Estate Markets," *Central Daily News*, 13 February 1987, p. 7.

133. *Central Daily News*, 15 February 1987, p. 7.

134. Kuo-shu Liang, "The Foreign Exchange Market and Managed Floating: The Experience of the Republic of China," *Industry of Free China*, July 1985, p. 1.

135. *Central Daily News*, 11 December 1986, p. 7.

136. Under the 1983 survey, 99.26 percent of the manufacturing industries were small and medium enterprises, which refers to the enterprises with NT$40 million paid-in capital or less. (Tzong-shian Yu, "The Relationship Between the Government and the Private Sector in the Process of Economic Development in Taiwan, Republic of China," *Industry of Free China*, October 1985, Table 2.)

137. *Central Daily News*, 22 February 1987, p. 7.

138. *Central Daily News*, 14 February 1987, p. 7.

139. *Central Daily News*, 24 February 1987, p. 7; Art Pine, "U.S. Economic Allies Indicate a Readiness to Intervene in Foreign Exchange Trading," *Wall Street Journal*, 23 February 1987, p. 140. The foreign-exchange reserves were estimated at US$46 billion at the end of 1986, and the imports and exports hit a record high of US$24.7 billion and US$39.7 billion respectively, with a surplus of US$16 billion. ("Statistical Data, R.O.C. on Taiwan," *Free China Journal*, 9 February 1987.)

140. "Balance of Payments," *Taiwan Statistical Data Book, 1990*, Table 11–1a. Taipei: Council for Economic Planning and Development, 1990.

141. Leung, "Taiwan under Fire," p. 1.

5

Lessons for Economic and Industrial Development

In reviewing the role of international capital movements in Taiwan's economic development, it is evident that the policies of encouraging foreign direct investment and restricting capital outflows have contributed significantly to the nation's successful economic development in the past thirty years. In the 1950s and 1960s, Taiwan was hungering for foreign capital inflows to help the nation rise from poverty at a time when the major exports were sugar and rice. An outward-oriented industrial policy has led the country to substantial economic growth after the rapid expansion of industries in the 1970s. Today, the problem of plenty has caused domestic concern for inflation and pressures of openness from abroad. Nonetheless, as one writer put it, "when a world where Third World poverty and unrest is the biggest single problem, Taiwan stands as a remarkable example of how a poor nation can raise itself by its bootstraps simply by adopting wise policies and sticking to them."[1]

The conclusions of this study will illustrate some lessons of the Taiwan experience with respect to the international capital movement controls (or encouragements). Meanwhile, the case of South Korea is similar to Taiwan in terms of successful economic development and has become one of the fastest newly industrializing countries. The competition between South Korea and Taiwan is keen on the international market because both countries have employed export-oriented industrial policies. Nonetheless, different policy approaches in South Korea have resulted in different levels of success and, of course, in somewhat different problems. For instance, the South Korean government has been borrowing heavily from abroad to finance its large domestic investment projects and conglomerates in contrast to the strong foreign direct investment and small but widely spread firms in Taiwan. Thus, some comparison between the two countries will be made to illustrate different policy options for developing countries.

FOREIGN INVESTMENTS

In Taiwan, foreign direct investment has played an important role in the nation's economic development. Foreign direct investment has brought technology know-how and marketing channels into Taiwan in addition to capital inflows. In the past, foreign direct investments were attracted by low costs and a well-educated labor force for developing export-oriented industries. Under export-oriented policies, the government consistently provided fiscal, financial, and other incentives, including protective tariffs and import bans to protect domestic production. Recently, the ill effects of the export-oriented policies have been criticized strongly as inviting protectionism abroad, distorting domestic resources, discouraging technology renovation, impeding economic efficiency, and as hurting domestic consumers.[2] Thus, a more pragmatic export-expansion and import-substitution policy has been initiated by the government.

The case of Korea is somewhat different; the Korean government, however, uses a similar scheme: tax holidays, duties and tax exemptions, accelerated depreciation, preferential loans, and export processing zones to encourage foreign direct investment. The total amount of foreign direct investment in Korea was US$532 and US$331 million in 1985 and 1986 respectively, which was lower than Taiwan's US$700 and US$770 million during the same period of time (due to Korea's more restrictive regulations and political unrest).[3] The major restrictions on foreign direct investment in Korea are equity requirements and export performance requirements. Nevertheless, the Korean government adopted a liberalized "negative list" on 1 July 1984 to offer easier access to foreign investors.[4] The equity requirements limit foreign equity to 50 percent of invested capital unless the investment projects fall into one of the following categories: (1) entirely export-oriented projects that will not compete with domestic firms in overseas markets; (2) technology-intensive projects that increase or reduce production of important export or import substitution products; (3) multinational projects that foreign investors only invest in the form of wholly owned subsidiaries in other countries; (4) projects that contribute to the rationalization of the domestic industrial structure and which are beyond the capacity of domestic investors because of the large capital or advanced technology requirements; (5) projects from a country that have made little investment in the past but which expect to increase investment in the future; (6) projects by Korean residents abroad; and (7) projects in the free export zones and some other specific industrial estates designated by the government. Moreover, in the following cases over 50 percent of local participation is required: (1) purely labor-intensive industries; (2) purely bonded-processing industries; (3) industries dependent on domestic resources for major new materials; and (4) industries oriented toward local market sales.[5] The export performance requirement is screened on a case-by-case basis. The failure of investors to meet the export ratio may cause the revocation of tax benefits. In the case of a less than 10 percent shortfall of the export target, the corporate and income taxes will be applied at the ratio of the shortfall. If the export shortfall exceeds 10 percent, property and acquisition tax exemptions will be canceled and the firm will be subject to corporate and income taxes by the ratio of its export shortfall. If the shortfall is incurred in two successive years, all taxes will be levied in full.[6]

The selective policies of the Korean government toward foreign direct investment emerged in the early 1970s due to the fear of foreign control over the domestic economy, and development strategy sifted to more high-technology industries to avoid the withdrawals of foreign capital during external shocks, and to the development of native industries.[7] As the result of domestic capital shortages and insufficient foreign direct investment, the Korean government has heavily depended on foreign borrowing to finance its investment projects. The Korean foreign debt load was estimated to reach US$50.1 billion by the end of 1985.[8] In 1986, however, the trade surplus and the deemphasis on foreign borrowing brought the total foreign debt down to US$44.5 billion.[9] In comparing the different approaches to foreign direct investment in South Korea and in Taiwan, the results suggest that a developing country can satisfy its needs for foreign capital either by attracting foreign direct investment or borrowing abroad.

One issue arising under the above comparison is whether a developing country should rely more upon foreign direct investment or more upon foreign borrowing to develop its domestic economy. The benefits of substantial borrowing abroad have been said to include the following points: (1) adjusting to a once-and-for-all income loss easily by deferring and offsetting from future income; (2) supplementing investment by borrowing foreign capital and repaying with the returns of the investment; (3) smoothing income cycles caused by temporary internal or external shocks; and (4) financing international trade with growth.[10] Most important, good economic management and an efficient use of invested capital, such as in the case of South Korea, show that a developing country can use foreign borrowing to its advantage.

On the other hand, there are arguments for the advantages of foreign direct investment as follows: (1) The repayments of foreign direct investment depend on the profit earned by the investing companies, thus it is more responsive to the host nation's economy; (2) the repatriation of foreign investing capital and earnings are regulated by the host country instead of deciding under contract terms of loans and international money-market interest rates which fluctuate under different worldwide economic conditions; (3) most of the foreign direct investments reinvest their earnings and repatriation of capital is less extensive than the case of foreign borrowing; and (4) the repayments of foreign direct investments are deferred until the maturity of the investment projects. Thus the goal of bringing short-term capital to finance long-term investment needs can be achieved without disrupting the current-account balance.[11] The experience of Taiwan, which introduced strong foreign direct investments, is an example of success. Nonetheless, a recent study conducted by the Council of Economic Planning and Development of Taiwan indicated that encouragement of foreign direct investment with some degree of restrictions, such as in South Korea, may better serve the nation's later development, that is, a more selective policy to encourage the development of high-technology industries.[12] For example, the Korean government has been able to finance target industries—export-oriented and high-technology industries—by borrowing abroad and using government-directed lending domestically,[13] thus creating an efficient use of foreign capital. And the Korean enterprises are able to acquire high technology through technology cooperation agreements, R&D projects (of the large conglomerates), and government institutions.[14] In South Korea, large credits were given to major conglomerates and government projects.[15] As a result, the Korean economy is dependent on the strength of its large conglomerates, the so-call *chaebol*, such as Daewoo, Hyundai, Samsung, and Lucky-Goldstar.[16] Nonetheless, these large conglomerates also have the advantages of economic scale and independent R&D projects, something badly needed in Taiwan.

Since the world debt crisis broke out in 1982, many developing countries borrowing heavily abroad through multinational banks have been strained. Developing nations also may attract foreign direct investment by providing a stable and welcome climate, something vital to a nation's economic development.[17] Nevertheless, a developing nation cannot depend on foreign direct investment solely to finance its domestic growth. Self-sustaining independent technology development must be added to the foreign direct investment process. Whether a stricter policy should be used to foster domestic industries and technology development, as in the case of South Korea, will vary from one country to another. Factors such as domestic savings, creditworthiness of previous foreign borrowing, and trade performance must be taken into consideration. South Korea and Taiwan are now working for the liberalization of foreign direct investment, with a view to fostering domestic competition and to introducing more high-technology investment. In a less-developed economy, it is not likely that the government will be willing to open all investment opportunities to foreign investors because the domestic economy is not yet mature enough to accept too much competition, and foreign direct investments usually dominate the labor-intensive industries. Thus, the more advanced an economy is, the greater the liberalization of foreign direct investment can take place.

Another similarity between the cases of South Korea and Taiwan is their export-oriented economies. Because Taiwan has enjoyed a trade surplus for a long period of time (since the early 1980s), a stronger balance of payments plus the high foreign-exchange reserve levels have spurred the consideration of import-substitution policies. In South Korea, 1986 was the first year in twenty years for which there was a surplus in current accounts. An import-substitution policy for South Korea will not gain support in the near future.[18]

With respect to the outward foreign direct investment, Taiwan's experience is somewhat new and incomplete due to strict controls on outward capital flows and the lack of coordination among small and medium enterprises. The Korean government has successfully used the Overseas Acquisition Corporation to purchase overseas enterprises, thus establishing international distribution networks and circumventing rising protectionism abroad.[19] In Taiwan, similar steps have been initiated by the Industrial Technology Research Institution to combine the manufacturers of machine tools to set up a metal corporation in the United States.[20] Restrictions on the capital outflows have been criticized as a barrier to outward direct investments and have been blamed as one important factor in worsening the influx of foreign-exchange reserves in Taiwan. Since outward foreign direct investments are interrelated to foreign-exchange controls, a nation with strong government support, such as South Korea, may achieve significant success in acquiring overseas firms.[21] And, in Taiwan where the government manages the economy with a "hands-off approach" to foster the prosperity of private enterprise, the outward direct foreign investment cannot be substantial without lifting more foreign-exchange controls.

Another side of the coin involving foreign direct investment is foreign portfolio investment. South Korea and Taiwan are using the same strategy in opening their capital markets to foreign investors—through the issuance of beneficiary certificates by investment and trust funds.[22] Thus, foreign investors are only allowed to invest on the capital market indirectly, reflecting the underdeveloped stock market.[23] Nonetheless, the Korean government has allowed its large conglomerates, the chaebol, to issue floating convertible bonds abroad.[24] The bond issuance again reflects the shortage of domestic savings to finance investment.[25] In contrast, for the case of Taiwan where the idle domestic money floods the financial system, overseas bond issuance has been considerably deemphasized by the government. Meanwhile, the openness of the stock market in Taiwan is based on a policy of internationalization of the stock market by introducing foreign capital to upgrade the securities exchange management and to enlarge the scale of the stock market instead of serving a borrowing purpose. A fully opened stock market to foreign investors will be the final goal. However, the timetable to allow foreign investors to invest on the stock market directly has yet to be set by the government.

The new outward portfolio investment channel opened to the public in Taiwan has not created a significant impact on the nation's economy because of the restrictive regulations and the appreciation of the New Taiwan dollar. Nonetheless, this represents a bold step toward the liberalization of foreign-exchange controls in terms of capital outflow restrictions. Until 1986, the government was hesitant to allow public investing abroad, fearing that the potential capital flight might cause a drain of the foreign-exchange reserves. It is evident that unless a developing nation has achieved substantial economic development, it is likely that such a country will retain its domestic scarce resources and capital for domestic investment instead of financing other countries' development.

In encouraging foreign direct investment inflows, the government of Taiwan has given more leeway to market forces by using a "hands-off approach." The liberal attitude toward the development of private entrepreneurs should not be overlooked. Particularly, small-scale economic entities have provided the dynamic power to push the economy ahead, though larger scales of operation may be more suitable in other developing countries. The strategy of introducing foreign direct investment rather than foreign borrowing has successfully contributed to domestic economic development and financial stabilization in Taiwan. But in South Korea, heavy foreign debts have been used to finance government investment projects or have been directed to the large conglomerates. This illustrates an example of managing foreign debt efficiently to achieve economic development. While large companies have contributed significantly to the nation's economic growth, the problems of the imbalance development of industrial sectors and unfair competition are growing. The Korean government has announced its plan to restrict the expansion of these conglomerates.[26] Moreover, in South Korea, a policy of deemphasizing foreign loans has been undertaken to reduce the foreign debt by paying off some loans and by seeking interest cuts.[27] In contrast, the government of Taiwan is pursuing policies to encourage the merger of small firms aimed to fight for more independent R&D, distribution networks, and larger economic scales of production. The policy shifts in these two countries indicate that more balanced development between large and small firms is necessary to achieve longer-run economic development.[28]

FOREIGN-EXCHANGE CONTROLS AND BANKING OPERATIONS

The comprehensive foreign-exchange control regulations in Taiwan have effectively prevented the leakage of capital flight in the past forty years. The main theme of those regulations is to regulate the inflows and outflows of capital with an emphasis on the controls of outward capital flows. The successful management of foreign-exchange reserves has contributed to the stabilization of the financial system and of exchange rates which are vital to maintaining public confidence and to smoothing out the expansion of international trade. The recent development in liberalizing foreign-exchange controls has not caused any adverse effects on the nation's economy. This has encouraged a further liberalization of foreign-exchange controls. The experience of Taiwan provides a lesson that at the early stages of economic development, foreign-exchange controls are crucial, and when the economy matures, the gradual liberalization of foreign-exchange controls for more efficient and sophisticated usage of capital may follow. In South Korea, the foreign-exchange control scheme is similar to that of Taiwan, with controls on inward and outward capital flows, prior-approval requirements, restrictions on the amount and uses of foreign exchange, surrender requirements, etc.[29] In fact, some of the recent moves in Taiwan to allow the payment of invisible transactions to be approved automatically were borrowed from the Korean regulations. Since Taiwan's balance of payments situation is better than South Korea's, given Taiwan's excessive foreign-exchange reserves, it is arguable that the liberalization of foreign-exchange controls should be reinforced despite considerations for national security needs. However, the painful consequences experienced in the Mainland since the 1940s have made a stable financial system highly valuable in Taiwan. Thus any further liberalization of foreign-exchange controls will depend on broader international developments and relative security.

One difference between the financial systems of South Korea and Taiwan is that the banking industry in Taiwan remains a state-run operation while the Korean government has privatized its banking industry, though with tight state planning. But directed policy loans in South Korea are even stricter than in Taiwan. The privatization of state-run banks in South Korea was initiated in 1983. Some problems have been noted since then as follows: (1) the intervention by larger conglomerate shareholders; (2) the privileges of large borrowers; and (3) the lack of a professional management system. The Korean government has employed the following measures to correct the malpractice: (1) restricting voting rights up to 8 percent per shareholder; (2) restricting the credit offered to no more than 50 percent of the net worth of any one enterprise and 25 percent of the net worth of any individual borrower; (3) the authorities in charge of finance may suggest a personnel change; and (4) the government may request that privately owned banks cooperate with specialized banks by making policy loans.[30] Because the private banks depended on the Bank of Korea's discount window to finance their excessive loans over deposits, their directed policy loans, and the appointment of high banking officials, the whole banking industry is still controlled by the state.[31] The state-run banks in Taiwan are working closely with the government to provide financing for the strategic industries, and the Korean government has been directing their policy lending to target industries as well. Thus, both governments, South Korea and Taiwan, consider that coordination between their financial system and industrial enterprises is important as a policy tool to guide economic development and to utilize their limited capital resources efficiently. In observing the privatization of the banking industry in Korea, it is evident that privatizing their banking industry is not equal to privatizing ownership of their banks. Full privatization will not be achieved without liberalizing the restrictions on banking operations.

With respect to foreign bank status as it relates to foreign direct investment and banking operations, the cases of South Korea and Taiwan are somewhat different because of the historical background of South Korea emphasizing foreign borrowing. Because of heavily borrowing from abroad in the past, the foreign banks "have enjoyed substantial advantages over the domestic banks, including guaranteed profit swaps and protection from excessive lending risk."[32] In 1986, the Korean government announced some measures of liberalization to allow the foreign banks access to the Bank of Korea's discount window, to engage in clearing house operations and trust business, and to issue certificates of deposits.[33] Under the principle of national treatment, foreign banks are required to reduce swap ceilings and provide 35 percent of new lending to small and medium-sized businesses in exchange for accessing the Bank of Korea's discount window.[34] The new measures coupled with the Korean government's efforts in reducing foreign borrowing have been criticized by the foreign banks as follows: "the reform is a masterstroke, the more for less."[35] Thus, the liberalization, even under the principle of national treatment, could have different impacts on the operations of foreign banks based on the different degree of government control over banking operations and whether there is adequate domestic capital to attract foreign banks.[36]

In the past thirty years, the government of Taiwan has been conservative and cautious toward the management of its financial system. The result of this attitude is a more stable financial system and exchange rates with negligible foreign debt.[37] Today, the government has shifted to internationalization and liberalization of the Taiwan economy. Although there are forty foreign bank branch offices operating in Taiwan, only three domestic banks have set up eleven overseas branch offices and five overseas representative offices. In comparison with Korean banks' forty-six overseas branch offices, sixty-one overseas representative offices, and five foreign subsidiaries, the banking operations in Taiwan have lagged behind the economic development needs because trade expansion required more worldwide financial services.[38] Furthermore, the internationalization of banking operations will be helpful in liberalizing domestic banking operations and in relaxing foreign-exchange controls.

One argument behind strict controls on the banking system is that the government could provide a bailout during any financial crisis and could save the industries involved. In 1985, the Cathy Crisis in Taiwan resulted in trouble for sixty-six major firms, and at least one-third of these troubled firms were restored to healthy operation due to the help of the state-owned banks.[39] By the same token, after the collapse of the Kukje ICC Group in 1985, the Korean government forced their commercial banks to take an estimated US$5 billion in guaranteed policy loans with the debt guaranteed by the Bank of Korea.[40] The carefully planned financial operations provide a stable financial system to support economic development without being interrupted by internal or external shocks. This probably is one of the most valuable assets of a developing country that seeks economic development with government backing.

However, the controls on financial operations are not sustained without costs. The costs of sustaining strict controls on financial operations have been severe in South Korea and Taiwan due to underground money-market activities.[41] The controls also encourage other underground activities through legal or illegal channels.[42] The adverse economic impacts of those underground activities are difficult to evaluate; nevertheless, a substantial amount of these activities will distort the legal economic activities and the government's policy function.[43] For instance, to prevent the underground financial market activities, the government of Taiwan has lifted the ban on the establishment of private banks. And the speculative capital inflows into Taiwan in 1986 have caused the government to regulate inward capital movements.[44] Since the nature of the regulatory controls inevitably invite circumvention of those very controls,[45] a policy of minimizing the adverse impacts of underground activities, including the liberalization or the strengthening of the audit function, is necessary to maximize the economic efficiency of capital and to avoid the distortion of the economy as a whole.

CONCLUSIONS

In sum, the more liberal attitude toward foreign direct investments has made the investment climate in Taiwan more attractive to foreign investors. The know-how technology has been employed by various small and medium businesses, thus contributing to successful economic development and a more equitable distribution of wealth among the people in Taiwan. Although the policy has shifted to emphasize more high-technology industries since the early 1980s, the basic principle of attracting more foreign capital has been sustained, and more industrial and service sectors have opened to foreign investors because of the needs of modern management technology and marketing skill, the necessity to head off rising protectionism abroad, and because of the demand for more competition in the domestic market in Taiwan. Thus, a more liberalized foreign direct investment climate in addition to other incentive measures have provided very attractive investment conditions for foreign investors.

Other types of international capital movement, such as inward and outward portfolio investment, and outward direct foreign investment are new phenomena in Taiwan. The impacts of these new policy measures have yet to be evaluated since the appreciation of the New Taiwan dollar has stimulated the inflows of foreign capital and has impeded outward capital flows. Nonetheless, under the recent principle of internationalization and liberalization of the Taiwan economy set by the government, the openness of the capital market for international investment will be helpful in attracting more foreign capital and in maximizing the returns of domestic savings. To attract more foreign capital is not the top priority of

domestic stock market needs, but rather, excessive domestic savings have
been of great alarm to the government. Thus, government policy is aimed
at establishing a sound capital market by fostering healthy capital flows.
Outward direct foreign investment will be encouraged as well to meet the
needs of trade expansion and to secure raw material supplies.

Taiwan has little problem in borrowing abroad either through multinational banking operations or through international bond issuance because
of a high performance in its international trade surplus. Nonetheless,
excessive domestic savings and large foreign-exchange reserves have
caused the fear of inflation, and it is argued that increasing foreign capital
inflows will make the situation worse than ever. Most important, however,
the government of Taiwan has pursued a policy of keeping high foreign-
exchange reserve levels to stabilize the financial system and to avoid
external shocks. More doubtful is borrowing from abroad, which in turn
could diminish public confidence and shake the economy because of
Taiwan's isolation in the international community.[46]

The excessive savings and foreign-exchange reserves in Taiwan due to
the nation's huge trade surplus have caused the appreciation of the New
Taiwan dollar and resulting inflation pressures. Although adverse impacts
on export-oriented industries are obvious, the situation also creates a
chance the nation never had before to relax foreign-exchange controls
because the restrictions on capital outflows have impeded outward investment which could have alleviated the influx of foreign-exchange reserves.
The surrender requirements have induced a burden on the Central Bank
to buy foreign exchanges which could have been avoided if the public had
been allowed to hold a portion of foreign exchange earned. And, the
expectation of the New Taiwan dollar appreciation has weakened the
willingness of the public to hold foreign currencies, thus the relaxation of
foreign-exchange controls may not cause a drain of capital. But measures
for relaxing the foreign-exchange controls have proven to have little effect
so far on the alleviation of the huge foreign-exchange reserves in Taiwan.
Given the fact that the government has few choices in sterilizing foreign-
exchange earnings,[47] further liberalization of the foreign-exchange controls and banking operations is necessary. But, this problem of plenty is
hardly typical of other developing countries' previous experiences and the
possible moves of the government remain to be seen in Taiwan.[48]

Two additional measures are being considered to implement the liberalization of the financial system in Taiwan. One is the establishment of
the deposit insurance system and the other one is the reinforcement of the
credit system. A deposit insurance system will provide a safeguard to the
public against any financial crisis where the government is no longer

needed to bail out collapsed financial institutions. The credit rating system can enhance bank loans based on the accountability of borrowers rather than based on the collateral provided. Thus, the banks' risk of lending will be reduced and the financial strains[49] of the small and medium business will be alleviated, that is, it will create a more efficient use of capital. The systematization of financial operations will assure a successful transition to further liberalization of financial operations and eventual privatization of the banking system. After all, the government is imposing controls to protect the public interest rather than to gain profits from controls.

In Taiwan, the import and export values accounted for the most important part of the nation's balance of payments.[50] The importance of trade-related service rendered, foreign direct investment, and other capital flows also are vital to Taiwan's economic development. For instance, export-oriented foreign direct investment in Taiwan will foster the nation's export performance in the long run, and, as an import substitution, foreign direct investment will help the home country in penetrating the domestic market. The services rendered by the service industries, such as banking and insurance, can be regarded as commodities. The next round of GATT negotiations has put the service industries, investment, and intellectual property into the agenda to reinforce fair play in these areas. Also coordination among the GATT, IMF, and World Bank has been emphasized.[51] As a study pointed out, foreign-exchange controls and import restrictions in Taiwan had "thwarted the classical adjust mechanism for a balance of payment surplus: that mechanism would translate excess foreign exchange into increased domestic liquidity, lower market interest rates, higher consumption and domestic investment, private capital outflows, and greater import demand."[52] To restructure domestic industries and to foster further economic growth, more liberalization of capital flows has been undertaken particularly for the Taiwan economy which is closely interrelated to the international market. If Taiwan either fails to smooth the adjustment mechanisms, thereby causing inflation, or to invoke trade retaliation abroad because of unfair practices caused by controls, a disaster for the uneasily built-up economic miracle in Taiwan may loom up.

However, a small outward-oriented economy like Taiwan's is vulnerable to external shocks. At the moment, the government of Taiwan is blamed for accumulating too much foreign-exchange reserves and responding to changing economic conditions too slowly. A delicate problem is arising: To what extent should the government lift foreign-exchange controls by taking into consideration the danger of potential capital flight, the shrinkage of exports in light of growing protectionism abroad, restrictions on Taiwan's exports because of the influence of Mainland China in the international community, and other economic adversities?[53] Thus, the liberalization of foreign-exchange controls will come to naught if any destructive impact is forthcoming in its wake.

NOTES

1. Andrew Tanzer, "Taiwan Reaps the Rewards of Economic Virtue—but Virtue Can Become Fanaticism: The Trouble with Mercantilism," *Forbes*, 11 August 1986, pp. 36–46.

2. *Central Daily News*, 4 July 1986, p. 7.

3. "Korean Business Brief," *Asian Wall Street Journal*, 5 January 1987, p. 4.

4. Of the 999 total industrial sectors in Korea, 237 sectors were on the negative list, of which 53 were banned and 184 were restricted up to the end of 1985. (American Institute in Taiwan, *Foreign Economic Trends and Their Implications for the United States* [Washington, D.C.: U.S. Department of Commerce, International Trade Administration, January 1986].)

5. Bohn Young Koo, "The Role of Direct Foreign Investment in Korea's Recent Economic Growth," in *Foreign Trade and Investment, Economic Growth in the Newly Industrializing Asian Countries*, ed. by Walter Galenson (New York: Praeger, 1985), pp. 178–79.

6. "Korea," in *A Business International Asian Research Report: World Sourcing Sites in Asia, Manufacturing Costs and Conditions in Hong Kong, Korea, Singapore, and Taiwan* (Hong Kong: Business International Asia Pacific, November 1979), p. 159.

7. Koo, "Role of Direct Foreign Investment," p. 178.

8. See Table 1.2.

9. "Korean Financial Outlook," *Business Asia*, 26 January 1987, p. 30.

10. Nicholas C. Hope and David W. McMurray, "Loan Capital in Development Finance, the Role of Banks, and Some Implications for Managing Debt," *Problems of International Finance, Papers of the Seventh Annual Conference of the International Economics Study Group*, ed. by John Black and Graeme S. Dorrance (New York: St. Martin's Press, 1984), p. 93.

11. Constantine Michalopoulos, "Private Direct Investment, Finance and Development," *Asian Development Review*, Vol. 3, no. 2 (1985), p. 59.

12. *Central Daily News*, 10 November 1986, p. 7.

13. Joseph P. Manguno and Hyung-Soo Kim, "Korean Banks Suffer Ill Effects from Years of State Planning," *Asian Wall Street Journal*, 5 January 1987, p. 4.

14. Korean manufacturers can benefit from some of the national research institutions: the Korean Institution of Science and Technology, the Korean Advanced Institution of Science, the National Industrial Research Institution, the National Construction Research, the Korean Marine Industry Development Corporation, the Radiation Research Institution for Agriculture, the Atomic Energy Research Institution, and the Radiological Institution. ("Korea," in *World Sourcing Sites in Asia*, p. 142.)

15. Willard D. Sharpe, "Four Tigers May Yet Reproduce Economic Miracles," *Wall Street Journal*, 27 January 1986, p. 20.

16. Louis Kraar, "Reheating Asia's Little Dragons," *Fortune*, 26 May 1986, p. 135.

17. One study by the IMF indicated that "foreign direct investment can help a country maintain sufficient resource inflows to support an adequate growth rate, as well as to reduce vulnerability to any future deterioration in economic conditions." (*Foreign*

Private Direct Investment in Developing Countries, IMF Research Department, Occasional Paper Series No. 33, Washington, D.C.: IMF, January 1985, p. 26.)

18. A *Business Asia* report indicated that a nationalistic backlash to liberalization of foreign direct investment is possible in South Korea. It illustrated the example of opening foreign tobacco imports under U.S. pressures, causing the delayed approval of several foreign investment projects in the second half of 1986. (*Business Asia,* 26 January 1987.)

19. For instance, the Hyundai Automobile Company has set up a distribution network in the United States and sales have reached 10,000 units annually. (*Central Daily News,* 13 August 1986, p. 7.)

20. The project remains in the planning stages, but the idea of setting up branch offices was borrowed from Korea's experience. (*Central Daily News,* , 6 December 1986, p. 7.)

21. In 1986, the Korean overseas projects abroad totaled 150 cases, of which US$46 million was invested in the United States and US$44.2 million in the Middle East. (*Asian Wall Street Journal,* 3 March 1987, p. 3.)

22. Up to 1986, there were five open-ended and one closed-ended mutual funds available to foreign investors in Korea. One different feature between South Korea and Taiwan is that the Korean funds are operated by local investment and trust companies only. ("Year of the Equity (Again) in 1987," *Far Eastern Economic Review,* 8 January 1987, p. 98.)

23. The value of the Korean stock market is thin and the transaction costs are high, according to a report of the World Bank. The stock market as a proportion of total securities shrunk from 76.5 percent in 1975 to 40 percent in 1982, thus reflecting the declining importance of the stock market. (World Bank, *Korea: Development in a Global Context,* A World Bank Country Study, Washington, D.C.: World Bank, 1984, p. 36.)

24. "Year of the Equity (Again) in 1987," p. 98.

25. During the periods of both 1971–76 and 1977–83, domestic savings as a percentage of domestic capital formation were 76 percent. (Asian Development Bank, *Key Indicators of Developing Member Countries of the Asian Development Bank,* Manila: Asian Development Bank, April 1984.)

26. The plan will restrict the conglomerates to invest over 40 percent of their net worth outside their respective groups. Some objections were reported on the grounds of industrial restructuring needs and possible government interventions. ("Seoul Plans to Rein in Korea's Big Conglomerates by Restricting Investment," *Business Asia,* 13 October 1986, p. 322.)

27. Cheah Cheng Hye, "Seoul Requests Rate Cut on $500 Million Loan," *Asian Wall Street Journal,* 2 March 1987, p. 2.

28. It is argued that small firms have a comparative advantage in the earliest stages of innovative work and less expansive but more radical innovations. The large firms have a comparative advantage in the late stage, mostly development, and in improving technological breakthrough. (Terutomo Ozawa, "Entrepreneurship and Technology in Economic Development," *Asian Development Review* 3, no. 2, 1985, p. 99.)

29. International Monetary Fund, "Korea," in *Annual Report on Exchange Agreement and Restriction, 1986* (Washington, D.C.: IMF, 1986), p. 327.

30. National Construction Committee, *A Study and Recommendation on the Reinforcement of Financial Policy and Economic Development,* Occasional Paper No. 43 (in Chinese) (Taipei: National Construction Committee, June 1985), p. 40.

31. Manguno and Kim, "Korean Banks Suffer Ill Effects," p. 5.

32. The swap arrangements allow foreign banks to bring in foreign exchange and swap it at the Bank of Korea for local currency lending. (Joseph P. Manguno, "Foreign

Banks in Korea Left Embittered by Government Policy of Liberalization," *Asian Wall Street Journal*, 29 December 1986, p. 2.) The report also cited the restrictions on foreign bank operations in South Korea as follows: (1) restrictions on foreign banks from engaging in banking activities that involve the taking of securities in real estate; (2) prohibitions against investment in their financial institutions, such as merchant banks and short-term finance companies; (3) limits on lending; (4) prohibition on land ownership which raises both overhead and costs for staff housing; (5) restrictions on engaging in the securities business; and (6) denial of access to special accounts that provide additional liquidity to local banks. Nonetheless, the swap transactions between the Central Bank of Korea and the foreign banks are most important and profitable for foreign banks because of the heavy foreign borrowing of the Korean government.

33. "Financial Outlook: Korea," *Business Asia*, 3 November 1986, p. 351.

34. Some disadvantages of this change have been cited as follows: inadequate discount ratios, higher rediscount rates, lower special swap fund ceilings, burdens of contributing to credit guarantee funds (for small and medium business) and higher risks of lending to small and medium firms. ("Foreign Banks in Korea Get Full Rediscount Access in Exchange for Privileges," *Business Asia*, 25 August 1986, p. 270.)

35. Manguno, "Foreign Banks in Korea Left Embittered." To avoid the risks of lending to small and medium business, Morgan Guaranty has downgraded its branch office to a representative office and concentrated its business on investment consulting, the Bank of America has reduced its number of customers, and Wells Fargo has adopted the so-called "California strategy"—to deal only with the firms doing business between California and Korea, thus minimizing the risks. (Joseph P. Manguno, "Foreign Banks Try to Adapt to Korea's Shrinking Needs, Lenders Lower Profile, Shift Tack, as Seoul Trims Its Borrowing; Wells Fargo's California Plan," *Asian Wall Street Journal*, 2 March 1987, p. 2.)

36. In Taiwan, the foreign banks are seeking to operate the New Taiwan dollar savings accounts as well as trust and investment businesses because the excessive domestic savings are attractive to foreign banks.

37. Up to the end of 1985, the total foreign debt amounted to US$5.2 billion, according to official statistics. (Central Bank of China, *Balance of Payments, Republic of China*, Taipei: Economic Research Department, Central Bank of China, September 1986, Annex Table.)

38. National Construction Committee, *A Study and Recommendation on the Reinforcement of Financial Policy and Economic Development*, pp. 30–31.

39. Anthony Risks, "All That Money is Being Bought Dearly," *Far Eastern Economic Review*, 15 May 1986, p. 82.

40. Manguno and Kim, "Korean Banks Suffer Ill Effects."

41. As aforementioned, over 30 percent of the financial sources of small and medium business in Taiwan came from the black market. In South Korea, the speculative money flow into Korea's Kerb money market has been sharply contracted because of the government's antispeculation measures. ("Year of the Equity (Again) in 1987," *Far Eastern Economic Review*, 8 January 1987, p. 96.)

42. Other capital flow leakages to circumvent controls are cited as follows: smuggling, falsified invoices, parallel loans, simulated currency loans, and currency swap. The latter three activities are most often used by multinational enterprises. (Michael R. Rosenberg, "Foreign Exchange Controls: An International Comparison," in *International Finance Handbook*, Vol. I, ed. by Abraham M. George and Ian H. Giddy, New York: John Wiley & Sons, 1983, p. 46.)

43. Theodore Morgan, "The Shadow Economies: Step toward Estimating Their Size in Asian Countries," *Asian Development Review* 3, no. 2 (1985), p. 72.

44. Currently, outward remittances and inward remittances of under US$3 million in one year are not subject to the prior-approval requirement.

45. Exchange control regulations have been characterized with "built-in incentive for violation" nature. (Leland B. Yeager, *International Monetary Relations: Theory, History, and Policy*, 2nd ed., New York: Harper & Row, 1976, p. 151.)

46. However, in 1986, the banking industry in Taiwan borrowed over US$4.6 billion abroad to finance exports because the New Taiwan dollar appreciation made the future repayment of the loans more profitable. (*Central Daily News*, 25 February 1987, p. 7.)

47. Other measures for sterilizing foreign-exchange earnings have been used by the Korean government as follows: (1) raising foreign-exchange handling fees from 0.5 percent to 0.9 percent; and (2) cutting the maturity of usance bills and documents acceptance from 90 to 60 days. ("Korea Moves to Check M2," *Business Asia*, 25 February 1987, p. 27.)

48. One report from Taipei indicated that the government had decided to allow the public to hold foreign exchanges and to buy foreign stocks. However, the report did not reveal the timing and details of the possible measures. ("Surplus Solvable Problem," *Free China Journal*, 23 March 1987, p. 2.)

49. According to a recent survey, 75 percent of the credits extended by the financial institutions went to the 5 percent large businesses, and the remaining 25 percent of loans went to small and medium businesses, which account for 95 percent of the enterprises in Taiwan. (National Construction Committee, *A Study and Recommendation on the Reinforcement of Financial Policy and Economic Development*, p. 17.)

50. "A Nation of Traders" was used by Lawrence Minard to emphasize the degree of the Taiwan economy's dependence on foreign trade. (Lawrence Minard, "A Major Transition Is under way in the Economy of Taiwan—with Important Consequences for U.S. Business: The China Reagan Can't Visit," *Forbes*, 7 May 1984, p. 36.)

51. See Gary Clyde Hufbauer and Jeffrey J. Schott, *Trading for Growth: The Next Round of Trade Negotiations* (Washington, D.C.: Institute for International Economics, September 1985), pp. 41–82.

52. "The Asian NICs and U.S. Trade," *World Financial Market*, January 1987, p. 7.

53. The issue has been widely debated. Some arguments have been posited as follows: allowing the public to hold part of their foreign-exchange earnings, encouraging imports instead of lifting foreign-exchange controls, freeing capital flows except for the outward capital flows, lifting foreign-exchange controls fully and empowering the government to restore controls when necessary, and lifting the export and import licensing requirements.

Bibliography

BOOKS

Bentley, Philip, ed. *A World Guide to Exchange Control Regulations*. London: Euromoney Publications, 1985.

Billerbeck, K., and Y. Yasugi. *Private Direct Foreign Investment in Developing Countries: Policy Issues for Host and Home Governments and for International Institutions*. World Bank Staff Working Paper, No. 348. Washington, D.C.: World Bank, July 1979.

Black, John, and Graeme S. Dorrance, eds. *Problems of International Finance*. Papers of the Seventh Annual Conference of the International Economics Study Group. New York: St. Martin's Press, 1984.

Bloomfield, Arthur I. *Capital Imports and the American Balance of Payments, 1934–39: A Study in Abnormal International Capital Transfers*. Chicago: University of Chicago Press, 1950.

Business International Asia. *World Sourcing Sites in Asia: Manufacturing Costs and Conditions in Hong Kong, Korea, Singapore, and Taiwan*. A Business International Asian Research Report. Hong Kong: Business International Asia Pacific, November 1979.

Carlip, Vivian, William Overstreet, and Dwight Linder, eds. *Economic Handbook of the World*. New York: McGraw-Hill, 1982.

Chang, Hu-wang. *The Financial Industry in Taiwan: Practices and Cases Analysis* (in Chinese). Taipei: Hei Ten, June 1984.

Charles, George E. *Developing Venture Capital in the Republic of China: An American Banker's Viewpoint*. Taipei: Industrial Development and Investment Center, June 1984.

Coats, Warren L., Jr., and Deena R. Khatkhate, eds. *Money and Monetary Policy in Less Developed Countries: A Survey of Issues and Evidence*. Oxford, U.K.: Pergamon Press, 1980.

Conference on Economic Development Experience of Taiwan and Its New Role in an

Emerging Asian Pacific Area. Taipei: Institution of Economics, Academia Sinica, June 1988.

Conwitt, Philip P., ed. *1984 World Currency Handbook.* Brooklyn, N.Y.: International Currency Analysis, 1985.

DaCosta, Michael. *Finance and Development: The Role of International Commercial Banks in the Third World.* Boulder: Westview, 1982.

Dam, Kenneth W. *The Rules of the Game: Reform and Evolution in the International Monetary System.* Chicago: University of Chicago Press, 1982.

David, Wilfred L. *The IMF Policy Paradigm: The Macroeconomics of Stabilization, Structural Adjustment, and Economic Development:* New York: Praeger, 1985.

Dell, Sidney. *On Being Grandmotherly: The Evolution of IMF Conditionality.* Essays in International Finance, No. 144. Princeton, N.J.: Department of Economics, Princeton University, 11 October 1981.

Dillon, K. Burke, C. Maxwell Watson, G. Russell Kincaid, and Chanpen Puckahtickom. *Recent Developments in External Debt Restructuring.* Occasional Paper No. 40. Washington, D.C.: IMF, October 1985.

Dunn, Angus, and Martin Knight. *Export Finance.* London: Euromoney Publications, 1982.

Dunning, John H., ed. *Multinational Enterprises, Economic Structure and International Competitiveness.* New York: John Wiley & Sons, 1985.

Edwards, Richard W., Jr. *International Monetary Collaboration.* Dobbs Ferry, N.Y.: Transnational Publisher, 1985.

Enke, Stephen, and Virgil Salera. *International Economics.* New York: Prentice-Hall, 1947.

Fanno, Marco. *Normal and Abnormal International Transfers.* Minneapolis: University of Minnesota Press, 1939.

Frame, J. Davidson. *International Business and Global Technology.* Lexington, Mass.: Lexington Books/D. C. Heath, 1983.

Frankel, Jeffrey A. *The Yen-Dollar Agreement: Liberalizing Japanese Capital Markets.* Policy Analyses in International Economics No. 9, Washington, D.C.: Institute for International Economics, December 1984.

Fry, Earl H. *The Politics of International Investment.* New York: McGraw-Hill, 1983.

Galenson, Walter, ed. *Economic Growth and Structural Change in Taiwan: The Postwar Experience of the Republic of China.* Ithaca, N.Y.: Cornell University Press, 1979.

————. *Foreign Trade and Investment, Economic Growth in the Newly Industrializing Asian Countries.* Madison: University of Wisconsin Press, 1985.

George, Abraham M., and Ian H. Giddy, eds. *International Finance Handbook,* Vol. I. New York: John Wiley & Sons, 1983.

————. *International Finance Handbook,* Vol. II. New York: John Wiley & Sons, 1983.

Gold, Joseph. *Legal and Institutional Aspects of the International Monetary System: Selected Essays,* eds. Jane B. Evenson and Jaikeun Oh. Washington, D.C.: IMF, 1979.

Gorostiaga, Xabier. *The Role of the International Financial Centers in Underdeveloped Countries,* trans. Annette Honeywell. New York: St. Martin's Press, 1984.

Haberler, Gottfried von. *Prosperity and Depression: A Theoretical Analysis of Cyclical Movement,* Enl. ed. New York: United Nations, 1946.

————. *The Theory of International Trade with Its Applications to Commercial Policy,* trans. Alfred Stonier and Frederic Benham. New York: Macmillan, 1937.

Ho, Samuel P. S. *Economic Development of Taiwan, 1860–1970* (A Publication of the Economic Growth Center, Yale University). New Haven, Conn.: Yale University Press, 1978.

Horsefield, J. Keith, ed. *The International Monetary Fund, 1945–1965: Twenty Years of International Monetary Cooperation*, Vol. III. Washington, D.C.: IMF, 1969.

Hsiung, James C., et al., eds. *Contemporary Republic of China, The Taiwan Experience, 1950–1980.* New York: Praeger, 1981.

Hufbauer, Gary Clyde, and Jeffrey J. Schott. *Trading for Growth: The Next Round of Trade Negotiations.* Policy Analyses for International Economics, No. 11. Washington, D.C.: Institute for International Economics, September 1985.

International Monetary Fund. *IMF Annual Report on Exchange Agreement and Restriction, 1986.* Washington, D.C.: IMF, 1986.

———, Research Department. *Foreign Private Investment in Developing Countries.* Occasional Paper Series No. 33. Washington, D.C.: IMF, January 1985.

Killick, Tony, ed. *Adjustment and Financing in the Developing World: The Role of the International Monetary Fund.* Washington, D.C.: IMF/Overseas Development Institute, 1982.

Kindleberger, Charles P. *International Money: A Collection of Essays.* London: George Allen & Unwin, 1981.

———. *International Short-term Capital Movements*, Reprint. New York: A. M. Kelley, 1965.

———. *Keynesianism vs. Monetarism, and Other Essays in Financial History.* London: George Allen & Unwin, 1985.

Kuo, Shirley W. Y. *The Taiwan Economy in Transition.* Boulder, Colo.: Westview Press, 1983.

Kuo, Shirley W. Y., Gustav Ranis, and John C. H. Fei. *The Taiwan Success Story: Rapid Growth with Improved Distribution in the Republic of China, 1952–79.* Boulder, Colo.: Westview Press, 1981.

Lessard, Donald, and John Williamson. *Financial Intermediation beyond the Debt Crisis.* Washington, D.C.: Institute for International Economics, September 1985.

Lindert, Peter H., and Charles P. Kindleberger. *International Economics*, 7th ed. Homewood, Ill.: Richard D. Irwin, 1982.

Lovett, William A. *World Trade Rivalry: Trade Equity and Competing Industrial Policies.* Lexington, Mass.: Lexington Books/D. C. Heath, 1987.

Machlup, Fritz. *International Trade and the National Income Multiplier.* Philadelphia: Blakiston, 1943.

Machlup, Fritz, Walter S. Salant, and Lorie Tarshis, eds. *International Mobility and Movement of Capital, A Conference of the Universities—National Bureau Committee for Economic Research.* New York: Columbia University Press/National Bureau of Economic Research, 1972.

Makin, John H. *The Global Debt Crisis, America's Growing Involvement.* New York: Basic Books, 1984.

Mayer, Emilio. *International Lending: Country Risk Analysis.* Reston, Va.: Reston Financial Services, Division of Reston Publishing, 1985.

Nurkse, Ragnar. *International Currency Experience: Lessons of Interwar Period.* Princeton, N.J.: League of Nations, 1944.

Oman, Charles. *New Forms of International Investment in Developing Countries.* Paris: OECD, Development Centre Studies, 1984.

Organization for Economic Cooperation and Development. *Code of Liberalization of Capital Movements.* Paris: OECD, March 1986.

————. *Controls on International Capital Movements: The Experience with Controls on International Financial Credits, Loans and Deposits.* Paris: OECD, 1982.

————. *Controls on International Capital Movements: The Experience with Controls on International Portfolio Operations in Shares and Bonds.* Paris: OECD, 1980.

————. *Industry and Trade in Some Developing Countries, The Philippines, and Taiwan.* London: Oxford University Press, 1971.

————. *International Investment and Multinational Enterprises: Investment Incentives and Disincentives and the International Investment Process.* Paris: OECD, 1983.

————. *Investing in Development Countries: OECD/DAC Member Countries' Policies and Facilities with Regard to Foreign Direct Investment in Developing Countries,* 5th Rev. ed. Paris: OECD, November 1982.

Please, Stanley. *The Hobbled Giant: Essay on the World Bank,* a Westview Replica ed. Boulder, Colo.: Westview Press, 1984.

Root, Franklin R. *International Trade and Investment,* 5th ed. Cincinnati: South-Western Publishing, 1984.

Schreiber, Jordan C. *U.S. Corporate Investment in Taiwan.* New York: Dunellen Publishing, 1970.

Southard, Frank A., Jr. *The Evolution of the International Fund.* Essays in International Finance, No. 135. Princeton, N.J.: Department of Economics, Princeton University, December 1979.

Swidrowski, Jozef. *Exchange and Trade Controls, Principles and Procedures of International Economic Transactions and Settlements.* Cambridge, U.K.: University Printing House, 1975.

Swoboda, Alexander K., ed. *Capital Movements and Their Control—Proceedings of the Second Conference of the International Center for Monetary and Banking Studies.* Geneva: Institute Universitaire de Hautes Etudes Internationales, 1976.

Taiwan's Foreign Trade Conference (in Chinese). Taipei: Institution of Economics, Academia Sinica, August 1981.

Thomas, Lloyd B., Jr. *Money, Banking, and Economic Activity,* 2nd ed. Englewood Cliffs, N.J.: Prentice-Hall, 1982.

Transnational Corporations in World Development, Third Survey. London: Graham & Trotman, 1985.

Tsoukalis, Loukas, ed. *The Political Economy of International Money, In Search of a New Order.* London: Sage, 1985.

Vincze, Imre. *The International Payments and Monetary System in the Integration of the Socialist Countries.* Dordrecht, Holland: Kluwer Academic Publishers, 1984.

Watson, Maxwell, Donald Mathieson, Russell Kincaid, and Eliot Kalter. *International Capital Markets, Developments and Prospects.* IMF Occasional Paper No. 43. Washington, D.C.: IMF, February 1986.

Williamson, John, ed. *IMF Conditionality.* Cambridge, Mass.: MIT Press/Institute for International Economics, 1983.

World Bank. *Korea: Development in a Global Context.* A World Bank Country Study. Washington, D.C.: World Bank, 1984.

————. *The World Bank Annual Report 1986.* Washington, D.C.: World Bank, 1986.

————. *World Bank Atlas: Population, Per Capita Products, and Growth Rates.* Washington, D.C.: World Bank, June 1983, June 1986.

Wu, Yuan-li. *Becoming an Industrialized Nation: ROC's Development on Taiwan*. New York: Praeger, 1985.

Yeager, Leland B. *International Monetary Relations, Theory, History, and Policy*, 2nd ed. New York: Harper & Row, 1976.

Yoshihara, Kunio. *Foreign Investment and Domestic Response: A Study of Singapore's Industrialization*. Singapore: Eastern Universities Press, 1976.

JOURNAL AND NEWSPAPER ARTICLES AND UNPUBLISHED PAPERS

"An Interview with Hu Yaobang, Peking Lashes Out at Washington-Taipei Link." *Far Eastern Economic Review*, 24 July 1986.

"Annual Report of 1985 of the Fund's Executive Board." *IMF Survey*, October 1985.

"The Asian NICs and U.S. Trade." *World Financial Markets* (Morgan Guaranty Trust Company of New York), January 1987.

Bangslerg, P. T. "Taiwan Pledges Further Cuts in Import Tariffs." *Journal of Commerce and Commercialism*, 12 February 1987.

Bowring, Philip. "Individual Can Play Too." *Far Eastern Economic Review*, 26 March 1987.

"Dealers Say Tax Is Killing Gold Trade, Despite New Rules." *Free China Journal*, 23 August 1986.

"Deputies of the Group of Ten Issues Report on Functioning of the Monetary System." *IMF Survey*, July 1985.

"Developments in International Banking and Capital Markets in 1985." *Bank of England Quarterly Bulletin* 26, no. 1 (March 1986).

Edwards, Sebastian. "Sequencing Economic Liberalization in Developing Countries: The Order of Policy is an Important, But Difficult, Aspect of Adjustment." *Finance and Development* (A Quarterly Publication of IMF and the World Bank) 24, no. 1 (March 1987).

"Enhanced Surveillance." *IMF Survey*, September 1986.

"An Essential Review . . . Article IV Consultations Provide Framework for Surveillance of Fund Member's Policy." *IMF Survey*, September 1986.

"Executive Board Warns of Harmful Effects Arising from Multiple Currency Practices." *IMF Survey*, 24 June 1985.

Feder, Barnaby J., "Capital Flight Adds to Burden of Debtor Nations." *New York Times*, 9 June 1986.

"Financial Outlook: Korea." *Business Asia*, 3 November 1986.

"Financial Outlook: Taiwan." *Business Asia*, 27 January 1986.

"Foreign Banks in Korea Get Full Rediscount Access in Exchange for Privileges." *Business Asia*, 25 August 1986.

"The Foreign Exchange Market and Managed Floating: The Experience of the Republic of China." *Industry of Free China*, July 1985.

"Fund Analysts Compare G-10 and G-24 Reports." *IMF Survey*, 30 June 1986.

Gerth, Jeff. "Mexico's Loss of Assets Threatening Debt Plan." *New York Times*, 9 June 1986.

Glad, James. "The ADB Slackens Its New Commitments, Last-Resort Lender." *Far Eastern Economic Review*, 15 May 1986.

Goldstein, Carl. "A Cash-Stuffed Case for Investment." *Far Eastern Economic Review*, 26 March 1987.

———. "Mountains of Green, Taipei Cannot Slow the Growth of Forex Reserves." *Far Eastern Economic Review*, 13 November 1986.

———. "The Question That Gets You Thrown Out." *Euromoney*, February 1987.

———. "Taiwan to Regulate Inward Cash Flows." *Far Eastern Economic Review*, 26 February 1987.

Ho, Ronald H. C. "The Financial System in Taiwan, Republic of China, Its Function and Operation." Unpublished paper. Taipei: October 1981.

Hou, Ching-ing. "The Features and Issues of Interest Rate Liberalization at the Current Stage" (in Chinese). *Industry of Free China*, March 1986.

"Hu's Dismissal Signals an Orthodox Backlash, Reforms in Jeopardy." *Far Eastern Economic Review*, 29 January 1987.

Hye, Cheah Cheng. "Seoul Requests Rate Cut on $500 Million Loan." *Asian Wall Street Journal*, 2 March 1987.

"Investment in Taiwan Hit 770.4 Million Last Year." *Asian Wall Street Journal*, 12 January 1987.

"Investment Law Changes, Trim Forex Restrictions, Widen Scope in Taiwan." *Business Asia*, 9 June 1986.

Khan, Mohsin S., and Nadeem Ul Haque. "Capital Flight from Developing Countries: An Examination of the Phenomenon and the Issues It Raises." *Finance and Development* (A Quarterly Publication of IMF and the World Bank) 24, no. 1 (March 1987).

"Korea Moves to Check M2." *Business Asia*. 25 August 1986.

"Korean Business Brief." *Asian Wall Street Journal*, 5 January 1987.

"Korean Financial Outlook." *Business Asia*, 26 January 1987.

Kraar, Louis. "Reheating Asia's Little Dragons." *Fortune*, 26 May 1986.

"Leaders of Seven Major Industrial Nations Agree on Coordinations of Economic Policies." *IMF Survey*, 19 May 1986.

Lee, Lourales Z. "Foreigners' Hunger for Taiwan Stock, Seen in Success of Newest Overseas Fund." *Asian Wall Street Journal*, 22 December 1986.

Leung, Julia. "Taiwan Banks Suffer Huge Foreign Exchange Losses." *Asian Wall Street Journal*, 12 January 1987.

———. "Taiwan under Fire for Regulating the Rise in Its Currency, Government Intervention Sparks Speculation, Fear of Inflation, Quick Fix for Trade Friction?" *Asian Wall Street Journal*, 12 January 1987.

Li, K. T. "A Report on the Development of Science and Technology in the Republic of China, 1982–1986." *Industry of Free China*, June 1986.

Liang, Kuo-shu, "Financial Reforms Recommended by the Economic Reform Committee, Republic of China." *Industry of Free China*, March 1986.

Liang, Kuo-shu, and Ching-ing Hou Liang. "Trade, Technology and the Risk of Protectionism: The Experience of the Republic of China." *Industry of Free China*, January 1984.

———. "The Foreign Exchange Market and Managed Floating: The Experience of the Republic of China." *Industry of Free China*, July 1985.

Long-term International Monetary Reform: A Proposal for an Improved International Adjustment Process. Occasional Paper. Washington, D.C.: American Society of International Law, 1972.

"Managing Director's Address . . . Adjustment Process Not Inimical to Growth, Protect-
    ing Human Needs." *IMF Survey*, 14 July 1986.
"Managing Director's Statement . . . Resolution of Developing Countries Debt Problem,
    Demand Rapid Growth, Open Trading System," *IMF Survey*, 28 October 1985.
Manguno, Joseph P. "Foreign Banks in Korea Left Embittered by Government Policy of
    Liberalization." *Asian Wall Street Journal*, 29 December 1986.
————. "Foreign Banks Try to Adapt to Korea's Shrinking Needs, Lenders Lower
    Profile, Shift Tack, as Seoul Trims Its Borrowing; Wells Fargo's California
    Plan." *Asian Wall Street Journal*, 2 March 1987.
Manguno, Joseph P., and Hyung-Soo Kim. "Korean Banks Suffer Ill Effects from Years
    of State Planning." *Asian Wall Street Journal*, 5 January 1987.
"Manufacturers Assume Growing Role in Trade, Offering Promise for Developing
    Countries." *IMF Survey*, 15 December 1986.
Mendelson, M. S. "Baker on Trial." *Bankers*, September 1986.
Michalopoulos, Constantine. "Private Direct Investment, Finance and Development."
    Asian Development Review (Studies of Asian and Pacific Economic Issues,
    Asian Development Bank) 3, no. 2 (1985).
Minard, Lawrence. "A Major Transition Is under way in the Economy of Taiwan—with
    Important Consequences for U.S. Business: The China Reagan Can't Visit."
    Forbes, 7 May 1984.
————. "Taiwan's Stock Market Is Slowly Opening up to Foreign Investors and
    Promises to Become One of Asia's Hottest Exchanges—but for Now It Remains
    Definitely Not for Widows and Orphans." *Forbes*, 4 June 1984.
Morgan, Theodore. "The Shadow Economies: Steps toward Estimating Their Size in
    Asian Countries." *Asian Development Review* 3, no. 2 (1985).
Morgenthau, Henry. "Bretton Woods and International Cooperation." *Foreign Affairs*
    (Council on Foreign Relations) 23 (1945).
"New Bond Issue Hot—Sells Like Pancakes First Day of Offer." *Free China Journal*,
    1 December 1986.
"No Relief in Sight for Taiwan Wage Rates." *Business Asia*, 26 July 1985.
Norman, Peter. "Banks Increased Overseas Activity in Second Quarter." *Wall Street
    Journal*, 27 October 1986.
Norton, Robert E. "Trade War: A New Track, The Administration Objects to Taiwan's
    Plan to Export Cars." *Fortune*, 26 May 1986.
"Nuclear Energy Accident Hinders on New Plant." *Free China Journal*, 29 September
    1986.
"Occasional Paper 45 Examines Swiss Role as Financial Center." *IMF Survey*, 30
    September 1986.
Ozawa, Terutomo. "Entrepreneurship and Technology in Economic Development."
    Asian Development Review (Asian Development Bank) 3, no. 2 (1985).
Pine, Art. "U.S. Economic Allies Indicate a Readiness to Intervene in Foreign Exchange
    Trading." *Wall Street Journal*, 23 February 1987.
"Protectionist Pressures Persist, but Capital Controls Ease in '85." *IMF Survey*, Septem-
    ber 1986.
Raike, William M. "Computing in Taiwan." *Byte*, December 1985.
"Report of Group of 24 Calls for Basic Changes in International System." *IMF Survey*,
    September 1985.
Riedel, James. "The Nature and Determination of Export-oriented Direct Foreign Invest-

ment in a Developing Country: A Case Study of Taiwan." *Weltwirtschaftliches Archiv* 3 (1976).

Risks, Anthony. "All That Money Is Being Bought Dearly." *Far Eastern Economic Review*, 15 May 1986.

Sanders, Sol W. "Washington and Beijing Call a Truce on Taiwan." *Business Week*, 18 July 1983.

Sease, Douglas R. "The Other Deficit: Dollar's Decline Fails to Have the Intended Effects of Narrowing the Trade Gap." *Wall Street Journal*, 7 January 1987.

"Seoul Plans to Rein in Korea's Big Conglomerates by Restricting Investment." *Business Asia*, 13 October 1986.

Shao, Maria. "U.S. Food Chains Sprout in Taiwan, as Affluence Creates New Appetites." *Asian Wall Street Journal*, 9 September 1985.

———. "U.S. Steps Up Pressures on Taipei to Lift Curb on Trade and Investment." *Asian Wall Street Journal*, 14 October 1985.

Sharpe, Willard D. "Four Tigers May Yet Reproduce Economic Miracles." *Wall Street Journal*, 27 January 1986.

"Simplified Red Tape Lures Increased Venture Capital." *Free China Journal*, 8 September 1986.

"Slowly, Slowly, Taiwan Reforms Forex Controls." *Business Asia*, 25 August 1986.

Smith, Patrick. "Taiwan Rounds Off a Peak Performance." *Far Eastern Economic Review*, 11 March 1983.

"Statistical Data, R.O.C. on Taiwan." *Free China Journal*, 5 January, 9 February 1987.

"Surging Reserves Prompting Taiwan to Reexamine Its Currency Controls." *Asian Wall Street Journal*, 2 February 1987.

"Surplus Solvable Problem." *Free China Journal*, 23 March 1987.

"Taiwan, Banking on Change." *Economist*, 12 July 1986.

"Taiwan Bond Issue Aims to Stem Inflation." *Journal of Commercial and Commerce*, 27 March 1986.

"Taiwan Financial Outlook." *Business Asia*, 27 June 1986.

"Taiwan Funds" *Far Eastern Economic Review*, 8 January 1987.

"Taiwan Liberalizes Forex System." *Business Asia*, 1 September 1986.

"Taiwan Proposes Changes in Securities Law to Broaden Brokerages' Activities." *Asian Wall Street Journal*, 16 February 1987.

"Taiwan Tax Reformers Will Have Another Try." *Business Asia*, 15 December 1986.

"Taiwan Technology Plan Sets Ambitious Targets, Relies on Private Sector." *Business Asia*, 22 September 1986.

"Taiwan's Fair Trade Law Now under Deliberation Breaks New Ground." *Business Asia*, 6 October 1986.

"Taiwan's New Copyright Law: A Great Leap Forward, but Many Hurdles Remain." *Business International*, 19 July 1985.

"Taiwan's 1986/87 Budget Boosts Spending and Deficit, Emphasizes Development." *Business Asia*, 14 April 1986.

Tang, You-thon. "Interest Rates Fall, Idle Money Seeking Investment Opportunities, Blind Investment Shown on the Stock and Real Estate Markets." *Central Daily News* (in Chinese), 13 February 1987.

Tanzer, Andrew. "Taiwan Reaps the Rewards of Economic Virtue—but Virtue Can Become Fanaticism: The Trouble with Mercantilism." *Forbes*, 11 August 1986.

"Three Already Approved, Limit Lifted on Quota of U.S. Insurance Firm Branch in Taiwan." *Free China Journal*, 4 March 1987.

Tsai, Steve Shin-ting. "The Development of R.O.C.-U.S. Economic Ties." *Industry of Free China* 61, no. 4 (April 1984).

"U.S. Capital Flows." *World Financial Markets* (Morgan Guaranty Trust Company of New York), January 1986.

"U.S. Revaluation Pressure on Korea and Taiwan May Succeed—Modestly." *Business Asia*, 18 August 1986.

"WEO 1985 ... How Capital Flows and World Oil Prospects Affect the Outlook for Developing Nations." *IMF Survey*, 13 May 1985.

Wieman, Earl. "The Export Processing Zone System: Is What Foreign Investors Want." *Free China Journal*, 1 September 1985.

"World Debt Crisis: Special Report." *Wall Street Journal*, 22 June 1984.

"World Economic Outlook, 1986." *IMF Survey*, 5 May 1986.

Wu, Chia-loong. "Dissipating Foreign Exchange Reserves." *Central Daily News* (in Chinese), 22 December, 23 December 1986.

Wu, Yuan-li. "The ROC Foreign Trade and Investment Climate." *Free China Journal*, 4 August 1985.

Xafa, Miranda. "Export Credits and the Debt Crisis, Recent Trends, Current Policy Issues." *Finance and Development* (A Quarterly Publication of the IMF and the World Bank) 24, no. 1 (March 1987).

"Year of the Equity (Again) in 1987." *Far Eastern Economic Review*, 8 January 1987.

Yu, Tzong-shian. "The Relationship between the Government and the Private Sector in the Process of Economic Development in Taiwan, Republic of China." *Industry of Free China*, October 1985.

Yuan, Jian-pao. "Taiwan's Banks." *Taiwan Economics and Finance Journal* (in Chinese) (Economic Research Department, Bank of Taiwan) 21, no. 5 (20 May 1985).

INSTITUTIONAL PUBLICATIONS

Asian Development Bank. *Asian Development Review* 3, no. 2 (1985).

———. *Key Indicators of Developing Member Countries of Asian Development Bank*. Manila: Asian Development Bank, April 1984.

International Monetary Fund. *International Financial Statistics*. Washington, D.C.: IMF, various issues.

Morgan Guaranty Trust Company. *Morgan International Data*. New York: Morgan Guaranty Trust Company, International Economics Department, February 1987.

Organisation for Economic Co-operation and Development. *Financial Market Trends, Special Feature: Prudential Supervision in Banking*. Paris: OECD, August 1986.

———. *Financial Statistics*, Part 1: *Financial Statistics Monthly*. Paris: OECD, various issues.

———. *Statistics on External Indebtedness: Bank and Trade-related Non-bank External Claims on International Borrowing Countries and Territories, at End-June 1986, (together with revised data for End-June and End-December 1985)*. Paris: BIS/OECD, January 1987.

GOVERNMENT PUBLICATIONS

Central Bank of China. *Balance of Payments, Taiwan District, The Republic of China.* Taipei: Economic Research Department, Central Bank of China, December 1990.

————. *Financial Statistics Monthly, Taiwan District, The Republic of China.* Taipei: Economic Research Department, Central Bank of China, December 1990.

————. *Statistical Operation Data of Financial Institutions in Taiwan, Republic of China, 1983* (in Chinese). Taipei: Financial Examination Department, Central Bank of China, 1983.

Republic of China, Executive Yuan. *Annual Report of Government Administration, Republic of China, 1982–1983.* Taipei: Research, Development, and Evaluation Commission, Executive Yuan, November 1984.

————. *Four-year Economic Development Plan for Taiwan, Republic of China, 1982–1985.* Taipei: Council for Economic Planning and Development, Executive Yuan, December 1981.

————. *Monthly Bulletin of Statistics of the Republic of China* 56, no. 11 (November 1990), Directorate-General of Budget, Accounting and Statistics, Executive Yuan.

————. *Ninth Medium-term Economic Development Plan for Taiwan, 1986–1989* (in Chinese). Taipei: Overall Planning Department, Council for Economic Planning and Development, August 1986.

————. *The Report of the Executive Yuan Tax Reform Commission.* Part III, Special Research Topic, Vol. 1. Taipei: Executive Yuan, June 1970.

————. *Taiwan Statistical Data Book, 1990.* Taipei: Council for Economic Planning and Development, Executive Yuan, 1990.

————. *The Republic of China's Economic Development for 1990, Macroeconomic Development Targets.* Taipei: Overall Planning Department, Council for Economic Planning and Development, Executive Yuan, 1990.

Republic of China, Industrial Development and Investment Center. *A Brief Introduction to the Industrial Estates in Taiwan, the Republic of China.* Taipei: IDIC, June 1985.

————. *Investment Opportunities in Taiwan, the Republic of China.* Taipei: IDIC, October 1981.

————. *Legal Consideration for Investment in Taiwan, Republic of China.* Taipei: IDIC, 1985.

Republic of China, Interior Ministry. *Investigation Report of the Needs of Vocational Training* (in Chinese). Taipei: Vocational Training Bureau, Interior Ministry, 1985.

Republic of China, Ministry of Economics. *An Analysis of the Operations and Economic Effects of Foreign Enterprises in Taiwan.* Taipei: Ministry of Economic Affairs, Investment Commission, various issues.

————. *Investigation of Foreign and Overseas Chinese Investing Business Operation and Its Contribution to the Economic Development of the Republic: An Analysis Report* (in Chinese). Taipei: Investment Commission, Ministry of Economic Affairs, various issues.

————. *Statistics on Overseas Chinese and Foreign Investment, Technical Cooperation, Outward Investment, Outward Technical Cooperation, the Republic of*

China. Taipei: Investment Commission, Ministry of Economic Affairs, various issues.

Republic of China, National Reconstruction Committee. *A Study and Recommendation on the Reinforcement of Financial Policy and Economic Development* (in Chinese). Occasional Paper, No. 43. Taipei: National Construction Committee, June 1985.

U.S. Department of Commerce. *Foreign Economic Trends and Their Implications for the United States.* Washington, D.C.: U.S. Department of Commerce, International Trade Administration, January 1986.

————. *Survey of Current Business.* Washington, D.C.: U.S. Department of Commerce, various issues.

U.S. Department of State. "Background Note: Taiwan." Washington, D.C.: U.S. Department of State, Bureau of Public Affairs, September 1983.

Index

accelerated depreciation, 93, 94, 127, 168

Africa, 7, 21, 123 n.61

Asian Development Bank, 117

Austria, 23

balance of payments, 10, 11, 16, 18, 24, 26, 28, 32, 34, 35, 36, 37, 38 n.2, 40 n.36, 43 n.71; and Taiwan, 49, 50, 66, 152, 171, 173, 178

bank lending, xiv, 2, 3, 5, 15, 30, 36, 39 n.13, 49; in Taiwan, 77, 78, 97, 98, 104, 139, 140

Belgium, 23

beneficiary certificates, 104, 105, 131, 133, 156, 172

Brazil, 21, 35, 39 n.12

Bretton Woods, 20, 25, 27, 42 n.68, n.70, n.71, 54

Britain, 6, 9, 22, 35, 105

British pound, 81

Canada, 6, 14, 23, 71, 131

capital account, 12, 24, 25, 28, 33, 42 n.68, 82, 102

capital flight, 2, 3, 9, 10, 18, 27, 28, 31, 32, 37, 41 n.39, 49, 51, 52, 55, 87,

109, 117, 118, 146, 159, 172, 173, 178

capital flow, 1, 3, 8, 10, 11, 13–15, 24, 25, 27–29, 31, 32, 34, 37, 52, 55, 87, 104, 115, 126, 130, 145, 146, 153, 158, 173, 177, 181 n.42, 182 n.53

capital inflow, 2, 9, 13, 16–18, 29, 34, 35, 36, 39 n.23, 41 n.51, 53, 56, 83 n.15, 87, 88, 97, 104–9, 110, 115, 116, 118, 122 n.48, 126, 132, 134, 136, 137, 142, 145, 167, 172, 176–78

capital outflow, 11, 14–18, 24, 29, 31, 34, 35, 39 n.23, 44 n.96, 88, 102, 106, 109–17, 123 n.64, 134, 141, 142, 145, 155, 158, 167, 171, 172, 177, 178

capital market, 11, 14, 16, 33–38, 56, 132, 138, 146, 154, 172, 176, 177

Central Bank of China, 17, 66–69, 71, 73, 75–80, 96, 111, 112, 114–16, 122 n.49, 123 n.56, 134, 136, 138, 139, 144, 145, 154, 155, 157, 158, 160 n.39, 161 n.39, 169, 177

China: Taiwan, Republic of, 51, 149; Mainland, People's Republic of, 22, 55, 68, 83 n.25, 84 n.25, 99, 117, 118, 119, 159, 178

ABOUT THE AUTHOR

CHICH-HENG KUO is Section Chief of the Laws and Regulations Committee of the Executive Yuan (the cabinet) of the Republic of China. He has been a part-time Associate Professor at National Chung Hsing University and Soochow University and was formerly on the staff of the National Treasury Bureau of the Ministry of Finance of the Republic of China. The author of *Interpretation of Tax Law, in Theory and Practices* (in Chinese), he holds an S.J.D. from Tulane University.